CONFUCIANISM
The Dynamics
of Tradition

Published in cooperation with
The Harry S. Truman Research Institute
for the Advancement of Peace
The Hebrew University, Jerusalem

CONFUCIANISM
The Dynamics of Tradition

Edited by
Irene Eber

The Hebrew University, Jerusalem

MACMILLAN PUBLISHING COMPANY
NEW YORK

Collier Macmillan Publishers
LONDON

Macmillan Publishing Company
866 Third Avenue, New York, N.Y. 10022

Collier Macmillan Canada, Inc.

Library of Congress Catalog Card Number: 86-949

Printed in the United States of America

printing number
1   2   3   4   5   6   7   8   9   10

Library of Congress Cataloging-in-Publication Data
Main entry under title:

Confucianism, the dynamics of tradition.

Seven of the papers presented at the Vitaly Rubin
Memorial Colloquium on "Confucianism, the Dynamics of
Tradition," convened under the auspices of the
Harry S. Truman Research Institute for the Advancement
of Peace, the Hebrew University, Jerusalem.
    Bibliography: p.
    Includes index.
    Contents: Toward a third epoch of Confucian
humanism / Tu Wei-ming—The unfolding of early
Confucianism / Cho-yun Hsü—The K'ung-family-
masters' anthology and third century Confucianism /
Yoav Ariel—[etc.]

    1. Confucianism—Congresses.   I. Eber, Irene,
II. Vitaly Rubin Memorial Colloquium on
"Confucianism, the Dynamics of Tradition" (Harry S.
Truman Research Institute for the Advancement of Peace,
the Hebrew University, Jerusalem) III. Makhon
le-mehkar/al shem Harry S. Truman.
BL1852.C66   1986   299'.512   86-949
ISBN 0-02-908780-5

Contents

Contributors   vi

Preface   viii

Introduction, Irene Eber   x

**PART I   The Vitality of Confucian Concepts and Their
             Reinterpretations**   1

1   Toward a Third Epoch of Confucian Humanism:
    A Background Understanding, Tu Wei-ming   3

2   The Unfolding of Early Confucianism: The Evolution
    from Confucius to Hsün-tzu, Cho-yun Hsü   23

3   The *K'ung-Family-Masters' Anthology* and
    Third-Century Confucianism, Yoav Ariel   39

PART II   Spiritual Aspects of Confucianism   61

4   What is Confucian Spirituality?, Julia Ching   63

5   On Confucian, European, and Universal Aesthetics,
    Ben-Ami Scharfstein   81

6   Human Rites: An Essay on Confucianism and Human
    Rights, Wm. Theodore de Bary   109

PART III Confucian Protest and Moral Responsibility   133

7   Scholarship and Autobiography: A Review of Vitaly
    Rubin's Work on Confucianism, Irene Eber   135

8   A Chinese Don Quixote: Changing Attitudes to Po-i's
    Image, Vitaly Rubin   155

    Notes   185

    Glossary   213

    Index   231

Contributors

Yoav Ariel is lecturer in philosophy at Tel Aviv University. He has co-authored a translation of the *Tao Te Ching* into Hebrew and is currently working on a book-length study of *The K'ung-Family-Masters' Anthology (K'ung-ts'ung-tzu)*.

Julia Ching is Professor of Religious Studies at Victoria College, Toronto University. Among her studies in Confucianism and Neo-Confucianism is *To Acquire Wisdom, The Way of Wang Yang-ming* (1976).

Wm. Theodore de Bary is John Mitchell Mason Professor of the University at Columbia University. He is the author and editor of numerous books on Asian philosophy and Neo-Confucianism. His most recent work is *The Liberal Tradition in China* (1983).

Irene Eber is Associate Professor of Chinese History at the Hebrew University of Jerusalem. She specializes in Chinese intellectual history and has among her publications *Voices from Afar: Modern Chinese Writers on Oppressed Peoples and their Literature* (1980).

Cho-yun Hsü is University Professor of Chinese History at the University of Pittsburgh. His numerous studies on Chou and Han dynasty social history include *Ancient China in Transition* (1965) and *Han Agriculture* (1980).

Vitaly Rubin was, until his untimely death, Associate Professor of Chinese Philosophy at the Hebrew University of Jerusalem. He specialized in the classical period of Chinese philosophy. His last book was *Individual and State in Ancient China* (1976).

Ben-Ami Scharfstein is Professor of Philosophy at Tel Aviv University. He has published on the subjects of comparative philosophy, mysticism, aesthetics, and the psychology of philosophy. His most recent work is *The Philosophers: Their Lives and the Nature of their Thought* (1980).

Tu Wei-ming is Professor of Chinese History and Philosophy and Chairman, Committee on the Study of Religion, Harvard University. His recent publications include *Confucian Ethics: The Singapore Challenge* (1984) and *Confucian Thought: Selfhood as Creative Transformation* (1985) in addition to numerous publications on Chinese intellectual history and Confucian philosophy.

Preface

On 14–16 March 1983, the Vitaly Rubin Memorial Colloquium, on "Confucianism: The Dynamics of Tradition," convened under the auspices of the Harry S. Truman Research Institute for the Advancement of Peace, the Hebrew University, Jerusalem. The foreign and Israeli participants explored Confucianism and its changing relevance in Chinese history as well as in a wider philosophical context. The present volume includes seven of the papers presented at the colloquium and also an unfinished paper by Vitaly Rubin, on which he was working at the time of his sudden and tragic death.

Friends of Vitaly and Inessa Rubin are well acquainted with their struggle to leave Soviet Russia in the first half of the 1970s. Vitaly's plight came to the attention of the international academic community in mid-1972 after the Rubins were refused a visa to immigrate to Israel, and especially after his open letter "Is the Scholar Human?" was published on 5 October 1972, in the *New York Review of Books*. It took nearly four years and help from international scholars before the Rubins finally received permission in June 1976 to leave Russia.

They settled in Jerusalem, where Vitaly eagerly accepted the challenge of his new position as professor at the Hebrew

University. He and Inessa were happy; their adjustment to a new life, a new country, and new commitments was made with ease. Theirs was a success story worth the difficult struggle and painful waiting. Vitaly's untimely death in 1981, therefore, profoundly shocked all those who had been concerned with his plight as a "refusenik" and who had rejoiced in his good fortune after 1976. In planning this colloquium, the organizers attempted to reflect some of the major concerns that animated Rubin's work on Confucianism both in the Soviet Union and in Israel, in addition to treating the broader issues aptly termed by Tu Wei-ming "the Confucian project."

The effort to convene the Rubin Colloquium and to see this book into print could never have succeeded without the generous help of others. Acknowledgement for funding must be made to the Kadoorie Family Fund—A project of the Fund for Higher Education. The Harry S. Truman Research Institute for the Advancement of Peace of the Hebrew University hosted the meeting, and its office staff worked above and beyond the call of duty on behalf of the participants. Thanks are due to my colleagues at Hebrew University and from abroad who attended and contributed to the success of the Colloquium. Above all, I am grateful to Harold Z. Schiffrin, who co-chaired the meeting and has given unstintingly of his time throughout the preparation of the manuscript for print. Sarah Lemann expertly typed large portions of the manuscript, and Dora Shickman provided the Chinese calligraphy in the glossary. I was fortunate to have Norma Schneider's constant involvement at each stage of the preparation of the manuscript as well as her professional editing of all the contributions. Finally, I want to express my appreciation to Joan Pitsch, the editorial supervisor at Macmillan, and to Eva Shan Chou for her highly skilled copyediting.

Irene Eber
Jerusalem, 1985

Introduction

IRENE EBER

Like other ancient systems of philosophical thought and religious practice, Confucianism has been expressed on a variety of levels and has developed and changed in accordance with an inner dynamic and in response to outer circumstances. The roots of Confucianism reach far back into the beginnings of Chinese civilization, predating the life of Confucius (551–479 B.C.) by perhaps more than one thousand years. The recognition and exploration of these roots is still in its preliminary stages. However, there is convincing evidence that characteristics which were integral to Chinese culture and civilization and which later became associated with Confucianism emerged at an earlier time. For example, a forceful argument has been made that the Shang dynasty (1766–1122 B.C.) had religious concerns with order and hierarchy and established a congruence between religious beliefs and political culture.[1]

If, indeed, religious impulses informed the earliest stages of what is identified as the "Confucian tradition," the concept of Confucius as rationalizer of that tradition must be modified. For no matter how secular most of his ideas and those of his disciples apparently were, they were endowed as well with an earlier religious logic and perpetuated that logic.

Hence, the emergence of the Confucian tradition and its institutions can no longer be seen in purely secular terms, without considering the religious substratum.

The interweaving of religious value orientations with concern for action in the mundane world, whether as social or political ethics, informs the first great flowering of Chinese thought in the Warring States period (481–221 B.C.). By the same token, the development of Confucius' ideas by such men like Mencius (ca. 372–289 B.C.) and Hsün-tzu (ca. 300–237 B.C.), the religiously oriented ethics of Mo-tzu (ca. 490–403 B.C.), and the cosmological–naturalistic speculations of the Taoists also took place in response to changing circumstances and the emergence of a new social structure. Although in the end the Realists, or Legalists, the architects of the first unified empire in 221 B.C., won the day, their preeminence was short-lived. The social and political order of imperial China which emerged after the fall of the Ch'in dynasty in 206 B.C. was fashioned over the next two millennia by Confucians into an increasingly complex meshing of thought, practice, and religious concerns, a synthesizing practice that tended toward a "totalism" which Thomas Metzger defines for the last millennium as an "ethos of interdependence."[2]

In this early emergence of the Confucian order (the "first epoch" discussed in Tu Wei-ming's essay), some normative developments were significant both in the realm of thought and in socio-political life. First, as is emphasized by Hsü Cho-yun, there occurred the enlargement, or universalization, of the aristocratic code of norms and values, which Professor Hsü secs as taking place against the background of social and political change. Second, the Mencian conception of "moral fulfillment for every individual" assumed the existence of a moral autonomy and a community of morally autonomous individuals, whether this assumption was articulated or not. This Mencian conception was an ideal achieved only by the minority, the literate elite.[3] Statecraft, administrative skills, and above all literacy were the monopoly of this elite. Already in the Han dynasty (206 B.C–A.D. 220) a division of power emerged between the elite and the monarchy. The elite had the knowledge needed to legitimize the exercise of power; the monarchy possessed the symbols as well as the practical means. Ideally, this division of power assumed the harmonious functioning of state and society, but practically the relationship between monarch and elite was more often than not a tense one. The elite's vision and its task of creating a moral society were challenged by ambitious men and groups both within and without the court. Thus the literati's professed concern with the world frequently also reflected their anxieties about maintaining their positions, escaping exile, and avoiding death. They saw that disruptive forces in a world threatened with disorder impinged on the lives of individuals. Hsü Fu-kuan has noted that the confrontation with historical crises and the anxious concern with the world's problems can be regarded as a basic aspect of Chinese thought from the Chou period (1122?–221 B.C.) onwards.[4]

Prior to the Sung dynasty (960–1279), the "ethos of interdependence" was rooted in the idea of a pervasive relationship between the human and the natural orders, with the natural order conceived in materialist rather than in spiritual terms. The basic assumption was that all parts of both human and natural orders and Heaven—a force that made for harmony and balance—existed in a harmonious relation. Human beings were capable both of disrupting and of maintaining and restoring harmony. Whereas ignorance, selfishness, irresponsibility, and the absence of morality might disrupt the human and therefore also the natural order, wisdom and morally responsible action could restore it. Wisdom was obtained through study, specifically the study of the Classics,[5] but also by studying the histories and writings of great men of the past. Professor Hsü Cho-yun ascribes the beginning of the exegetical tradition to Confucius' followers who combined careers in government service with learning. Learning therefore conferred on the elite an awesome responsibility because the acquisition of wisdom required devotion and a readiness to sacrifice personal interests for the sake of larger goals. But learning alone did not lead to wisdom. Self-discipline and self-cultivation, which enabled a person to achieve the fullest manifestation of *jen* (humanity, goodness, or love), were ultimately necessary for acquiring wisdom and for becoming a sage. The goal of sagehood was not a matter of personal gratification. It was seen as vital for establishing and maintaining harmony and order. The idea of the interdependence of the socio-political and the natural orders, the harmonious relationship with Heaven and the human being's functioning, if not active, participation, amounts to a religious creed, held and perpetuated by the literary elite.

The political disruptions of the third to the sixth centuries, the large-scale dislocations, and the introduction and spread of Buddhism obscure the continuation and the nature of the development of the Confucian tradition during those centuries. But in spite of the dominant positions of Buddhist and Neo-Taoist philosophical schools, the eclipse of Confucian speculative thought and certainly of Confucian learning was less complete than might be assumed.[6] Yoav Ariel argues in his essay for the continued intellectual–philosophical activity of Confucians after the fall of the Han dynasty. His analysis of Wang Su's (A.D. 195–256) contribution to the ongoing Confucian dialogue reveals the importance attached to the transmission of texts as well as to the Confucian scholars' attempts to establish the texts' relevancy. He suggests, furthermore, that after a lapse of more than four hundred years, Confucians like Wang Su revived the dialogue form of disputation, a polemical and essentially rationalistic form that makes it possible to expose contradictions and faulty reasoning. Dr. Ariel highlights the need for a more precise definition of the content of Confucian scholarship during this period, including the question of spurious texts.

The persistence of Confucian norms among the elite and the continuity of Confucian scholarship can be assumed for most periods. This scriptural continuity was important, not only for preserving and perpetuating learning, but also for keeping alive the idea that the Classics contained spiritual values necessary for civilized existence. Arthur F. Wright has suggested that those families which maintained Confucian learning "felt themselves responsible for safeguarding and transmitting the unchallengeable moral truths laid down in the Classics—truths that were infallible guides to the conduct of life."[7] It was no doubt the upholding of these moral truths and the insistence that the Confucian tradition formed their repository that led T'ang dynasty (618–907) intellectuals in the eighth and ninth centuries to examine standard commentaries to the Classics with a new critical and rational spirit and to attempt to establish new standards of Confucian scholarship. Significant as these scholarly endeavors were in foreshadowing subsequent developments,[8] the intellectual revival, when it occurred, was nevertheless an unprecedented development in Chinese history. "The Confucian revival in the Sung," Wm. Theodore de Bary has written elsewhere, "was a broad historical process, and the Neo-Confucianism which emerged from it was neither a static philosophy nor a set of fixed doctrines, but a movement which grew precisely through successive efforts to redefine tradition and reformulate orthodoxy."[9] The scope and content of this revival, the towering figures it produced who in turn gave it shape, and the continuing dynamic of this revival have been explored in a number of significant studies. Thanks to scholarship of the past decades, our understanding of Sung, Yüan (1279–1368), and Ming (1368–1644) dynasty Confucianism has been enormously enlarged.

Most importantly, these seminal studies have emphasized "the inner life and dynamism" of Confucianism and Neo-Confucianism, and have effectively shattered the stereotype of an unchanging and, by implication, in the course of time, a stagnant Chinese tradition. They have similarly revealed the fallacy of considering this tradition only in terms of secularism.[10] Indeed, the revival of Confucianism and the development of Neo-Confucianism between the thirteenth and nineteenth centuries included the adaptation of both Confucianism and Neo-Confucianism to new circumstances and also a new, pronounced religious orientation. Recent studies by Hao Chang and others have stressed the importance of the spiritual content in Neo-Confucian thinking; they have stressed, for example, how self-cultivation and the attainment of sagehood were aimed at transcending merely mundane goals. While self-cultivation is morally significant, the stress on the unity of Heaven and the human being (t'ien-jen ho-i) endows this concept with religious significance as well.[11]

Julia Ching argues in her essay that the quest for sagehood has been a central idea in Confucianism and that this quest "can only be understood with reference to the 'interior life' of the spirit, to personal discipline, and sometimes to mystical experience." The spiritual qualities of Confucianism, specifically a language of spirituality and forms of meditation which insist neither on passivity nor on the cessation of intellectual effort, have complemented the secular character of Confucianism. Although the religious concern and commitment that emerged in Shang and Chou times was vastly transformed by the seventeenth and eighteenth centuries, the religious and spiritual values, "the horizon of spirituality," have continued to be significant. Therefore Professor Ching also argues that the quest for sagehood, which is at the heart of Confucianism, cannot be understood without reference to the individual's spiritual life.

The implicit assumption that the individual is a spiritual being, capable of transcending the demands of the purely mundane world, is also expressed in aesthetic theory, especially in speculation about the painter's act of creation. The Confucian aspects of aesthetic theory are often neglected in favor of stressing Taoist and Buddhist concepts of spontaneity in artistic creation. Yet, as defined by literati painters from the Sung dynasty onward, painting was considered an additional method for manifesting the mind and a means of self-cultivation, along with other modes of artistic expression.[12] Thus, Chinese aesthetic theory does not extol only craftsmanship, but also stresses the inner personal qualities which the artist must express and embody in the work of art. Thomé Fang, a present-day Confucian, has likened artistic inspiration to being in touch with cosmic "vibrations of vitality," the artist conveying in the work of art the sense of universal flux.[13]

Professor Ben-Ami Scharfstein's essay defines the spiritual content in artistic creation as the "need of the individual to live beyond himself." He therefore sees a spiritual motivation in the artist's desire to overcome existential loneliness and isolation. Accordingly, all art anywhere expresses an "aesthetic universal," and it is this aesthetic universal which allows the artist to communicate with his audience. Professor Scharfstein, however, does not conceive of art as something accessible to everyone at all times, in spite of the inherent presence of the universal aesthetic. Rather, art by necessity is always an individual expression; the artist's desire to have his creation transcend and "fuse" with the supra-individual arises precisely because of art's separateness and individuality.

In addition to the spiritual strivings, Neo-Confucianism also stressed participation in society and in public life. A balance was sought, though most often not easily achieved, between intellectual and moral training, between public service and contemplation. For the fact was that even the sage existed within a social setting where a balance had to be maintained between his inner and outer being. The question of human rights which Professor de Bary raises in his essay is concerned with the social existence of the individual, though from a broader perspective human rights also involve the inner freedom of the individual and his moral autonomy. To Vitaly Rubin human rights became in time a core issue that informed most of his scholarly work on early Confucianism. Thus Rubin saw human rights, as does Professor de Bary in his essay, not as a product of modern Western civilization, or as a Chinese import of Western liberal thought, but as a part of a Confucian tradition which raises the issue in conjunction with moral autonomy and moral action.

Professor de Bary suggests a novel approach to the problem of the locus of the awareness of and respect for human rights in Chinese tradition. There is no specific teaching or doctrine which guarantees such rights. Rather, the possibility of asserting them is found, on the one hand, in the family-centered outlook of traditional Confucianism with its emphasis on filiality and reciprocity, and, on the other, in the belief that the ritual order constitutes the basis of the social order. Professor de Bary stresses Chu Hsi's (1130–1200) practical elaboration of these ideas in his writings on local government and communal organization. According to Chu Hsi, the principles of the ritual order in society are inherent in the universe as the basic pattern (*li*) of the universe. Popular education, the practice of ritual and personal self-transformation, and voluntary communal cooperation—that is, voluntaristic mutuality and reciprocity—necessarily protect human rights. The idea of individual responsibility implies that each responsibility has its correlative right. In holding that human rights were embedded in the Confucian and Neo-Confucian tradition, Professor de Bary furthermore argues that authentic Confucians like Huang Tsung-hsi (1610–1695) recognized the importance of law for protecting the rights of man.

The all-inclusive nature of the Neo-Confucian experience between the thirteenth and nineteenth centuries, with its "ethos of interdependence"and its highly syncretic tendencies, should not obscure the internal changes and transformations which occurred during that long span of time. The Sung intellectual revival, itself not a uniform phenomenon within a specific historical situation, was subject to stresses and strains in subsequent centuries. The decline and collapse of the Chinese empire in the middle of the seventeenth century led to a profound intellectual crisis which in turn evoked different kinds of responses by Confucians like Huang Tsung-hsi, Ku Yen-wu (1613–1682), and Wang Fu-chih (1619–1692). Whereas it is true that the elite held a common body of assumptions and that Confucian orthodoxy was a pervasive and often strangulating phenomenon in the Ming and Ch'ing dynasties, it is also true that there were dissenters from and rebels against orthodoxy.[14] The tendency toward diversity and new intellectual directions might be seen, for example, in the School of Han Learning of the Ch'ing dynasty, with its philological and phonological studies aimed at the recovery of the exact meanings of classical texts.[15] Tu Wei-ming has labelled this enormously rich and intellectually lively and diverse period the "second epoch" of Confucianism.

But neither dissent nor certain forms of radicalism were sufficiently strong or pervasive to disrupt what was considered "the intelligible and moral universal order." That this disruption did not begin to occur until the end of the nineteenth century, under Western impact, raises a number of questions that are central to most scholarly discussions of the modern period. Crucial among these are: the relationship of the tradition to the modern period, its discontinuities and the persistence of continuities; the nature of the disruption; and the extent to which, as events pass into history, present perceptions must be revised to accommodate a changed perspective.

To begin with the last, it could be argued, for example, that "the death of the Confucian world view" in the late nineteenth and early twentieth centuries[16] was a valid assumption to make a decade and more ago. Similarly, Joseph Levenson's forceful paradigm of "the progressive abandonment of tradition by iconoclasts and the petrification of tradition by traditionalists" had seemed as convincing as his metaphor of the museum. Parts of the past, he argued, when shorn of their environment, their associations, their culture, and placed into a new context, become museum pieces.[17] It is suggested here, however, that Levenson's argument cannot be accepted with a sense of finality. From the vantage point of the post-Cultural Revolution period, and in view of, a continuing dialogue among Chinese philosophers outside as well as to some extent also within, the People's Republic of China, the Confucian world view seems less dead than it was once thought to be. The tradition seems less abandoned and less petrified than it was some years ago.

The question of continuities and discontinuities is at the heart of Levenson's thesis. Portions of the past can never equal the whole, for, he wrote: the "bricks of the old structure . . . [cannot] convey the essence of an invincible tradition."[18] In contrast to Levenson, Wing-tsit Chan has argued that, in spite of the abandonment of institutional Confucianism, traditional rites, and Confucian religious institutions in the twentieth century, Confucianism was not dealt a deadly blow. Confucianism was never expressed entirely through its institutions, and, according to Chan, the absence of a rigid organizational framework is one of Confucianism's strengths, allowing for change and transformation.[19] It may be that the relationship of tradition to modernity should be seen in terms of change and transformation, such as any living tradition must undergo, within which there will necessarily be continuities and discontinuities.

There can be no question, however, that nineteenth- and twentieth-century China has undergone cataclysmic sociopolitical changes. Wars and revolutionary upheavals, in addition to the Western impact on intellectual life, have characterized Chinese history in the past one hundred and fifty years. Numerous outstanding studies which have in recent years enlarged our understanding of this enormously complex period have tended to stress the all-pervasiveness of change, the rejection of the Confucian past, May Fourth iconoclasm and the destruction of tradition, and the submergence of traditional values brought about by Western ideas. It has also been suggested, however, that on the level of personal identity and the "assumed 'givens' of social existence" total displacement and total disruption is impossible, for a revolution that disintegrates also tends toward new integrations.[20] More recently scholars have pointed to the persistence of Confucian values in rural China in the post-Mao period.[21]

Both the last two decades of the nineteenth century and the intellectual revolution of the 1920's (commonly referred to as the May Fourth movement) are crucial moments in modern Chinese history. Did the first generation of radical intellectuals at the end of the nineteenth century begin a dismantling of the Confucian tradition that was completed in a violent onslaught by the second generation of the twenties? According to Hao Chang, both K'ang Yu-wei (1858–1927) and T'an Ssu-t'ung (1865–1898), men of the first generation, are significant for the complexity of their radicalism, which is not derived solely from Western sources or solely from Chinese cultural tradition. Rather, their vision of modernity, their reflections on their time and the future, represented an intellectual syncretism, or what might be called steps in a new transformation.[22] By the same token, many aspects of the May Fourth ideological ferment, rather than being "an invalidation of the core traditional values," might also be seen in terms of continued steps in a modern transformation.[23] Professor Tu, in his essay, points out that the attacks on Confucianism, though destructive on one level, also fostered a critical spirit that allowed some thinkers to develop new perspectives on Confucianism.

No doubt in scholarship the champions of iconoclasm will continue to wrestle with the advocates of transformative thinking. Continued studies of this important period may very well show that both are equally significant in explaining nineteenth- and twentieth-century intellectual trends. Ch'ien Mu's considered judgment regarding the integrative tendency of seeming opposites might also be noted. The divisions of Western thought, with the clash between religion and science, idealism and materialism, individualism and socialism, and old and new, are not part of Chinese thought, which sees things in terms of wholes. Western thought, writes Ch'ien Mu, can be a stimulus in giving new life to Chinese thought.[24]

How to evaluate the scholarship on Confucius and Confucianism in the first three decades of the twentieth century continues to be a problem. To be sure, the intent of most scholars of the time was no longer to safeguard and transmit "unchallengeable moral truths," but to rectify (*cheng-li*) a tradition that was seen as having become distorted. Nonetheless, Hu Shih's (1891–1962) work on the *Ju* ("Shuo Ju"), which attempted to reevaluate Confucius' religious position, and Fu Ssu-nien's (1896–1950) studies of Shang and early Chou religion and their relationship to Confucius' ideas both broke new ground. Similar pioneering efforts may be found among articles collected in the seven volumes of the *Discussions in Ancient Chinese History* (Ku shih pien).[25] There are, for example, the probing studies by Fung Yu-lan and Mei Ssu-p'ing (Tzu-fan) on Confucius' relationship to the Spring and Autumn periods, Ku Chieh-kang's (1893–1980) attempts to sort out the images of Confucius at various periods, and Ch'ien Mu's investigations of Confucius and the Classics, to mention only a few. Many of these studies have serious shortcomings, and Hu Shih's critical work in particular is often flawed by his tendency to search for Western values in Chinese tradition. Moreover, the positivistic approach taken by the *cheng-li kuo-ku* group entirely neglected the spiritual content at the core of the Confucian tradition.[26]

Tu Wei-ming argues persuasively that twentieth-century challenges concerning philosophical inquiry and scholarship were not taken up in an effective manner by either late nineteenth-century intellectuals or by the intellectuals of the May Fourth period. According to Professor Tu, this challenge has been met only in the last thirty years, in what he terms the "third epoch" of Confucianism. Scholars like T'ang Chün-i and Hsü Fu-kuan, who play a central role in the third epoch, are, however, concerned not only with the survival of the Confucian tradition and the continuity of traditional Chinese culture. Their concerns are subsumed "under a broader concern for the future of humankind." Nothing less than the well-being of humanity, both within the East Asian cultural sphere and beyond it, is at stake. Thus, Tu suggests, Confucianism must "universalize its perennial concerns."

Elsewhere Professor Tu has written that it is possible to conceive of Confucianism not only as political ideology, "or a kind of socio-economic ethic, but primarily as a tradition of religious philosophy. Confucianism so conceived is a way of life which demands an existential commitment on the part of Confucians . . .[like] that demanded of the followers of other spiritual traditions such as Judaism, Christianity, Islam, Buddhism or Hinduism."[27]

Today Confucianism as a spiritual–moral tradition has articulate adherents with broad philosophical–religious concerns in Taiwan and elsewhere. Men like Mou Tsung-san treat questions on the development of Chinese culture and thought, but Mou's outlook is not parochial, and a traditionalist label does not easily fit him when he deals with individual and political morality and with democracy and *jen* in human life and society.[28]

Can the same be said for the People's Republic? There are modest indications that the Confucian dialogue which was suspended for all practical purposes by the mid-sixties[29] has been diffidently resumed. Caution is evident in the way the subject of Confucius and Confucianism is handled and, according to one comment, recent articles do not differ substantially from those of the fifties.[30] On the other hand, Fung Yu-lan remains a central and stubbornly persevering figure in contemporary Chinese philosophy. Tu Wei-ming credits him with trying to establish "a creative synthesis between the identity and individuality of Confucian culture on the one hand and the emergence of a universal civilization defined in terms of science and technology on the other."[31] But, at present, systematic inquiries into Confucianism of earlier and later periods are only beginning to be evident in the People's Republic. Whereas scholars acknowledge that the study of Chinese history is impossible without critical explorations into the influence of Confucius, Marxist and Maoist formulations continue to dominate their discourse.[32] Wu An-chia is undoubtedly correct when he writes that Chinese Communist policy fluctuated between "critical inheritance" and "complete severance" until 1976, when, after Mao's death, the latter course was abandoned.[33] Although "critical inheritance" allows for a form of dialogue and may encourage the continuation of the "Confucian enterprise" on some level, it does not seem conducive to a genuine flowering of Confucian humanism as defined by Professor Tu.

Yet no final pronouncements can or should be made. The

example of Vitaly Rubin, a scholar of Confucianism who "thought not only with his head but also with his heart," is proof that the "Confucian enterprise" can be carried on in unexpected quarters and in unexpected ways. For Rubin, the study of early Confucianism posed both an intellectual challenge and, as Professor de Bary writes, a degree of involvement that in time became "inseparable from his personal struggle for human freedom and dignity." His increasing concern during the last twenty years of his life with human rights issues, questions of personal autonomy and, therefore, with dissent from whatever was inimical to such autonomy, characterizes his work on classical Chinese philosophy both before and after he left the Soviet Union. Although he did not raise the question of spirituality in Confucianism in the sense in which Julia Ching or Hao Chang have discussed it, he was increasingly concerned with personality and conduct, the inner imperative for action, non-conformity and dissent, and with how to retain moral purity while acting in the mundane world.

The subject matter of his final and unfinished study of Po-i and Shu-ch'i, which concludes this volume, clearly reveals Rubin's broadening perception regarding these topics, and adds the question of responsible participation versus protest and withdrawal. In his essay Vitaly Rubin develops these theoretical considerations around the figure of Po-i, who at the beginning of the Chou dynasty refused to enter the service of the Chou emperor Wu-wang, and analyzes the interpretations accorded Po-i's act in subsequent intellectual history.

Several aspects of the "dynamics of the Confucian tradition" are examined in the following essays. In the past, generations of scholar–officials explored this tradition for moral and spiritual affirmation in a world vastly different from ours, but for them it was a world probably no less complex than ours. Although their world is no more, and cosmopolitan influences have impinged on the tradition in the twentieth century, the Confucian tradition either as a source of moral guidance and spiritual sustenance or as a subject of scholarly inquiry is obviously not a stream run dry. Intellectual change, always complex, is never a case of simple discarding, borrowing, or substitution.

PART 1

The Vitality of Confucian Concepts and Their Reinterpretations

CHAPTER 1

Toward a Third Epoch of Confucian Humanism: A Background Understanding

TU WEI-MING

In his "Values of Confucianism," Vitaly A. Rubin observes that "the last decades have witnessed an extremely significant phenomenon in Chinese cultural and intellectual life outside Communist China: the revival of Confucianism. This movement, which is about thirty years old, has been called 'New Confucianism.'"[1] For those of us actively involved in the movement, Rubin's encouraging words are most precious. For me it is a rare, uplifting experience to hear a sympathetic echo in the wilderness where perpetual silence has been taken for granted. Although I never had the opportunity to speak to Rubin face to face, I have heard his inner voice in his written words and felt his brilliant intelligence and his searching mind. Rubin thought not only with his head but also with his heart, indeed with his entire body and soul.

In this essay I intend to discuss the authentic possibility of a third epoch of Confucian humanism, an issue that fascinated Rubin. I will first take the Levensonian interpretive

3

stance as a point of departure in order to identify the question. After a brief survey of the historical background, I will try to assess the contemporary situation in the perspective of the modern transformation of Confucian China. The essay ends with a look toward the future.

The Question

The question of whether or not a third epoch of Confucian humanism is possible has intrigued students of Chinese intellectual history for decades. Joseph Levenson's monumental attempt to understand the dilemma of the modern Chinese thinker responding to the impact of the West answers this question in the negative.[2] For those who were privileged to know Levenson personally, however, the statement that the "Mozartian historian"[3] makes about Confucian China and its modern fate is not only the verdict of a disinterested judge but also the lamentation of a poet–philosopher. Levenson is said to have been anguished over the demise of the Confucian amateur ideal. Yet, despite his admiration for the Confucian literatus, he concluded that, in an increasingly specialized and professionalized modern society, the scholar–official ideal was outdated. As the feudal society which has nourished Confucians degenerates, Levenson observed, Confucian humanism inevitably fades into the background.[4]

An important assumption in the Levensonian interpretation is Max Weber's characterization of the modern West as the triumph of rationality. An obvious implication of Weber's thesis is that traditional forms of life will all be destroyed as the modernizing process which originated in the Calvinist spirit of capitalism in Western Europe engulfs the whole world. The leveling power of science and technology will eventually render major historical religions inoperative as differentiating cultural factors. The technocrat, rather than the literatus, will rule the universe. Confucian humanism, in this Levensonian perspective, can only remain a faint memory in the minds of those who still cherish the ideal of the amateur who writes poetry and thinks great thoughts for pleasure.[5] To be sure, the Confucian heritage may still have a place in the "museum without walls,"[6] dominated though it is by what Weber refers to as "bureaucratic authority."[7] This remaining place, however, by no means contains the hope that Confucianism can reemerge as a dynamic intellectual force in the twentieth century.

Levenson's interpretation of the fate of Confucian China may be arbitrary. But this argument that Confucianism has only historical significance for contemporary China is widely accepted as self-evident and thus as true. A clear indication of the influence of the Levensonian interpretation is the common practice among Western students of modern China to label post-May Fourth (1919) Confucians as traditional, conservative, or reactionary. They take it for granted that the incongruity between Confucian traditionalism and rational, scientific modernism is so clear-cut that the rise of modernity in China entails the demise of the Confucian tradition.[8]

A number of scholars have tried to develop alternative explanatory models. A fruitful approach has been to explore the lives and thoughts of the so-called "traditionalists," "conservatives," and "reactionaries" in order to see how they wrestled with "modern" Western questions. In the collection of essays *The Limits of Change*, the perimeters of Confucian conservatism are extended to include spiritual values.[9] These essays serve as a corrective to the stereotypical image that Confucianism caused traditional Chinese political culture to be dominated by an authoritarian, gerontocratic, and male-chauvinist orientation. Guy Alitto's study of Liang Shu-ming vividly attempts to apply Confucian ideas to village governance in the twentieth century.[10] Liang may very well have been "the last Confucian," but the Confucianism that he advocated may outlast such influential modern ideologies as socialism, liberalism, democratism, and scientism in both theory and practice in China.

Thomas Metzger, in his thought-provoking reflection on the "predicament" of the Neo-Confucian personality, seriously challenges the Weberian explanation of the Confucian ethic as one of making "adjustment to the world."[11] Instead Metzger persuasively demonstrates that the dilemma of a typical Confucian, caught between self-cultivation and social service, is likely to generate an internal psychic dynamism comparable in intensity to that generated in the Calvinist under the influence of the Puritan inner asceticism. The Confucians, in this view, shape the world according to their cultural ideal. They do not simply submit themselves to the status quo. It is debatable whether the Neo-Confucians were inescapably constricted by what Metzger describes as the unpleasant state of affairs, given their ontological assumptions and existential conditions. Metzger's claim that the impact of the West actually provided an outlet by which the Neo-Confucians escaped their unbearable predicament is also debatable. However, his assertion that Confucian ethics is transformative in the Weberian sense is well founded.[12]

A concerted effort to investigate the inner logic as well as the internal dynamics of the Neo-Confucian tradition began in the United States in the early 1960s. Led by Wm. Theodore de Bary, a series of research conferences was held in America and Europe to engage scholars from both the East and the West to study the second epoch of Confucian humanism. The four collections of essays subsequently published represent a comprehensive attempt to probe the deep meanings embodied in the lives and philosophies of Neo-Confucian thinkers.[13] This attempt would have been impossible without the active participation of contemporary exemplars of the Confucian heritage, notably Wing-tsit Chan of the United States, T'ang Chün-i of Hong Kong, and Okada Takehiko of Kyūshū. Through their exemplary teaching, they inspired a whole generation of American scholars to undertake the difficult task of understanding and interpreting Confucian "codes" in terms of contemporary Western conceptual apparatuses.

On the surface, Levenson's assessment of the fate of Confucian China is diametrically opposed to de Bary's faith in the relevance of the Confucian project to the perennial concerns of our times. Political events since the untimely death of Levenson in 1969 suggest that the fate of Confucianism in China remains an open question. Few people doubt the relevance of the Confucian tradition to the emerging political culture in the People's Republic of China. Industrial East Asia's success in the last two decades in competing with the United States and Western Europe in manufacturing enterprises and high technology presents another situation. Its ingenious employment of culturally specific development strategies raises challenging questions about the relationship between Confucian ethics and the East Asian entrepreneurial spirit.[14] Some sociologists, fascinated by the economic performance of the so-called post-Confucian states (Japan, South Korea, Hong Kong, Taiwan, and Singapore), have even proposed new concepts such as "modern capitalism" and "second modernity" to describe the new phenomenon.[15] If Levenson were alive today, would he fundamentally revise his interpretive stance?

Levenson, as an intellectual historian dedicated to probing the thinking person in his total context, was particularly sensitive to the ability of the Confucian in contemporary China to produce original and creative perspectives. This he felt to be painfully deficient. He did not find the influential intellectuals who shaped the currents of thought in modern China to be creative or original. In fact, he found virtually no evidence of the originality and creativity required if Confucianism was to become a living tradition either through the active participation of an articulate Westernizer or in the contemplative reflection of an erudite classicist. One wonders, however, whether he would have changed his perception had he encountered the writings of an unusual metaphysician such as Hsiung Shih-li, of a philosopher of culture such as T'ang Chün-i, or of a concerned intellectual such as Hsü Fu-kuan, or of an idealist thinker such as Mou Tsung-san.

As our knowledge about the lives and thoughts of the Sung-Ming Confucian masters increases, thanks to de Bary and his colleagues, the Levensonian outlook becomes even more poignant. The days of Chu Hsi and Wang Yang-ming (1472–1529) are gone forever. Even the glory of Tai Chen (1723–1777) is hardly visible in the philosophical writings of modern Confucians. Many of the alleged followers of the Confucian Way are more reminiscent of the characters in Wu Ching-tzu's *Ju-lin wai-shih* (*The Scholars*): petty, superficial, selfish and irrelevant. Lu Hsün's (1881–1936) apparent cynicism about Confucian ritualism realistically identifies much in the Confucian practice that is callous, insensitive, and outmoded. The more we learn about the Confucian tradition, the more we are convinced that its modern expression is not what it is supposed to be.

A comparison of the *t'i-yung* (substance–function) dichotomy in Chu Hsi's thought with Chang Chih-tung's (1837–1909) formula ("Chinese learning as substance and Western learning as function") clearly shows how the subtlety of a dynamic category can become an excuse for nonthinking. This, of course, does not mean that Chang's conscious effort to bring categories in traditional Chinese philosophy such as *t'i-yung* to bear upon the modern situation is not significant. Indeed, his formula may have been an ingenious way of softening the Western impact. Nevertheless, in regard to creative thought, Chang's dichotomy is indicative of the paucity of the Confucian response to the intellectual challenge presented by the West. Levenson was right in characterizing much of the wishful thinking among contemporary Chinese literati as an index to the identity crisis of the modern mind of China.[16]

In a deeper sense, Levenson's negative response to the question of whether there is an authentic possibility for the development of a third epoch of Confucian humanism serves as an excellent point of departure for exploring the narrow ridge where a positive response might be found. To put it differently, the concrete procedure by which this authentic possibility might be realized must begin with the recognition that the Confucian world studied by de Bary and his colleagues is no more. De Bary himself and some of his colleagues are critically aware of the intellectual challenge. This, however, does not imply that the only hope for a Confucian revival in modern China is resurrection. Reanimating the old to attain the new is surely still possible in Confucian symbolism, but to do so the modern Confucian must again be original and creative, no matter how difficult the task and how strenuous the effort.

To retrieve the meaning of a tradition after the naive certainty of its universal truth has been thoroughly criticized is no easy task. The effort required to overcome the sense of estrangement and to bridge the gap between classical texts as dead letters and as living messages is no simple effort.

The systematic inquiry into the lives and thoughts of the Sung–Ming Confucian masters is only the first step. Scholarly endeavor alone may not bring about an intellectual renaissance. Egyptologists, or for that matter Buddhologists, cannot by themselves breathe vitality into ancient scripts. Nor can Sinologists alone bring about a new epoch in Confucian learning. Numerous political, social, and cultural factors are involved. The upsurge of interest in Confucian ethics in the 1980s, sharply contrasted with the anti-Confucian sentiments of the 1960s, was not predicted by futurologists. Nor has there been a sophisticated explanatory model to help us appraise its seemingly far-reaching implications. The veil of ignorance is so extensive that we are at the mercy of external forces which are often beyond our comprehension.

This psychology of uncertainty, verging on a deep sense of perplexity, is not at all alien to the Confucian experience. Confucius himself is said to have constantly worried about the fate of his teachings, although he was not particularly worried about his own lot.[17] His concern for the well-being of the cultural tradition, for a form of life that was thought to have been inherited from King Wen and the Duke of Chou, was shared by Mencius, Hsün-tzu, and virtually all subsequent Confucian masters. The idea that the line of transmission has been broken and that extraordinary measures must be taken to ensure the proper transmission of the Way (*tao-t'ung*) began long before Han Yü's (768–824) famous essay on the subject. Han Yü's unique contribution lies in his definition of the *tao-t'ung* as the human way, in contradistinction to the Buddhist dharma.[18] The Neo-Confucians, since Chang Tsai (1020–1077), have taken this identity of the Confucian Tao as their ultimate concern. A fear that "this culture" (*ssu-wen*)[19] would perish if they did not continue to embody the Tao in their ordinary daily existence was pervasive among the Neo-Confucian thinkers.

Historical Background

Han Yü's claim that the transmission of the Confucian Way had been broken since Mencius was widely accepted by

Confucians of the Sung-Ming period, but historically it is a gross exaggeration. The claim overlooked the fact that it was in the Han dynasty (206 B.C.–A.D. 220) that the Confucian polity became firmly established. The interplay between the Confucianization of the Legalist bureaucracy and the politicization of Confucian moral values characterized much of the dynamics of the Han governing mechanism.[20] It is true that the following Wei (220–265) and Chin (265–420) periods are commonly known in intellectual history as the age of Neo-Taoism, and it is often assumed that after the fall of the Han empire, the Confucian method (*ju-shu*) was also eclipsed. Yet, as Yü Ying-shih and others have pointed out, the Confucian form of life at the societal level not only continued but also flourished. The emergence of lineage organizations, clan cooperatives, and family rules in this period, all defined in Confucian terms, clearly indicates that, despite the disintegration of the Confucian polity, Confucian norms played an important role in society.[21]

Even during the Sui (581–618) and T'ang (618–907) dynasties, when Buddhism was the predominant spiritual force in Chinese society, Confucian classics, history, and ritual studies developed further. The completion of the commentaries and subcommentaries of the Thirteen Classics, the compilation of the T'ang codes, the composition of great works in historiography and in institutional history, and the elaborate effort to analyze Confucian rituals signify the high level of T'ang scholarship in Confucian studies.[22]

What we see from Mencius to Han Yü, then, is a broadening of the Confucian project to include political and social practices in its overall concern. Ironically, it was the Confucian institutionalization of polity and the Confucian ritualization of society that enabled Han Yü to make his lamentation that the true message of Confucian humanism had been lost for more than a thousand years. What Han Yü and the defenders of the Confucian Tao wanted was not the minimum survival of Confucian ethics, but the maximum expression of Confucian truth; they wanted the most authentic manifestation of the Confucian way of life. This quest for a holistic vision grounded in Confucian spirituality led to a redefinition of the Confucian project. The defenders of the Confucian Tao were no longer satisfied with Confucianism as a political ideology and a social norm. They wanted to make the teachings of the sages the center of their form of life. To be sure, they were deeply concerned about politics and society, but they took Confucian self-realization as their ultimate concern. A new priority was clearly set: political and social practicality had to radiate from self-cultivation. The classical Confucian ideal, "inner sageliness and outer kingliness,"[23] became a defining characteristic of their rediscovered "learning of nature and destiny" (*hsing-ming chih hsüeh*).

Undoubtedly, without the rise of Buddhism in China and the Chinese transformation of Buddhism,[24] the second epoch of Confucian humanism could not have come about. Despite the broadening of the Confucian project, the Chinese intellectual scene from the third to the tenth century was dominated by the introduction, growth, maturation, and transformation of Buddhism.[25] Viewed from a comparative perspective, it is one of the most significant chapters of intercultural communication in human history. The scope, depth, and lasting effect of the Indian influence on China represent a phenomenon laden with far-reaching implications.[26] It signifies, for one, the universality of the Buddhist message and the receptivity of the Chinese mind.

The emergence of Neo-Confucian thought as a conscious response to the challenge of Buddhism has often been portrayed as a departure from the cosmopolitan spirit of the T'ang. The rise of narrowly defined official orthodoxy may give the impression that Neo-Confucianism as a political ideology was inextricably linked with a form of xenophobic culturalism. The history of China from Sung to Ch'ing is a story of conquest dynasties. Neo-Confucianism, with its emphasis on legitimacy in historiography and authenticity in culture, aroused interest in ethnicity and proto-national sentiments. However, it is ill-advised to associate Neo-Confucianism with exclusivistic Chineseness, let alone with a particular Chinese dynasty, be it Sung or Ming (1368–1644). The historical record speaks for itself. As the story of Neo-Confucianism unfolds, we see that the term is a generic one covering not only Sung–Ming Confucianism but Chin (Jurchin, 1115–1234) Confucianism, Yüan (1271–1368) Confucianism, and Ch'ing Confucianism. By stretching the term, we may also include Yi Dynasty (1392–1910) Confucianism in Korea, Tokugawa (1600–1867) Confucianism in Japan, and Later Le Dynasty (1428–1789) Confucianism in Vietnam. As our awareness of the complexity sharpens, we may even find the term "Neo-Confucianism" misleading.

A distinctive feature of the second epoch of Confucian humanism is the spread of Confucianism to Korea, Japan, and Vietnam. As Shimada Kenji implies, it is parochial to describe Confucianism as Chinese; it is Korean, Japanese, and Vietnamese as well.[27] To be sure, Confucianism has never extended beyond East Asia. Unlike Buddhism, Christianity, Judaism, or Islam, Confucianism is not a world religion. It has not yet transcended the linguistic boundary. Even though Confucian classics are now available in English translation, the Confucian message still seems inextricably entwined with written Chinese. However, it is at least conceivable that, if there is an authentic possibility for the development of a third epoch of Confucian humanism, its message will be communicable in languages other than Chinese.

Levenson's analogy of the relationship between vocabulary and language is particularly pertinent in this connection.[28] The revival of Confucianism in the tenth century ushered in a new epistemic era partly because it created a new language, indeed, a new grammar of action. The Sung Confucians absorbed much from Taoism and Buddhism. Their vocabulary of self-cultivation was greatly enriched by Taoist and Buddhist ideas. A strong and yet open sense of identity enabled them to take advantage of symbolic resources in other ethico-religious traditions without losing the main thrust of their own spiritual direction. Since they advocated an all-inclusive human way which neither denies nor belittles nature and heaven, they tried to incorporate a wide range of experience as a constitutive part of their ultimate concern. They firmly believed that their thought engaged reality and characterized what they taught as "real learning" (shih-hsüeh).[29] To them, "nature and destiny," "body and mind" (shen-hsin), and "principle and vital force" (li-ch'i) were all real. The moral metaphysics[30] that they constructed as a collective enterprise provided the final justification for their teaching. Prior to the impact of the West, East Asian polity, society, and, to a great extent, psychology were shaped by Confucian values. The language and, indeed, the grammar of action of the East Asian people was distinctively Confucian.

Modern Transformation

Since the mid-nineteenth century, Confucian China has undergone unprecedented transformation. The Opium War of the 1840s and the Taiping Rebellion of the 1850s signaled a perpetual pattern of "domestic trouble and foreign invasion" in modern Chinese history. The abortive Self-Strengthening Movement which followed was symptomatic of the impotence of the Chinese leadership in dealing with Western aggression. The encroachment of the Western powers from the coast to the interior and the total collapse of the Chinese defense occurred in one generation. By the time of the Reform Movement in 1898, Wei Yüan's (1794–1857) recommendation, "learn their superior technology in order to control them,"[31] made more than half a century previously, had been tried, it was thought, and had failed. The T'ung-chih Restoration (1862–1874), depicted by Mary Wright as the last stand of Chinese conservatism, did not yield sufficiently fruitful results to turn the tide.[32] K'ang Yu-wei's (1858–1927) radical attempt in 1898 to reform all the institutions, military, economic, political, and educational, lasted for only one hundred days. His vision for the Age of the Great Unity was truly utopian, for it was "nowhere" and, for all practical purposes, irrelevant.[33]

Liang Ch'i-ch'ao (1873–1929), K'ang Yu-wei's disciple, described his teacher's "New Text" interpretations of the Confucian tradition as "a cyclone, a mighty volcanic eruption, and a huge earthquake."[34] The furor that K'ang created among conservative scholars marked an important change in Confucian rhetoric. We may not accept Liang's glorification of K'ang Yu-wei as the Confucian Martin Luther, but K'ang was revolutionary in his action as well as in his vision. K'ang's speculations about the ideal state significantly changed Confucian discourse. If Confucius was a reformer in K'ang's sense, Confucianism was not only a reformist ideology but also a comprehensive utopia. For K'ang, Confucianism had little to do with differentiation and hierarchy. It was universalism through and through. In order to modernize Confucianism, K'ang felt free to draw inspiration from many sources—Taoist, Buddhist, Christian, social Darwinian, and scientific sources, as well as common sense. His eclecticism supplied a significant new context for Confucian scholarship. His deliberate attempt to undermine the scholasticism of the Ch'ien–Chia (1736–1820) period aroused much resentment among the "Old Text" scholars, notably Chang Ping-lin (T'ai-yen, 1868–1936). Thanks to K'ang's unrestrained imagination, the shape of the Confucian tradition became indeterminate and thus susceptible to a wide range of interpretations.[35] As the Confucian repertoire expanded, however, its core curriculum became problematic.

This becomes apparent in the case of Liang Ch'i-ch'ao. Levenson defines Liang's intellectual predicament as one of being emotionally attached to Chinese history and intellectually committed to Western values.[36] This is a controversial judgment. As Benjamin Schwartz's subtle analysis of Yen Fu (1854–1921) shows, the dichotomy of China and the West, or the dichotomy of history and value, is too simplistic a scheme to account for how an intellectual mind like Liang Ch'i-ch'ao's actually works. Often the truth lies somewhere in between. Its elusiveness can only be overcome through nuanced investigation.[37] Nevertheless, Liang's seemingly unlimited selection of sources may well have been a reflection of his inability to find a niche in which to build his intellectual enterprise. This sense of spiritual homelessness must have been acutely felt by the sensitive minds of his generation.

The concerted effort to criticize Confucianism by some of the most influential intellectuals during the May Fourth period (1917–1921) was on the surface the result of an existential choice by progressive Chinese youth to make a clear break with China's feudal past: familialism, authoritarianism, antiquarianism, passivity, submission, and stagnation were their targets. However, underlying an elated sense of liberation was an extremely persistent and destructive cynicism. The slogan "wholesale westernization" was probably embraced by only a small minority of the iconoclasts, but it was symptomatic of a widespread attitude. The demand for radical change was so overwhelming and the inability of the political structure to make any adjustment so obvious that the level of frustration among concerned intellectuals became unbearable. The situation was not at all conducive to quiet reflection and deep thinking. The tendency toward action was so strong that the very act of writing was transformed into a weapon for effecting concrete changes in society. Escapism became rampant merely as a reaction to this collective impulse to be *engagé*. The political question dominated the intellectual scene.[38] When Wei Yüan offered his advice on how to deal with urgent matters on the coast in the 1840s, the issue of cultural identity was not even raised. Chang Chih-tung's wishful thinking in the 1890s was at least a compromise between identity and adaptation. The May Fourth Westernizers accepted the survival of the Chinese race and nation as the supreme goal; for them, cultural identity consisted of its instrumental value in helping China to adapt to a new order defined in Western terms.

Ironically, at the time that Chinese youth, especially students, demonstrated great patriotism and nationalism, Confucianism was thoroughly criticized as a defining characteristic of Chineseness. What had made China, and indeed East Asia, a society of ritual and music was now blamed as the cause of backwardness in the Chinese economy, polity, society, and culture. Hu Shih was not being entirely serious when he ridiculed the Chinese cultural essence as foot-binding and opium-smoking.[39] Lu Hsün, however, was absolutely serious in his scathing attack on "Confucius and Sons."[40] Ch'en Tu-hsiu's (1879–1942) short-lived magazine *New Youth* was not particularly informative in its promulgation of science and democracy, but its devastating comments on Confucianism were most effective.[41] Mao Tse-tung's depiction of the "three bonds" (*san-kang*) as the authoritarianism of the ruler, the father, and the husband was in perfect accord with the May Fourth appraisal of the Confucian heritage.[42]

The writers of *New Youth* believed that the introduction of Western ideas to China was predicated on a fundamental turnabout of Chinese attitudes toward Western currents of thought, and that the rejection of the Confucian mode of thinking was a precondition for China's modernization. For the brief period when virtually all major intellectual trends in vogue in America and Europe found a sympathetic audience in China, the sense that China was on the verge of an enlightenment was truly contagious. John Dewey and Bertrand Russell were personally affected by the excitement during their sojourns in China.[43] Liberalism, pragmatism, vitalism, idealism, socialism, anarchism, evolutionism, positivism, and scientism all seemed to have a brilliant future in the thirsty mind of the Chinese youth. In retrospect, it seems extraordinary that Marxism-Leninism emerged as the predominant ideological force less than two decades after the founding of the Chinese Communist Party in 1921. Li Ta-chao (1888–1927), the nationalist who saw the Leninist theory of imperialism as a way for China to become independent, was for years a lone voice hailing "The Victory of Bolshevism!"[44]

This description of the May Fourth intellectual ethos may give the impression that the Westernizers failed to make any positive contribution to a fair-minded appraisal of Confucian tradition. This is not the case, for by formulating an all-out attack on Confucius and his followers, the Westernizers rendered it virtually impossible for any reflective literatus to embrace the Confucian heritage uncritically. They forced the small coterie of thinkers who were committed to a living tradition of Confucianism to introduce fresh perspectives on their chosen tradition. Thus the Westernizers of the May Fourth generation paradoxically performed a great service: by their concerted effort to prove the incompatibility between the Confucian value orientation and the spirit of modernization, they helped purify Confucian symbolism.

The most serious damage to the public image of Confucianism did not come from the frontal attack organized by the liberals, anarchists, socialists, and other Westernizers. It came from the extreme right, specifically from the warlords and collaborating traditionalists who used Confucian ethics to stabilize their control. The notorious attempt of Yüan Shih-k'ai (1858–1916) to revive the state cult of Confucius for the purpose of realizing his own imperial ambitions must have provoked much anti-Confucian sentiment among the revolutionaries. Yüan's monarchical fiasco of 1915, as J. K. Fairbank calls it,[45] was most detrimental to the Confucian cause. Those who saw a gleam of a Confucian revival in Yüan's monarchical movement were totally disillusioned. Those who were directly involved were shown to have been either fools or knaves. Unfortunately, this corruption of Confucian symbols from within was continued by other warlords for at least another generation. Lu Hsün, for example, was repeatedly surprised by the haunting power of the Confucian ghosts throughout China.[46] The vicious circle of frontal attack and internal corruption made Confucianism either a scapegoat of China's sins or a sinister ideology for beguiling the innocent.

Contemporary Situation

Needless to say, circumstances made it painfully difficult for a conscientious intellectual to philosophize in the true spirit of Confucian humanism. The few Confucian thinkers who managed to do so, not infrequently with originality and brilliance, deserve our particular attention. Methodologically, two sources of inspiration contributed to the revival of creative thinking in the Confucian tradition in the post-May Fourth era. One was the critical spirit of the West. In 1921 Chang Chün-mai (Carsun Chang, 1886–1969), who had accompanied Liang Ch'i-ch'ao to the Paris Peace Conference after World War I, proposed a new way of reexamining the national heritage in the perspective of a philosophy of life.[47] He later devoted himself to the task of forming the Democratic Socialist Party as a way of integrating Western liberal democracy with Confucian socialism.[48] Although his "third force" made little impact on the Chinese political scene, he was a pioneer in using comparative philosophical methods to analyze Neo-Confucian thought.[49] Carsun Chang turned his attention to scholarship in the 1940s, but by then Fung Yu-lan and Ho Lin had reinterpreted the Confucian project in the light of Western philosophy. While Fung reformulated Chu Hsi's system in the light of New Realism, Ho interpreted

Wang Yang-ming's philosophy of mind from the viewpoint of German Idealism.[50]

Another source of inspiration came from Buddhism, specifically from the Yogācāra (or the Consciousness-only) School. The revival of this Buddhist tradition, under the leadership of Ou-yang Ching-wu (1871–1943) and Abbot T'ai-hsü (1889–1947), stimulated a great deal of original thinking among Chinese intellectuals.[51] The analytical method of the Yogācāra, particularly its psychoanalytical technique, helped sensitive minds in China to study human life and the world holistically. Although there is no clear evidence that Liang Shu-ming, Alitto's "last Confucian," directly benefited from the Yogācāra methodology, he was deeply influenced by Buddhism. His *Eastern and Western Cultures and Their Philosophies*, published in 1921, "championed Confucian moral values and aroused the Chinese to a degree seldom seen in the contemporary world,"[52] by comparing the Sinic world view with the Indian view on the one hand, and with the Western on the other. Hsiung Shih-li, who also drew inspiration from Buddhism, received his analytical training in a Buddhist institute under the tutelage of Master Ou-yang. Considered one of the most profound and original thinkers in contemporary China, Hsiung reconstructed Confucian metaphysics on the basis of a penetrating critique of Yogācāra presuppositions.[53]

It has been argued that Hu Shih's pragmatic approach to the vital issues of contemporary China failed partly because of his strong stand against "isms."[54] The triumph of Marxism in filling the ideological vacuum left by "bourgeois" scholars preoccupied with academic pursuits and a problem-solving mentality seemed inevitable. Yet the Chinese Communist movement, significantly shaped by nationalist sentiments, undertook the task of Sinicizing Marxism from the beginning. As a result, Confucianism figures prominently in this supposedly materialist interpretation of Chinese history and society. The shape of Confucian thought in Chinese Marxism is, however, one-sided. Because of its insistence on a simplistic and highly partisan view of history as a struggle between materialism and idealism, it relegates to the background such great architects of the Confucian project as Mencius, Tung Chung-shu (ca. 179–ca. 104 B.C.), Chu Hsi, and Wang Yang-ming. Confucian thinkers with a perceived materialist predilection, such as Hsün-tzu, Wang Ch'ung (27–100?), Chang Tsai, and Wang Fu-chih (1619–1692), receive much attention. Nevertheless, the Confucian question, whether concerned with evaluating the historical role of Confucius or with determining the proper line of cultural inheritance for socialist China, continues to occupy the center stage in intellectual debates.[55] As the Cultural Revolution unfolded, Levenson began to wonder how his earlier thesis that the Confucian heritage had been relegated to a museum of the past could be compatible with the fanfare of anti-Confucian campaigns. He had to accept that, beyond doubt, Confucian symbolism was relevant to contemporary Chinese political culture.[56]

The last thirty years have witnessed a significant development of Confucian humanism in Taiwan and Hong Kong. The New Asia College in Hong Kong, founded on the principle of revitalizing the true spirit of Confucian education, played a key role in coordinating individual efforts to promulgate Confucian learning. Under the leadership of Ch'ien Mu and the aforementioned T'ang Chün-i, the college trained a generation of scholars in the study of various dimensions of Confucian culture. Especially noteworthy in their scholarship is their philosophical focus. Ch'ien and T'ang, later assisted by two intellectual luminaries from Taiwan, Mou Tsung-san and Hsü Fu-kuan, provided the most comprehensive curriculum for the study of Confucian thought in recent memory.[57] Even though the college has been incorporated into the Chinese University of Hong Kong, its position as a center of Confucian studies has remained strong.

The situation in Taiwan is less focused. Since the most prestigious institute of higher learning on the island was dominated in the 1950s and 1960s by refugee scholars from Peking University, the intellectual atmosphere was not congenial to Confucian learning. Mou Tsung-san, first at Taiwan Normal University and later at Tunghai University, and Hsü Fu-kuan at Tunghai University were involved in a lonely struggle to deliver the Confucian message. The situation in the 1970s, however, was considerably different. Fang Tung-mei's (Thomé Fang) impassioned lectures on Chinese philosophy at Taiwan and Fu-jen universities aroused a generation of young scholars to enthusiasm for investigating the spirit of Confucian culture.[58] The surge of interest in Confucian studies in Taiwan in recent years, however, has been complicated by a lack of differentiation between official ideology, which promotes Confucianism as an anti-Communist weapon, and genuine scholarly pursuit. Surely, Confucian learning, by definition, is more than a genuine scholarly pursuit. Yet the distinction between the Confucian intention to moralize politics and the politicization of Confucian values for ideological control is not only meaningful intellectually but also significant politically.

The question of a third epoch of Confucian humanism has been addressed by scholars such as T'ang Chün-i, Hsü Fu-kuan, and Mou Tsung-san. Indeed, their life-long work has been to demonstrate that the authentic possibility not only exists in their own minds and in the minds of those who share their vision but has also been realized in the acts of philosophizing, in the practices of writing, and through the exemplary teachings of numerous like-minded intellectuals around the world. The real challenge to them is how a revived Confucian humanism might answer questions that science and democracy have raised. While these questions are alien to traditional Confucianism, they are absolutely necessary for China today. In a deeper sense, these scholars perceive the challenge to be the formulation of a Confucian approach to the perennial human problems of the world: the creation of a new philosophical anthropology, a common creed, for humanity as a whole. They are fully aware that concern for the survival of the Confucian tradition and for the continuity of traditional Chinese culture must be subsumed under a broader concern for the future of humankind. To them, what is at stake is not the relevance of the popular idea of the Confucian literatus to a functionally differentiated modern society, but a much larger issue, the well-being of humanity as the locus for meaningful existence in our world, present and future.[59]

The Future

There is no way to predict the future direction of Confucian humanism as envisioned by T'ang, Hsü, and Mou. However, given the fruitful indications to date, we can suggest the steps by which such a project can be further developed. If the well-being of humanity is its central concern, Confucian humanism in the third epoch cannot afford to be confined to East Asian cultures. A global perspective is needed to universalize its perennial concerns. Confucians can benefit from dialogue with Jewish, Christian, and Islamic theologians, with Marxists, and with Freudian and post-Freudian psychologists. The conscious attempt to analyze Confucian ideas in terms of Kantian and Hegelian categories, an attempt that has yielded impressive results, will have to be broadened to accommodate new philosophical insights in the twentieth century.

The Confucian response to the West must not weaken its roots in East Asian cultures. Interregional communication among Confucian scholars in Japan, South Korea, Taiwan, Hong Kong and Singapore may lead to a genuine intellectual exchange with scholars in the People's Republic of China. The internal dynamics of China in the post-Cultural Revolutionary era are likely to generate unprecedented creativity in Confucian studies. Confucian scholars in North America and in Europe can take an active role in bringing all these dialogues into a continuing conversation.[60] Such conversation may bring about a communal critical self-consciousness among concerned Confucian intellectuals throughout the world. Original thinking from Confucian roots, the kind that Levenson felt no longer possible, may very well re-emerge to stimulate and inspire productive scholarship. Vitaly Rubin's prophetic insight, in the Levensonian sense, is historically significant.

CHAPTER 2

The Unfolding of Early Confucianism: The Evolution from Confucius to Hsün-tzu

CHO-YUN HSÜ

The ideas of early Confucianism developed against the background of vast social and political changes. In an attempt to comprehend their changing world, successive generations of thinkers evolved and elaborated these ideas in confrontation with intellectual trends both inside and outside the Confucian schools of thought. My primary concern in this essay is to trace the reasons for and the ways in which Confucians shaped a number of key concepts that have remained axiomatic to Confucian thinking about the individual and society. The concepts which I have selected as most significant to this topic are: humanity, or benevolence (*jen*); righteousness (*i*); and ritual, or propriety (*li*).

The Time of Confucius

Confucius lived at a time when the feudal social structure had reached a state of almost complete disintegration. The

23

Chou dynasty's hierarchical order of power distribution and division of territory among men who were related by kinship ties and a common code of aristocratic conduct had gradually broken down after two centuries of continuous internecine struggle. But by Confucius' time wars between the states had become less frequent. During the years 552–543 B.C., the decade of Confucius' birth, there were no significant interstate conflicts for five of the ten years, and there were eighteen years of peace during his lifetime. In comparison, there were only six relatively peaceful years during the entire preceding century, and only thirty-eight during the 259 years covered by the *Tso chuan*.[1] The relative tranquility of Confucius' time indicates that the redistribution of power had been almost completed; the ministers of the various states had taken control of political power, although a new group of intellectual bureaucrats had yet to appear.[2]

In Lu, Confucius' own home state, the duke had become a puppet in the hands of the families of three powerful ministers who had virtually divided Lu into three sub-states. The new power-holders respected Confucius as a learned man and employed his disciples to facilitate consolidation of the new post-feudal sociopolitical structure. They did this despite Confucius' support of the old order and his preference for stability over struggle and unrest.

Confucius did not want to reestablish feudalism per se, but he was interested in restoring its values, in particular civility and propriety (*wen* and *li*), which he believed necessary to the maintenance of a stable society. In a sense he infused these values—part of the old aristocratic code—with new meaning by claiming a moral basis for them. I have argued elsewhere[3] that the first breakthrough in the creation of Chinese civilization came with the notion of a moral god, at the beginning of the Chou dynasty, and that this affirmation of morality led to the development of humanism and rationalism. Thus while archeological excavations from Shang dynasty sites still reveal the practice of human sacrifice, there are no examples of human sacrifice from Chou sites. Some form of humanity must have arisen even prior to the time of Confucius, and the humanity that he espoused was related to these incipient notions of morality. The goal of Confucius' teachings was not social reform; rather, his efforts were directed toward transforming society by attempting to improve the individual human being.

Confucius believed that the aristocratic code had universal validity when applied to civilized behavior and to the common humanity that he thought existed in human nature. He developed humanity (*jen*) as a key notion in organizing his whole creed with values such as loyalty, sincerity, and propriety. Confucius' definition of the quality of humanity is: "In retirement, to be sedately grave; in the management of business, to be reverently attentive; in intercourse with others, to be strictly sincere."[4] Or, "It is, when you go abroad, to behave to everyone as if you were receiving a great guest; to employ the people as if you were assisting at a great sacrifice; not to do to others as you would not wish done to yourself; to have no murmuring against you in the country and none in the family."[5] Confucius considered every individual potentially capable of becoming a superior man (*chün-tzu*), a moral aristocrat. And he downgraded the importance of status conferred by aristocratic position. Although a person's social status might be low, his confidence in the efficacy of virtuous conduct will lead him to be on equal terms with people of high social status. Virtuous conduct knows no boundaries; it should be honored in China as well as abroad;[6] it should transcend social classes. In short, when Confucius advocated civility (*wen*), he wanted to extend to all people the civility which had been part of the aristocrats' code.

Confucius practiced what he preached, for he gave instruction to everyone who aspired to learn. His curriculum taught human values (ethics and morality) in terms of their appeal to all members of society, regardless of social status, but it emphasized pragmatic knowledge useful to members of the ruling class (e.g., archery, charioteering, knowledge of rituals, and literacy). Although it was within reach of every individual[7] to be a man with the quality of humanity (*jen*), it was nevertheless a virtue that must be attained through self-cultivation. Humanity is not easily attained, and even Confucius was sometimes known to state that one can do no more than aim for it. He once claimed, "The sage and the man of perfect virtue—how dare I rank myself with them?

It may simply be ... that I strive to become such without satiety, and teach others without weariness."[8] The latter sentence refers to Confucius' conviction that he did not innovate, but only transmitted. However, as a transmitter, he in fact transformed contemporary ideas of humanity.[9] He stipulated a perfect personality, the *chün-tzu*, the man of noble mind and noble conduct. And by giving a new meaning to the term *chün-tzu* (which originally referred only to aristocrats) Confucius effectively transformed older, aristocratic notions.[10]

The Time of Confucius' Disciples

Confucius' disciples can be divided into two groups: an older generation and a younger one. Most of the older ones were only a few years junior to Confucius and spent their lives in the employ of various states or aristocratic households. These disciples may have been the ones who spread Confucius' reputation, but they themselves spent little time either in teaching or in intellectual pursuits. The younger group, represented by men like Tseng Tsan, were primarily teachers, and were the ones responsible for elaborating Confucianism. Both groups of disciples lived during the transitional period from the late Spring and Autumn to the early Warring States period. This was a time during which the old feudal order completely disappeared and a new society organized around a consolidated state and a professional bureaucracy emerged, in other words, a time of great social mobility.[11]

The new professional bureaucracy (*shih*) was drawn primarily from the ranks of the lower aristocratic warrior-courtier group. Men from this group put their newly acquired skills and expertise in the service of the rulers of the reorganized states. The social and occupational transformation of the warrior-courtier group into experts in government coincided with their acceptance of Confucius' teaching that knowledge and character are more important than social status.[12] To internalize this new belief, the *shih* had to develop a different kind of self-image and a new sense of self-esteem.

Their model was Yen Hui, Confucius' favorite disciple, who distinguished himself by self-cultivation and by his internalization of Confucian moral values. Although, like Confucius, Yen Hui did not have a prominent political career, we can surmise from the little information available about early Confucians that he, as they, did admire political achievement along with personal integrity.[13] Since the early Confucians tended to become members of the *shih* group, following careers in government service, they emphasized the importance of moral principles in politics.

The intellectual tradition which the early Confucians inherited also emphasized the study of the Classics transmitted from past generations of learned men. The books of *Poetry, Documents, Changes,* and *Rites* all existed before Confucius. They were, I believe, common knowledge among the scribes, archivists, and secretaries whose task it was to preserve ancient traditions at the court and in the palace. But it was the Confucian scholars who abstracted the implications of these ancient works. An example is their discussion of the poem, "The pretty dimples of her artful smile!/The well-defined black and white of her eyes!/The plain ground for the colors." When Tzu-hsia asked about the meaning behind these words, Confucius' reply indicated that ceremonies should be a "subsequent thing,"[14] meaning that decoration and ornament should only be supplementary to a substantial base of real feeling. If the *Doctrine of the Mean* truly reflects the thought of Tzu-ssu, the grandson of Confucius and, it is held by some scholars, a disciple of Tseng Tsan, it may be assumed that early Confucians concerned themselves with the philosophical problem of cultivating sincerity and intelligence.[15] However, their approach remained individualistic, and the linkage between individual and society was still missing.

The exegetical tradition probably became an important part of Confucian teachings in the various schools established by Confucius' disciples. More than one hermeneutic tradition evolved;[16] after Confucius died, the Confucians were divided into at least eight schools, each of which claimed to be true to the master. The main concern of these schools seems to have been either ritual details, such as appropriate dress at a funeral,[17] or the practice of moral conduct, which can be called the internalization of Confucian values.

Mencius and his Time

Mencius (ca. 372–289 B.C.) lived in the middle of the Warring States period, when the prevailing sociopolitical conditions differed drastically from those experienced by the earlier generations of Confucius' disciples. Although the Chou royal house still existed in name, it no longer exercised power or controlled the several states and their rulers. The numerous feudal domains of the earlier period had been reorganized into less than a dozen states, each of which controlled large territories. By this time the parochial mentality often associated with the *gemeinschaft* condition of small, tightly knit communities had disappeared; frequent interaction in war or peace had created a condition of translocalization in anticipation of the creation of a universal state. Mencius himself discussed the unification of the whole world (i.e., the world known to him) under one political order as if it were inevitable.[18] And indeed, in Mencius' lifetime, rulers of at least eight states laid claim to the title of king and some kind of universal sovereignty.[19]

The old aristocrats had been replaced by a ruling group consisting of the rulers with their centralized power, expert professional bureaucrats, and soldiers. That there continued to be social mobility in the upper echelons is evidenced by many of the public figures listed in the historical records who are of obscure origins. According to my statistics, for the whole Spring and Autumn period, 26% had no known antecedents; for the Warring States, the figure was 55%, more than twice as much; and this figure rose to 57% in Mencius' lifetime.[20] We see that the Warring States period was a time of drastic change in the course of which the old social system was totally transformed. As Mencius' time was entirely different from that of Confucius, the intellectuals of Mencius' day were accordingly concerned with finding a new set of values for reestablishing an orderly world. They sought values with wide social implications rather than the simple virtues of good individuals.

During this period intellectuals—Mencius among them—and military men routinely travelled from one state to another seeking opportunities and employment in public life. For years Mencius travelled with an entourage of tens of chariots filled with disciples and followers, visiting the courts of various states, including such important ones as Wei (or Liang) and Ch'i. Such interstate travel inevitably broadened the concern of Mencius' group to include social units larger than their immediate community or kinship group. In this way the problem of kinship ties versus obligation to the state was raised. Here the differences between Mencius and Mo-tzu are instructive.

Vitaly Rubin correctly pointed out that one of the basic differences between Confucians and Mohists was that the former placed kinship ties above obligation to the state. According to Rubin, Mohists thought the state should function as a machine aimed at achieving first the general welfare of its own people and eventually the general welfare of all peoples of the world (*t'ien-hsia*).[21] Indeed Mo-tzu's concept of "general benefit" (*i*), translated by Rubin as "justice," was not concerned with people in a neighborhood, a state, or even the world, but rather with a more general benefit.[22] In the chapter "Heavenly Will" (*T'ien-chih*), Mo-tzu defined this as the concern of Heaven, and Heaven as the origin of *i*.[23] Rulers who were concerned with the general benefit were thought to have achieved *i*, while those who did not were labelled as unfaithful to the principle of *i*. Mo-tzu also stated that rectifying regulations adds to the general benefit (*cheng*), using as an illustration the standard in the hands of the craftsman. The social standard, he indicated, must have an objective base.[24]

Mo-tzu's wide following explains why Mencius spared no effort to argue against Mohism. In fact, he responded to Mo-tzu's arguments so frequently that he modified Confucius' views by discussing humanity (*jen*) and justice, or righteousness (*i*) in combination, although in the *Analects* humanity was the central virtue and righteousness was discussed only occasionally. Mencius emphasized that humanity was the innate virtue of men; he argued that no person could bear to see others suffer, and that the feeling of commiseration or compassion was the beginning of the principle of humanity.[25] According to Mencius, righteousness and other related virtues were closely associated with humanity. Therefore, after arguing for the innate existence of humanity, he simply related it to other virtues in human nature.

Mencius repeatedly posited that the principle of righteousness (*i*) was opposed to that of profit (*li;* not to be confused with a different *li*, propriety). And he understood *li* to mean private profit whereas he interpreted *i* as righteous benefit to the public.[26] The debate between Mencius and Mo-tzu as to whether righteousness was external to human nature or was an inner attribute can perhaps be traced to the concept *i* having, at an earlier time, signified some type of public benefit and social justice. In Mo-tzu's interpretation, since the origin of righteousness was the will of Heaven, it was external. Mencius asserted that righteousness should also be "internal," that is, it was innate in human nature. Although this assertion was based on the assumption that righteousness existed in all human beings, Mencius also believed in yielding to one's senior in situations where righteousness played a role.[27] Thus, righteousness was a part of the social order and was to be applied whenever differences of obligation were involved.

Mencius defined *i* explicitly on two occasions: (1) "How to take what one has not a right to is contrary to righteousness,"[28] and (2) "if [one] can give full development to the feeling which refuses to break through, or jump over a wall [that is, commit a robbery], his righteousness will be more than can be called into practice."[29] I would like to suggest that Mencius defined righteousness to mean "the concern to take part in a social order by sharing [a common benefit] with others." He considered righteousness both as innate and as an external social standard.

Although Mencius hesitated to delimit righteousness as being solely innate, he was responsible for opening a new dimension in Confucianism. For, according to Confucius, since humanity (*jen*) consists of the utmost self-assertion, sincerity (*chung*), and forgiveness or sympathy (*shu*), it was a complex of virtues that was concerned with relationships between (normally two) individuals. For Mencius, however, righteousness was a complex of virtues that was concerned with relationships between the one and the many and between an individual and his group, that is, between the individual and his social environment. Therefore, to Mencius righteousness was also an external, social standard, one which is used to rectify individual conduct, for the group and the social environment into which an individual is born have prior existence.

Under Mencius, the concept of *i* underwent three important developments: by defining righteousness as one of the four innate virtues, Mencius raised it to the level of humanity; by defining righteousness as a social standard, he stipulated that it is both external and innate; and by considering righteousness as external, he incorporated into Confucianism, despite his vigorous rejection of Mohist ideas, the Mohist concern for the general public good. It was no doubt Mencius' acceptance of the Mohist idea of benefiting society which led him to constantly preach the importance of the people's livelihood, and thence to advocate that the people should be allotted a fair share of available resources.[30]

In developing the notion of righteousness, both Mo-tzu and Mencius were responding to the demands of their time, which they viewed in terms of regulating the behavior of individuals within their social context. In the Warring States period, society was in the process of being reshaped from the ruins of the localized feudal community into a new translocal society in which the divisions as well as the stratification had yet to be decided. Mencius believed that simple principles, such as Confucius' humanity, which governed relationships between individuals should be replaced with more stringent regulations. Inscriptions on a set of bronze bells from ca. 310 B.C. recently excavated in Hopei province, site of the ancient state of Chung-shan, include seven appearances of *i*, all of them rendered by its homonym, meaning proper or appropriate.[31] The fact that *i* could be rendered to mean proper or appropriate indicates that during the time of Mencius, the term was related to standards used in regulating the place and share that an individual was allotted in society. Thus, the two definitions of *i* by Mencius cited above probably reflect his appreciation of such a standard and his effort to incorporate it into Confucianism. Mencius explained, more explicitly than can be found in the *Analects*, that the values he discussed were universally contained in human nature, regardless of birth or social background. His teaching that human nature is good was the logical outcome of this concept. To illustrate this idea, he pointed out that everyone was potentially a sage as long as he was willing to exert himself in the effort to attain such a level of accomplishment.[32]

Mencius enlarged the Confucian code of virtues regarding relationships between individuals to include society at large. The new social order which he envisioned was predicated on social virtues developed on the basis of righteousness that, with him, became a universal principle governing the general fairness and well-being of society.

Hsün-tzu and his Time

Hsün-tzu (ca. 298–238 B.C.) lived in the generation after Mencius, during which the struggle for supremacy among the seven major Chinese states neared its conclusion. Efforts at political reform, which took place in practically all the states, resulted in the increasing centralization of power and the development of bureaucratic government. A model in miniature of the later imperial bureaucracy gradually emerged in each of the states, although with varying degrees of success.[33]

As the conflict among them drew to an end, Ch'in, the state which had hired the most foreigners to serve in its court, appeared to be the most likely winner. Under the leadership of Shang Yang (d. 338 B.C.) and a series of capable ministers, the Ch'in government was subjected to such a thorough transformation that it came to be regarded as the most efficient state during the late Warring States period. When Hsün-tzu visited Ch'in, he was favorably impressed, recording his observations in the chapter "Strengthening a State" (*Ch'iang-kuo*):

> Its common people live simply: the sound of their music displays no tendencies toward the licentious. Their dress

is not fanciful. They are greatly in awe of the officials and are obedient. . . . The staffs of officials are decorous and respectful: there are none among them who are not reverential and temperate, earnest and sincere, loyal, trustworthy and not rude. . . . Entering the capital, I have observed the scholars and great officials. . . . They were involved in no private matters; they are not partisan and cabalistic; they do not form cliques or factions. Dignified in manner, none among them are not intelligent and understanding and equitable in their actions. Observing the court [I note that], in the administering and judging of government business, all matters are disposed of readily and quietly, as if there were no governmental business there at all.[34]

Of course, what impressed Hsün-tzu in Ch'in was the product of an authoritarian Legalist theory in action!

Born in Chao, in the former state of Chin, where the most important legalist schools flourished, Hsün-tzu was no doubt aware of the legalist ideals of political rationalism and functionalism. Indeed, Hsün-tzu was well versed in the theories of many contemporary schools of thought: In one chapter of the *Hsün-tzu* he reviewed the tenets of all the major schools,[35] including the naturalism of Taoism and the pragmatism of Mohism. He criticized most of his fellow Confucians, particularly Mencius, and ridiculed the schools of other Confucian disciples as frivolous and formalistic. The challenges from these schools led him to devise a system of Confucian thought very different from that of Mencius.

Hsün-tzu's social theory closely resembles that of Hobbes. He argued that, since individual desires are always greater than the resources available, these resources must be distributed so that every member of society will enjoy an adequate share. In order to do this, it is necessary to establish a social order under a political leadership.[36] Hsün-tzu's views may have been influenced by Mo-tzu's idea that the absence of political leaders leads to chaotic social conditions.[37]

In addition to Mohist social ideas, Hsün-tzu was probably influenced by Taoist naturalism, according to which nature is objective reality, with no will of its own, and the functioning of nature is governed by its own rules. Hsün-tzu too held that nature runs its own course, with no will, and it is up to human beings to harness it to their use. His cosmological notions were similarly rational and naturalistic: he did not consider Heaven a divine power, and he therefore denied the efficacy of worshipping it.[38]

But an impersonal nature could not guarantee the presence of righteousness (*i*), which was Mencius' principle for keeping human society in order as well as Hsün-tzu's principle for safeguarding the orderly sharing and distribution of resources. To meet this problem, Hsün-tzu stipulated the existence of four levels for materials and creatures: (1) water and fire are forces without life; (2) plants are lives without sensual feelings; (3) animals have sensual feelings but no righteousness; (4) only human beings are capable of attaining all these attributes. He went on to say that, although men live in groups in order to overcome their physical limitations, righteousness, which governs the life of the group, causes its members to recognize the necessity of sharing.[39] To Hsün-tzu, therefore, the function of righteousness is almost identical to its function as described by Mencius: righteousness should be the principle for organizing individuals in any social entity, whether primary group, state, or all of human society.

Nonetheless, Hsün-tzu and Mencius did not agree on the nature of righteousness. This disagreement may be defined as the difference between nature and nurture. Aside from its function as a social value, Mencius suggested that righteousness is also innate in all human beings. Indeed, Mencius' optimistic assumption that human nature is good was based on this axiom. Hsün-tzu, however, in essence rejected this hypothesis when he stipulated that since men have desires, peaceful coexistence within society is arbitrary. On the one hand, he affirmed the principle of righteousness, but on the other, he viewed it as an acquired and cultivated virtue.

Since righteousness as an acquired virtue does not suffice to guarantee civilized behavior, Hsün-tzu invoked the principle of rites and ceremonies, or propriety (*li*), as a regulating and rectifying principle. But Hsün-tzu was not concerned with the formality of ritual as practiced in some Confucian schools. Indeed, he sometimes ridiculed scholars of the Tzu-hsia and Tzu-yu schools for paying too much attention to outer trappings. What he was concerned with was broadening the definition of rites and ceremonies to include the institution of the rite and its regulation, as well as deportment during the rite.[40] I would therefore like to suggest that to Hsün-tzu *li* meant "norms and modes of society." For he believed that by establishing norms and adhering to the principle of righteousness,[41] the human tendency toward contending could be rectified.

The differences between Mencius and Hsün-tzu are significant: Mencius, who argued that humanity and righteousness are regulated and rectified by ceremonies and propriety, subscribed to the circumscribed definition of *li*;[42] Hsün-tzu emphasized the interdependence of humanity or love (*jen*), righteousness, and propriety. To Hsün-tzu, human love (*jen*) was sentimental, justice (*i*) was rational, and these two virtues were coherently regulated by means of the principle of propriety (*li*). True love (*jen*) was just love, true justice was manifested through appropriateness, and the function of the principle of propriety linked these together.[43]

Since not everyone was capable of establishing the norms or mode of society, Hsün-tzu assigned this task to the sages. Ancient "sage kings" had, he felt, designed the institutions necessary to regulate social life.[44] Nonetheless, he did not advocate restoring ancient civilization and institutions, stating that there were some things and phenomena which the sage kings could not conceive of, and that there were some cases in which people of one place could not understand those of another place. He therefore urged that the norms and modes of human society be created only by contemporaries, presumably by learned gentlemen of good will who were capable of interpreting their time and place by means of rational deduction.[45] On this point Hsün-tzu departed from both Confucius' and Mencius' ideal, in which a golden age of the past would be somehow projected into the future. Indeed, Hsün-tzu not only warned against rigidly institutionalizing the past, he was equally cautious in praising the authoritarian Legalist regime of Ch'in. Although he did have good words for the state of Ch'in, Hsün-tzu also suggested that it had embarked on a dangerous course. Ch'in, Hsün-tzu argued, evolved a single and complex system of

governmental techniques that required a capable king of
great reputation to operate it. Hsün-tzu feared that such a
king did not exist.[46]

It is commonly assumed that there is a connection between
Hsün-tzu's ideas and Legalist practice. But, in spite of Hsün-
tzu's praise for the Ch'in order, I am led to conclude that
Legalist theory did not have a marked impact on the main
tenets of his thought, which remained thoroughly Confucian.
It is true that Han Fei (d. 233 B.C.), the most important
Legalist, and Li Ssu (ca. 280–208 B.C.), the chancellor of Ch'in
who helped the First Emperor turn China into a Legalist
authoritarian empire, were both students of Hsün-tzu. Nonetheless, in his lifetime, Legalist theory was not highly developed. Earlier Legalists, like Kuan Chung (d. 645 B.C.),
Shang Yang, and Shen Pu-hai (d. 337 B.C.), were practical
men who instituted reforms in government structure and
techniques. They did not bequeath to posterity abstract
notions. At the same time, we cannot dismiss some stone
stele inscriptions attributed to the First Emperor, which read
as if Hsün-tzu's ideas, especially those concerning humanity,
righteousness, and propriety (*jen*, *i*, and *li*), were at last being
put into practice by Legalist institutions. According to the
inscriptions, a world formerly engaged in war had been
unified by a sage king, who created exemplary order; conflict
had ceased because all the people lived safely and well under
the law; a hierarchy between senior and junior and divisions
between occupations were now clearly established.[47] Whether
this was in fact the case must remain an open question.

Conclusion

In this essay I have traced the development of several
Confucian concepts in order to show how attitudes toward
the individual and society gradually evolved. The essence of
Confucian human relations was presented in the *Analects* as
the principle of humanity (*jen*), which is based on the personal
feelings of one individual toward another individual. Confucius
himself did not discuss the relationship between the individual
and the group. This question was taken up by Mencius, who

developed the notion of righteousness and with it explained the relationship between the individual and society. His emphasis on righteousness as a social and individual value must be seen within the context of the deterioration of the old society and his attempt to envision a new society based on new values. Hsün-tzu developed this idea further by dividing the social sanction into two parts, with righteousness as the guiding principle and propriety and rites as the functional aspect. However, the development and elaboration of these Confucian concepts did not take place in isolation. Not only rival Confucian schools, but non-Confucian thinkers as well, challenged accepted assumptions, thereby stimulating Confucians to reexamine and reinterpret their propositions. Both Mencius and Hsün-tzu responded to the challenges of other schools of thought and integrated some of their assumptions into their own systems of thought. Mencius responded to the Mohist challenge to benefit society by incorporating the idea of righteousness into his system. Hsün-tzu's response to Taoist naturalism and Legalist rationalism was to evolve a rationalistic Confucianism. Indeed, the whole process was somewhat dialectical. It may not be mere coincidence that the Han dynasty scholars who catalogued the ancient books commented that the difference between the contending schools resembled the activity of water and fire, for water and fire both mutually overcome each other and cooperate. By the same token, humanity and righteousness are both opposites and complementary.[48]

CHAPTER 3

The K'ung-Family-Masters' Anthology *and Third-century Confucianism*

YOAV ARIEL

The present essay is an attempt to provide some new data concerning Confucianism at the beginning of the third century A.D. by discussing one of the Confucian texts of the period, the *K'ung-ts'ung-tzu* (The K'ung-Family-Masters' Anthology, hereafter *KTT*).[1] A preliminary examination of the *KTT* within the context of Confucianism of the Wei and Chin dynasties (220–420) will, it is hoped, shed new light on the state of Confucianism in the immediate post-Han period, as well as contribute fresh insights into the nature of Chinese philosophical forgeries.

Scholars have frequently expressed views rather doubtful of Wei–Chin Confucianism. They have questioned the genuineness of its philosophical nature and doubted its viability. They have questioned what was called the revival of the Hundred Schools of Philosophy at the beginning of the period and have been reluctant to consider Confucianism a major feature of this "revival." This skepticism does not imply the period has been understood. On the whole, inquiries related to Confucianism in the post-Han period have not been able to overcome the enormous gaps which still exist in present day scholarship.

According to some major Western studies,[2] Confucianism indeed appeared to have reached a low ebb during the period in question. It is argued that orthodox Confucianism, which had dominated Chinese intellectual life for centuries, had lost its prestige.[3] The fall of the Han empire and the failure of Confucianism to cope with the resultant social and political upheavals were accompanied by a revival of various older schools of thought. The long-forgotten theories of the Legalist, Taoist, Mohist and even Sophist schools suddenly seemed relevant to the burning questions of the day. These schools, which had been absorbed into the Confucian synthesis during the Han, now tended to go their own way; by combatting each other's ideas they sought to replace the doctrine that had failed.[4] The Confucian response to this new fragmentation of Chinese philosophy seemed weak. Chi-yun Chen, for example, argued that Confucianism had become apolitical and evasive and had gradually absorbed metaphysical ideas from other schools of thought.[5] This resulted, first, in a new trend of thought, a mixture of Confucianism and Taoism known by the name *hsüan-hsüeh* (Dark Learning), and secondly, in the pursuit of *ch'ing-t'an* (Pure Conversation) by elite Confucians.[6]

The philosophical picture of the Wei-Chin period, as well as the portrait of a declining Confucianism which emerge from these studies, must be evaluated with some caution. Whereas many of the conclusions appear correct, others should be modified or even discarded when additional evidence is considered, especially bibliographical evidence. Table 3.1 below makes use of the bibliographies in three works—the *Hou-Han i-wen-chih* (*HHIWC*) for the Later Han dynasty,[7] the *San-kuo i-wen-chih* (*SKIWC*) for Wei,[8] and the *Pu-Chin-shu i-wen-chih* (*PCSIWC*) for Chin[9]—to give a relatively complete account of the number of titles credited to every school of philosophy from the Later Han to the Chin period. It can therefore be regarded as a concise catalogue of the textual story of Chinese philosophy between the years 25 and

Table 3.1

PCSIWC	SKIWC	HHIWC	
40	34	38	Confucianism (Ju-chia)
45	21	7	Taoism (Tao-chia)
4	7	5	Legalism (Fa-chia)
1	0	0	Mohism (Mo-chia)
1	5	0	School of Names, Logicians (Ming-chia)
41	9	10	Analects (*Lun-yü*)
64	18	35	*The Three Li* (San-li)

420. The table also includes the commentaries written on four major Confucian Classics in these centuries, that is the *Analects* and *The Three Classics of Li* (*san-li*). The figures for the latest period are given first.

Let us now reexamine, in light of this table, the philosophical scene at the beginning of the Wei-Chin era by posing the following questions: Was Confucianism still viable?[10] Was there a Mohist revival?[11] Was the interest in logical problems on the increase?[12] In other words, what was the nature of Chinese philosophy in the Wei-Chin period? The table reveals four significant facts. First, the so-called mini-renaissance of the Hundred Schools may be exaggerated. Second, considering the number of texts produced, Confucianism was not dead but quite alive. Third, no text was ascribed to the followers of Mohism, and Legalism in Wei produced only two more works than it did in the Later Han period. Fourth, the increase in the number of texts in the field of Logic and Taoism indicates that there was a distinct shift in philosophical concerns.

The table has, however, some serious shortcomings which must be noted. Often the connections assumed between title and subject are not definitive, as the dividing line between schools of thought is not always clear. Furthermore, the table makes no reference to the content of the texts, many of which are now lost. Such is the case with the *Chou-tzu hsin-lun*, considered one of the 34 Confucian works of the San-kuo period.[13] It had disappeared before the Sui dynasty, and its contents are practically impossible to know today. The table, following the bibliographies of the official histories, also does not include many texts attributed to antiquity whose actual authors lived in the Wei-Chin era. For example, the *Yin Wen-tzu* was most likely forged in the third century A.D. and no doubt represents the philosophy of a *Ming-chia* (School of Names) scholar of that period.[14] Nonetheless, the text is not included in the *SKIWC* list of the five School of Names' works of the period[15] because it was, until recently, attributed to the pre-Han philosopher Yin Wen-tzu, who was a member of the famous Chi-hsia academy (fl. 360 B.C.) at Lin-tzu. As a result of this and other omissions the figures for the School of Names in the third century A.D. are not altogether reliable.

But these reservations aside, the vigor of Confucian scholarship in this period cannot be doubted. In this environment the *KTT*, a third-century Confucian work, deserves special attention. Listed as a work of the Three Kingdoms period,[16] it is an often aggressively polemical text which attempts to refute the theories of all other non-Confucian schools. The *KTT* may therefore be representative of a type of polemical Confucianism which flourished at the beginning of the Wei-Chin era. In addition the *KTT* is almost certainly a literary forgery by Wang Su (195–256), who was an eminent Confucian personality in his day. Wang Su's purpose in producing a spurious work of this kind may be at least in part adduced from his methodology. As the *KTT* is only one of a considerable number of spurious works in this period, it to some extent mirrors the period's intellectual concerns.

Format and Content of the *KTT*

The *KTT* is about the same length as the *Mencius*. It was first listed in the bibliographical section of the *Sui-shu*[17] under the general category of the Classics (*ching*), in the *Analects* (*Lun-yü*) section, as a work of 7 *chüan* or "books." Its table of contents usually lists 23 titled *p'ien* or "chapters." It is made up of a mosaic of some 200 sections, mainly in the form of anecdotes about or dialogues between members of Confucius' family.

These sections form a sort of anthology that purports to recount the philosophical and political activities of various members of the K'ung family from the end of the Spring and Autumn period in the fifth century B.C. to the middle of the Later Han. It is likely the mosaic form of the text that has caused it to be attributed to no single author; it gives the impression of being a cumulative compilation by the K'ung family over six and a half centuries. The cumulative effort is also reflected in the title, *The K'ung-Family-Masters' Anthology*, or, as it was called in the third century and very often during other periods up to the T'ang, *K'ung-ts'ung*, that is, *The K'ung-Family Anthology*. The *KTT* starts with Confucius and ends with Chi-yen (d. 124), who was Confucius' descendant of the twenty-first degree. Table 3.2 below gives a genealogical table of the 21 generations of the K'ung family based on the *KTT* and other sources. Members of the family of whom the *KTT* says little are marked with one asterisk, while those who play major roles are marked with two asterisks. Members of the family whose existence we learn of from the postscript of *K'ung-tzu chia-yü* (The School Sayings of Confucius), the *Shih-chi*, and the *Han-shu*, but who are not mentioned in the *KTT*, are left unmarked. The table also gives the chapter number in the *KTT* in which the K'ung family member plays a role.

We now turn to a description of the 23 chapters of the *KTT*:

1. **"Chia-yen"** (Words of Praise), in 8 sections. This chapter begins with an introductory dialogue which shows Confucius' role in Chinese history. The Confucius of the opening section is portrayed as the new sage and savior of the declining Chou culture. The chapter also includes several dialogues between Confucius and his disciples and rulers. The subject matter varies, but is mostly concerned with rites, morals, and politics. The chapter ends with a short philosophical discourse by Confucius, in which he labels the nature of the argumen-

Table 3.2

GENERATION	PERSONAL NAME	ADULT NAME	KTT CHAPTER NO.
0 **	Ch'iu (Confucius)	Chung-ni	1–5
1 --	Li	Po-yu	—
2 **	Chi	Tzu-ssu	5–10
3 *	Po	Tzu-Shang	6–7
4 --	Ch'iu	Tzu-chia	—
5 --	K'o	Tzu-chih	—
6 **	Ch'uan	Tzu-kao	12–14
7 **	Wu	Tzu-shun	15–17
8 **	Fu	Tzu-yu	18–21
8 --	—	Tzu-hsiang	22
8 --	—	Tzu-wen	22
9 *	Tsui	Tzu-ch'an	22
10 **	Tsang	—	22
10 *	An-kuo	—	22
11 *	Lin	—	22
12 *	Huang	—	22
12 *	Mou	—	22
13 *	—	Tzu-kuo	22
14 *	—	Tzu-ang	22
15 *	—	Chung-huan	22
16 *	—	Tzu-li	22
17 *	—	Tzu-yuan	22
18 *	—	Tzu-chien	22
19 *	Jen	—	22
19 **	—	Tzu-feng	22
20 **	—	Tzu-ho	23
21 *	—	Chang-yen	23
21 **	—	Chi-yen	23

tation mere verbosity and discusses the values of his own methods with his disciples.

2. **"Lun-shu"** (Discussion of the *Book of Documents*), in 16 sections. The general pattern of the chapter is monotonous: A disciple asks a question concerning a specific extract from the *Book of Documents* (Shu-ching), and Confucius replies, adding references to a number of political and moral issues.

The chapter is therefore a set of comments on various parts of the *Documents*, together with Confucius' views on political and moral issues.

3. **"Chi-i"** (Record of Righteousness), in 10 sections. One of the major themes of this chapter, whose general mode is paradigmatic, is righteousness. Anecdotes about Confucius provide a paradigmatic framework for elucidating such concepts as "righteousness" (*i*) and "virtue" (*te*). It also includes a section on music as a mirror of the performer's state of mind, and a section in which Confucius discusses portions of the *Book of Poetry* (Shih-ching).

4. **"Hsin-lun"** (On Punishment), in 8 sections, discusses some basic tendencies of Chinese political thought by contrasting Confucianism and "harsh" Legalism. Confucius represents the Confucian school, the central principles of which are portrayed in culturally oriented terms. He declares his preference for a moral government which relies on the cultural symbolism of the rites for educating the people. In such a climate, Confucius argues, people gradually become moral agents; following the inspiring example of the virtuous ruler, they are forced to confront their own conscience. Confucius concludes that the concept of "shame" (*ch'ih*) provides the only sanction against immoral behavior. The Legalist school is represented by a general from the state of Wei who extols a government that controls behavior by strict rules and punishments. The chapter also deals with laws, punishments, crime, and the possible methods for hearing and dealing with criminal cases.

5. **"Chi-wen"** (Recorded Questions), in 8 sections. The main purpose of this chapter is to introduce Tzu-ssu and to reaffirm that he received his philosophical education from Confucius; this chapter ends Confucius' part in the anthology. Among topics discussed are rites versus law and the moral responsibility of descendants to keep family heritage alive. Toward the end of the chapter the dialogue form is abandoned, and Confucius uses poetry to express his feelings. The main theme of his poems is his longing for the Tao of the Sage Emperors which, according to him, has been lost forever.

6. **"Tsa-hsün"** (Various Doctrines and the Teachings of the Sage), in 9 sections. In the first section of this chapter Tzu-ssu

argues for the supremacy of the teachings of the sage over all other doctrines. Mencius is introduced as one of the disciples Tzu-ssu trained in philosophy. Among the topics discussed are mourning rites, politics, and the adoption of the Hsia (2183–1752 B.C.?) calendar. The chapter ends with a curious debate between Tzu-ssu and Mencius, in which the former refutes Mencius' belief in the supremacy of *jen* and *i* (benevolence and righteousness) over *li* (profit).

7. **"Chu-Wei"** (Living in Wei), in 9 sections, relates anecdotes from the life of Tzu-ssu in the states of Wei, Ch'i, and Sung. Most of the sections are politically oriented. The dialogues are between Tzu-ssu and his son, Tzu-shang; and Tzu-ssu and Mencius, Yin Wen-tzu, and Ts'eng-tzu. The dialogue with Tzu-shang is a short discourse in which Tzu-ssu puts forward the Taoist notion that the mental state of no-desire is man's greatest aspiration, meaning that the philosopher should express his ideas in an atmosphere of total freedom, and develop commitments in terms of his personal ideals. Tzu-ssu is, however, forced to admit that total freedom can be achieved only by eliminating those aspects of reality that are governed by needs and desires. This chapter also contains two dialogues with Mencius. In the first Tzu-ssu states that sagehood can be attained by ordinary people. The second raises a dilemma which appears repeatedly in the *KTT*: The fullest realization of the philosopher's personal aspirations eventually leads to solitude, but the philosopher who tries to escape solitude by neglecting his own aspirations renders his life meaningless. Tzu-ssu suggests that the philosopher function on two levels: he should never stop developing his individuality, but he should also appeal to the rites as a framework of socio-cultural contact. The last section of this chapter portrays Tzu-ssu in the state of Sung, facing serious difficulties and coping with them in what he regards as "a K'ung-family manner." In this manner he is able to transcend his objective state of affairs and concentrate on the composition of the *Chung-yung* (*Doctrine of the Mean*) in forty-nine chapters.

8. **"Hsün-shou"** (Tours of Inspections). This is a one-section chapter consisting of a relatively long dialogue in which Tzu-ssu explains how the Sage-Kings of ancient times performed their tours of inspection.

9. **"Kung-i"** (A Man Called Kung-i), in 9 sections. Aspects of Confucius' personality, his inner life, decisions, goals, achievements, and the frustrations of the non-conformist philosopher are discussed.

10. **"K'ang-chih"** (Adhering to One's Personal Ideals), in 17 sections. The central theme of this chapter is the importance of criticism for creative government. Tzu-ssu argues, with considerable sophistication, that an uncritical attitude on the part of intellectuals will lead to decadence and corruption. This is the last chapter in which Tzu-ssu takes part, and in it the motif of the hardships and fate of the lonely Confucian philosopher is carried to an extreme. In its last section Tzu-ssu meets Lao Lai-tzu, who raises the issue of Taoist principles of behavior. Lao Lai-tzu suggests that Tzu-ssu model himself after the tongue, which is soft but never wears out, rather than after the teeth, which are hard but perish by being ground down. Tzu-ssu responds that he cannot accept these principles and that he prefers to accept the consequences of his attitude toward life.

11. **"Hsiao Erh-ya"** (The Concise Erh-ya). This chapter, clearly different from the remainder of the text, may be a later interpolation; it contains no discourses, dialogues, or personages. It is a set of lexical comments modeled after the dictionary of the Former Han, *Erh-ya,* one of the Confucian canonical texts.

12. **"Kung-sun Lung"** (The Philosopher Kung-sun Lung), in 3 sections, marks a watershed in the development of the critical mood of the anthology. In the first ten chapters Confucius and Tzu-ssu criticized people, rulers, and officials who advocated or represented types of teachings or actions which the philosophers found unacceptable. From now on, however, the major philosophical confrontation is with non-Confucians. Tzu-kao, Confucius' descendant of the sixth generation, who lived in the Warring States period, plays a central role. He meets Kung-sun Lung twice in public debate and succeeds, at least formally, in demolishing the force of his arguments. Bitterly attacking Kung-sun Lung's doctrine of a "white horse," he rejects the whole philosophical enterprise of the dialectician, considering it irrelevant for the principal truths of life.

13. **"Ju fu"** (The Confucian Robe), in 7 sections, has no

specific theme but deals with several topics including Confucianism, rites, politics, the mutual commitment of scholars, and historical tales and morals.

14. **"Tui Wei-wang"** (Answering the King of Wei), in 5 sections, is the last chapter in which Tzu-kao appears. Mostly concerned with political philosophy, it extols the virtue of nonselfishness as appropriate for both officials and the entire bureaucracy, praises the Confucian, human-oriented approach, and denounces the Legalist approach, which argues for the advantages of brutal punishment.

15. **"Ch'en shih-i"** (Recounting Scholars' Righteousness), in 10 sections. Tzu-kao's son, Tzu-shun, makes his appearance in the anthology. The topics discussed are politics and morals. Tzu-shun refers to his forefather, Confucius, thus reaffirming that the anthology contains a line of thinking perpetuated through the ages by succeeding members of the K'ung family. The most interesting feature of this chapter is its sarcastic criticism of those Taoists who advocate the possibility of achieving immortality by means of special techniques. To Tzu-shun this is absurd and is only noteworthy as a joke.

16. **"Lun shih"** (Discussion of Crucial Conditions), in 9 sections, focuses on political maneuvers in crucial times.

17. **"Chih-chieh"** (Holding Fast to Moral Integrity), in 14 sections, deals mainly with measures of expedience and attitudes of flexibility. The sixth section deals with borrowing titles from canonical books such as the *Ch'un-ch'iu* and using them for contemporary books. Tzu-shun, who makes his exit from the *KTT* in this chapter, justifies the borrowing of titles by arguing that the sages do not have a monopoly over their book titles.

18. **"Chi Mo"** (Criticizing Mo-tzu), in 9 sections. The purpose of this chapter is the refutation of Mo-tzu's ideas or, more accurately, the refutation of Mo-tzu's criticism of Confucius. Each section contains a single quotation from the *Mo-tzu*, which is aggressively criticized by an unidentified Confucian, and its blatant fallacies are revealed. Unlike other chapters of the *KTT*, the Mohist position here is not defended. Most striking is the fact that some of the statements which the *KTT* attributes to the *Mo-tzu* are clearly spurious for they do not appear in the *Mo-tzu* at all. Only in the last section of this

chapter is the identity of the Confucian disclosed: He is Tzu-yu, that is K'ung Fu, Confucius' descendant of the eighth generation, to whom the composition of the *KTT* was traditionally ascribed.

19. **"Tu chih"** (Superlative Mastery), in 6 sections, gives detailed biographical data on K'ung Fu, who is portrayed as a unique individualist motivated by the ambition to protect his family's cultural heritage. The chapter stresses the motif of the nonconformist philosopher and the solitary individual. One section ascribes to K'ung Fu the plan to hide the canonical books from the First Emperor of Ch'in (259–210 B.C.), who wanted to destroy them.

20. **"Wen chün-li"** (Questions about Military Rites), in 1 section. The sole subject of this chapter is military rites in warfare.

21. **"Ta wen"** (Answering Questions), in 5 sections, the last chapter of the *KTT* proper, deals largely with politics. The opening section attacks Han Fei-tzu and the book that bears his name. Nevertheless the promise of a resounding clash between Confucianism and Legalism ends in a minor argument in which the inaccuracies in Han Fei-tzu's book are said to disqualify him as a philosopher of Confucius' caliber. The last section of the chapter describes K'ung Fu's death: he gathers his disciples around him, delivers his spiritual testament, and names a successor.

22. **"Lien-ts'ung-tzu shang"** (Appendix to the *Masters' Anthology*, Part A), in 11 sections. This chapter and the next were sometimes taken to be later interpolations. However, although their headings might indeed suggest a later supplement, their structure, nature, and content indicate that they are part of the original text. The chapter starts with a genealogy of the K'ung family and continues with brief references to no fewer than 14 family members in the Former Han period. The main figure of this chapter is K'ung Tsang, whose letters and poems make up almost its entire first half. Among the letters is one from K'ung Tsang to his cousin, K'ung An-kuo, in which he violently attacks the "Vulgar Confucians," that is, the *Chin-wen* (Modern Texts) scholars. The end of the chapter focuses on the activities of Tzu-feng, Confucius' descendant of the nineteenth generation, about

whom it is stated that he dismissed the writings of the various philosophers and devoted himself to the study of the classical heritage; his preface to the *Tso chuan i-chieh* is included. The chapter also contains anecdotes dealing with politics, morals, and rites.

23. **"Lien-ts'ung-tzu hsia"** (Appendix to the *Masters' Anthology*, Part B), in 10 sections. This last chapter of the *KTT* contains many anecdotes describing the K'ung family in the Later Han period. It has two central figures, Tzu-ho and Chi-yen, and makes a final survey of the major activities of the K'ung family throughout the ages. It also emphasizes the merits of classical learning and denounces the study of the works of the non-Confucian philosophers. The last line of the text records the death of Chi-yen, Confucius' descendant of the twenty-first generation, in A.D. 124.

Several prominent features as well as a coherent basic structure can be discerned in this chapter-by-chapter description of the *KTT*. It is a family chronicle of the K'ung family from the year 500 B.C. to A.D. 124, and is subdivided into three major parts. The first part, chapters 1–10, deal with the activities of Confucius and his grandson Tzu-ssu prior to the development of the Hundred Schools. The second part, chapters 12–21, takes place in the Warring States period. Tzu-kao (sixth generation), Tzu-shun (seventh generation), and Tzu-yu (K'ung Fu, eighth generation) play central roles. The third part of the text, the last two chapters of the *KTT*, narrate the story of the K'ung family during the first three hundred years of the Han period. This part focuses on the activities of K'ung Tsang (tenth generation), Tzu-feng (nineteenth generation), Tzu-ho (twentieth generation), and Chi-yen (twenty-first generation). The *KTT* discusses numerous topics and subjects, of which the following appear most frequently: politics, or political criticism; the moral character of rulers and officials; administrative corruption; methods of governing the people; essential steps in diplomacy; rites such as mourning rites, rites of warfare, and rites obtaining in personal relations between people of various ranks and classes. The *KTT* also includes historical anecdotes, and discussions of penology, music, education, tactics of warfare, economics, and the Confucian classics. The central

motif of the work and its major subject, however, is the
supreme excellence of the K'ung family's world view, ideals,
and values, as compared with the ideals and values of their
rivals and opponents. Following is a list summarizing several
of the *KTT*'s targets of philosophical criticism:

1. The method of ruling the people by means of
   punishment

2. The method of countering philosophical problems
   with sophisticated arguments

3. Heterodox teachings (*tsa-shuo*)

4. Taoists who teach immortality

5. The method that advocates the supremacy of
   administrative techniques (*shu*)

6. Vulgar Confucians—the Modern Texts scholars

7. Students of non-Confucian texts.

8. Non-Confucian philosophers (*chu-tzu*)

9. Kung-sun Lung

10. Han Fei-tzu

11. Mo-tzu

Some Scholarly Evaluations of the *KTT*

In spite of its obvious importance, the *KTT* text has not
fared well in Chinese intellectual history. Reactions to it have
varied for the past thousand years. Although the bibliographical section of the *Sui-shu* attributed the text to K'ung Fu,[18]
Confucius' descendant of the eighth generation, after the rise
of textual criticism in the Sung dynasty, the *KTT* was often
considered a late forgery and therefore of no value. Chu Hsi
(1130–1200), for example, described the *KTT* as an inferior
Later Han forgery,[19] and Hung Mai (1124–1202) labeled it "a
ridiculous fabrication composed in the fourth century A.D.
by people who had nothing better to do."[20] Yet during the

same period, Sung Hsien wrote the first commentary to the text (preface dated 1058) in which he stated that the *KTT* was a genuine anthology of the K'ung family.[21] Despite an occasional author like Sung Hsien, in most cases the *KTT* received only cursory treatment. Many commentators neglected it altogether, and those who discussed its contents wrote notes that were too brief to stimulate readers' interest. From the seventeenth century on, attitudes toward the text underwent a slight change. Tsang Lin (1650–1713) pointed out that there were striking similarities between the *KTT*, the *School Sayings of Confucius*, and other forged works which bear the imprint of Wang Su.[22] In 1720 Chiang Chao-hsi reedited the *KTT*,[23] arguing that it was a true embodiment of the heritage of the K'ung family. And in 1795 the Japanese scholar Tsukada Tora wrote an elaborate commentary to the text in which he accused Chu Hsi of doing injustice to an authentic and insightful work of the K'ung family.[24] But still one would hardly call the *KTT* one of the famous texts. It is barely mentioned by Western scholars,[25] and its title is sometimes erroneously rendered.[26] Obviously, the *KTT* is not a part of the mainstream of Chinese philosophy as it is established in major compilations of Chinese philosophy. And until recently scholars both in China and in the West have dealt only with selections of Chinese philosophical literature, that is, with the selections dictated by traditional Chinese scholarship. And as long as Chinese traditional scholarship denied the text a place in Chinese philosophy, it was hard to justify calling the *KTT* a notable text. Indeed why should a scholar of Chu Hsi's caliber devote himself to the mastery of a text that is most probably a fabricated anthology of the K'ung family?[27]

Problems of Authorship

Without question, the text contains absurdities that a traditional scholar could not have tolerated. The philosophical conversations between Confucius, Tzu-ssu, and Mencius are a good example: How could Tzu-ssu engage in conversation with both his grandfather Confucius and his disciple Mencius when Mencius was born at least a hundred years after the death of Confucius? Anachronisms are the rock on which counterfeit works run most risk of shipwreck, and it was on that rock that the value of the *KTT* was historically belittled. Nevertheless, twentieth-century scholarship can make new and exciting use of a text such as the *KTT* precisely because it is a forgery.

First, we should be reminded that the practice of writing under a distinguished name is universal and that the forged literature of the world makes a spectacular library. Moreover, spurious literature flourishes in times of great political upheaval, as forgers attempt to change somehow the course of events. Thus, it is not surprising to find that large numbers of spurious works flooded China from the Later Han to the Sui period. But these have not yet been studied seriously, and their dating, authorship, and the forgers' motives are but little understood.

Second, the study of the *KTT* as a forgery is especially interesting because it is unlike other forgeries. The *Yin Wen-tzu*, the *Teng Hsi-tzu*, or the *Ho Kuan-tzu* are attributed to famous individuals and cover a limited period of time. In contrast, the *KTT* deals with many personages, and its historical period spans 650 years. The work pretends to have resulted from the combined efforts of many individuals lasting for twenty-one generations. Surely the third-century author's attempt at recapitulating, transmitting, and interpreting the development of Confucian thought is of major significance in the post-Han intellectual setting.

Third, and perhaps most interesting with regard to the *KTT* as a forgery, is that the work allows us a glimpse into the third-century intellectual milieu and into the mind of the forger. The fact that the author consciously chose to conceal his identity, thus denying all signs of his personal identity to history, might cause us to wonder about his notions of individuality, creativity, and uniqueness.

Chang Hsin-ch'eng's masterful *Wei shu t'ung-k'ao*, which deals with literary forgers, is of help on this last point. Following a monumental description of literary forgeries, Chang constructs a twelve-item list of motives of literary forgers. I summarize them as follows:

1. Books were forged for the sake of honor, fame, or profit attainable only by writing under the name of a celebrated figure or the title of a famous, lost book;

2. Authors preferred to conceal their identity and to manipulate the reputation of distinguished ancient figures in order to change the course of events;

3. The making of a forgery was sometimes the outcome of an insecure person who dared not risk criticism;

4. The production of forgeries is, in some cases, only an intellectual game.[28]

The *KTT*'s author, too, has expressed views on the subject of forgery. According to him, the concealment of authorship actually serves a higher purpose. Following are two passages from the *KTT*.

> Duke Mu said to Tzu-ssu, "There are some people who suspect that Confucius' words which are recorded in your book are actually your own words." Tzu-ssu answered, "What I recorded in my book are my ancestor's words. Some of them I heard myself and some I heard from others. Though my book contains words that I heard from others and therefore cannot be regarded as the precise words of my ancestor, it still seems that my book does not miss [my ancestor's] line of thought. Now tell me, what more there is in my book that has led you to cast doubt on it?" The duke said, "In fact there is nothing wrong with the book." Tzu-ssu said, "There is nothing wrong with my book because it really consists of my ancestor's line of thought. Assuming that what you previously claimed was true, and that the words in my book are actually my own words, and if, as well, there was nothing to be criticized in them, they would also be appropriate to serve as a standard and to be honored. Nevertheless, this is not the case here [and the words of my book are my ancestor's words], so what is the point in casting doubts on them?"

Yu Ch'ing wrote a book and entitled it *Ch'un-ch'iu*. Ch'i [the premier of Wei] said to him, "Don't! *Ch'un-ch'iu* was the name given by Confucius, the sage, to a classic book. Now your book mainly consists of discussions, and that is all. Why did you choose that very name?" Yu Ch'ing answered, "The term 'classic' refers to anything the relevance of which is lasting. If a book has a lasting relevance, it becomes a classic. Moreover, the fact that a book was not written by Confucius does not mean it cannot become a classic, does it?" Ch'i brought the question to Tzu-shun. Tzu-shun said, "There is no harm in doing so. The records of the state of Lu are named *Ch'un-ch'iu*, hence the title of this classic. The book of Yen-tzu was also entitled *Ch'un-ch'iu*. I have heard that there were seventy-two rulers who officiated at the ceremony of worshiping Heaven and Earth on top of Mount T'ai, but of the seventy-two, fewer than ten remained celebrated. This is called the situation in which the honorable and the lowly do not object to being classified under the same name."[29]

The idea expressed in these two passages is this: One should not be concerned with the external framework of a book for the true value of a book is conveyed by its ideas. In the first passage Tzu-ssu in effect says that he would justify the attribution of words to Confucius, even though Confucius might have never said them, provided that the attributed words convey Confucius' line of thought. In the second passage an equally radical statement is made: The sages do not have a monopoly over their books' titles, nor should they be considered the only ones capable of producing everlasting masterpieces. Viewed in the light of these statements, the author of the *KTT* is not really a forger attempting to deceive. On the contrary, he now becomes the sage, a K'ung family member, who can shape and transmit the heritage of his adopted family. The forger of the *KTT* is therefore something of a rebel who by attempting to master his cultural heritage, also assumes the responsibility of transmitting and interpreting it. In his anthology the historical figures of the K'ung family become philosophical treasures, to be drawn on as a source or added to in the course of history.

The *KTT* is, hence, not merely a spurious work, and its author not simply a forger. The evidence indicates that the work was produced by Wang Su, a major Confucian scholar of his age whom Kramers describes as "the general of forgers."[30] Wang Su's philosophy has not yet been the subject of a comprehensive study. Although he was the author of more than thirty philosophical works, most of these are not mentioned by others.[31] Kramers' distinguished study of the *School Sayings of Confucius* contains a translation of the *San-kuo chih* (Three Kingdoms Chronicle) biography of Wang Su and a discussion of his intellectual activities in connection with his debate about the Classics with the followers of Cheng Hsüan (127–200).[32] But Kramers' work is mainly concerned with the *School Sayings of Confucius* and translates only its first two *chüan*. Clearly any assessment of third-century Confucianism must begin with a reevaluation of both Wang Su as a Confucian philosopher and the *KTT* as a so-called spurious literary and philosophical work.

Conclusion

I have already pointed out the extent to which the *KTT* has been neglected by traditional Chinese scholarship. No doubt the continued study of Wei–Chin Confucianism and of Wang Su's contribution will provide a deeper understanding of why the *KTT* text never became part of mainstream Confucianism. My study of the text so far leads me to conclude that the *KTT* represents a polemical tradition within Confucianism that was either overlooked or ignored by later Confucians.

Scholars are generally agreed on the escapist nature of third-century Confucianism and on the fact that it absorbed alien elements from other, newly revived schools of thought. Confucianism was, so runs the consensus, on the whole moribund. However, a survey of then-existing texts (Table 3.1) has introduced us to a rather different picture. Furthermore, after considering the structure and contents of this lively Confucian text, the generally held view of third-century Confucianism might have to be drastically modified.

The Confucianism of the *KTT* is decidedly aggressive. The author of the text regards the Way (*Tao*) of Confucianism as an inexhaustible mine of eternal truths, while, at the same time, he bitterly attacks almost every other school of ancient Chinese thought. He attacks Legalism as a political method which propagates reliance on punishment and he castigates Han Fei-tzu as a second-rate philosopher. He denigrates immortality and jokes about its aspirations. He labels Kung-sun Lung "a petty sophist," and refers to the students of the "Modern Texts School" as vulgar Confucians. He even launches an attack on Mo-tzu, whose views were hardly current at the time. The K'ung family members in his anthology invariably silence their opponents, or force them to admit failure; on occasion the K'ung family members resort to decisive (though certainly not always convincing) counterarguments. In short, the *KTT* appears to perpetuate a polemical and "authentic" type of third-century Confucianism that has not been sufficiently noted until now. The author's purpose in writing the *KTT* is to answer contemporary critics of Confucianism. Toward this end, he uses a pseudoepigraphic framework, consisting of reconstructed debates between members of the K'ung family and other philosophers. The following passage illustrates his method:

> Meng K'o [Mencius] asked what ought first to be done in leading the people. "First, to profit them," answered Tzu-ssu. Meng K'o said, "What is the point of mentioning the word 'profit' when all that matters in the teaching of the *chün-tzu* is benevolence and righteousness and that is all." Tzu-ssu said, "Benevolence and righteousness are certainly the means by which one profits the people. If superiors are not benevolent, then inferiors will not get a proper place. If superiors are not righteous, then inferiors will enthusiastically cause disorder. These are instances of a great loss of profit. Therefore *The Book of Changes* says, 'Profit is the

harmony of righteousness;'[33] and again it says, 'Function profitably and calm the self in order to exalt virtue.'[34] These are all instances of great profit."[35]

This well-known passage is a reversal of the argument in the opening section in *Mencius*,[36] where Mencius forced King Hui of Liang to admit that only *jen* and *i* (benevolence and righteousness), and not *li* (profit), should guide human actions. Is it possible that the author of the *KTT* decided to abandon these basic principles of Confucianism and declare the supremacy of *li* over *jen* and *i*? No, he did not. Rather, the author of the *KTT* in this instance carried on the critical (and interpretative) tradition first raised to a fine art by Wang Ch'ung, the famous critical philosopher of the Later Han. Concerning the opening section in *Mencius*, Wang Ch'ung made the following comment:

> Now, there are two kinds of profit, the one consisting in wealth, the other in quiet happiness. King Hui asked how he could profit his kingdom. How did Mencius know that he did not want the profit of quiet happiness, and straightaway took exception to profit by wealth?[37]

Wang Ch'ung presents in this passage an analytical criticism of Mencius' understanding of the concept of "profit" which does not allow one to distinguish between two possible meanings of "profit." Now, the author of the *KTT* was no doubt familiar with Wang Ch'ung's writings. To reply on Mencius' behalf to Wang Ch'ung's criticism, he wrote the dialogue between Tzu-ssu and his "disciple" Mencius. Mencius' silence at the end of Tzu-ssu's argument strongly suggests that he agreed with the latter's view, which sees no necessary contradiction between *jen, i* and *li*, provided the concept of *li* is seen only in terms of its moral implications. Apparently the author of the *KTT* assumed that the reader of Wang Ch'ung's criticism of Mencius, on turning to the *KTT*, would realize that Mencius had been instructed by Tzu-ssu on this issue. The *KTT* passage, furthermore, indicates that Mencius was aware of the distinction between the two kinds of profit, and that his reproof of King Hui of Liang was, therefore, based on a knowledge of the king's one-dimensional concept of the word profit.[38]

If we assume that the *KTT* author's intention was to perpetuate and interpret Confucianism for his day, he certainly
succeeded in his project by continuing the dynamics of the
Confucian polemical tradition. Thus, at the beginning of the
third century, he infused with new life the dramatic announce-
ment made by Mencius some five hundred years earlier:

> I am not fond of disputation. I have no alternative.
> Whoever can, with words, combat Yang and Mo, is the
> true disciple of the sage.[39]

PART II

—◆—

Spiritual Aspects of Confucianism

CHAPTER 4

What Is Confucian Spirituality?

JULIA CHING

In the Introduction to his *History of Chinese Philosophy*, Fung Yu-lan discusses the relative absence of concern for philosophical methodology, and the presence, on the other hand, of much concern for practical "methods of self-cultivation" in the field of Chinese philosophy. To use his own words:

> Chinese philosophers for the most part have not regarded knowledge as something valuable in itself, and so have not sought knowledge for the sake of knowledge; and even in the sense of knowledge of a practical sort that might have a direct bearing upon human happiness, Chinese philosophers have preferred to apply this knowledge to actual conduct that would lead directly to this happiness, rather than to hold what they considered to be empty discussions about it.[1]

According to Fung, the Chinese philosophical ideal has been traditionally that of attaining "sageliness within and

kingliness without." In other words, the ideal was to become
a wise and humane person with a sagely disposition and, as
well, with the ability to give order to the world—even if that
means only the smaller world of the would-be sage's own
human relationships. Fung writes:

> Because Chinese philosophers pay special attention to
> the way of becoming "sagely within," their methods of
> self-cultivation (*hsiu-yang*), that is, the so-called
> "methods of study" (*wei-hsüeh*) are very detailed and
> complete. Although these may not be called philosophy
> in the Western sense, China truly has a contribution
> to make in this respect.[2]

Such reflection on methods of self-cultivation which
Chinese philosophy has to offer is also found in the Western
tradition, but much more often in its strictly religious development than in its philosophical treatises. I refer here specifically
to the *spirituality* of Western religious traditions, which has
not been adequately integrated into philosophy itself, even if
religious—and mystical—experience has served as the basis of
much philosophical reflection. The English word "spirituality"
is relatively little used and often misunderstood, sometimes
confused with the word "spiritualism," which has to do with
making contact with the spirits of the deceased. "Spirituality"
has usually been associated with theology, "spiritual theology"
being sometimes used as another designation for what is also
called "ascetical and mystical theology," and that usually
within the context of Christianity. Here, the meaning has to
do with the life of the *spirit,* including the ascetic and mystical
life. More recently, the word is also being used in the study
of the spiritual teachings of non-Christian religions, including
not only Judaism and Islam, but also Hinduism and Buddhism.
But what about Confucianism and Neo-Confucianism?

Confucius the Model

Confucius was not only a philosopher; he was also a great
spiritual personality, a paradigmatic individual. To a large
extent, he personified his philosophical message: he *was* his

message. Thus he remains the model and inspiration even though his philosophy today no longer enjoys the protection of the state. His central doctrine is that of *jen*, translated variously as goodness, benevolence, humanity, or human-heartedness. This was formerly a particular virtue, the kindness which distinguished the gentleman in his behavior toward his inferiors. Confucius transforms it into a universal virtue, that which makes the perfect human being, the sage. He defines it as loving others, as personal integrity, and as altruism. Confucius' philosophy is clearly grounded in religion—the inherited religion of the Lord on High or Heaven, the supreme and personal deity. This is so even though Confucius is largely silent regarding God and the afterlife (*Analects* XI.11). He makes it clear that it was Heaven which protected him and gave him his message (*Analects* VII.23). He believes that human beings are accountable to a supreme being (*Analects* III.13), even if he does show a certain skepticism regarding ghosts and spirits (*Analects* VI.20). Confucius' emphasis on rituals is significant, as they govern human relationships, especially among the aristocrats. The word for ritual, *li*, is related etymologically to the words "worship" and "sacrificial vessel," both of which have definite religious overtones. The ancestral cult was surrounded with ritual; so was the worship offered to Heaven as supreme lord (*Shang-ti*, i.e., Lord on High). But the term *li* came to include all social, habitual practices, even to the extent of partaking of the nature of law as a means of training in virtue and of avoiding evil. It refers also to propriety, that is, to proper behavior. Propriety carries a risk of mere exterior conformity to social custom, just as a ritual might be performed only perfunctorily, without an inner attitude of reverence. But Confucius is careful to emphasize the importance of the correct inner disposition without which propriety becomes hypocrisy (*Analects* XV.17). In offering moral and spiritual perfection as the human ideal, Confucius has bequeathed a legacy that is perennial and universal, even if his cultural assumptions have their inherent limitations.

As a teacher of disciples, Confucius practiced the art of spiritual guidance, exhorting his followers to moderate the excesses of their temperaments by certain efforts of self-control, aided by the practice of self-examination. He gives this general advice: "When you meet someone better than yourself, think about emulating him. When you meet someone not as good as yourself, look inside and examine your own self" (*Analects* IV.17). His disciple Tseng-tzu describes three counts of daily self-examination: "In my undertakings for others, have I done my best? In dealings with my friends, have I been faithful? And have I passed on to others what I have not personally practiced?" (*Analects* I.4). Confucius said of his own spiritual evolution:

> At fifteen I set my heart on learning [to be a sage]; at thirty I became firm; at forty I had no more doubts; at fifty I understood Heaven's Will; at sixty my ear was attuned to truth; at seventy I could follow my heart's desires, without overstepping the line" (*Analects* II.4).

This is the description of a man who consciously cultivated an interior life, who trained his mind to apprehend the truth and his heart to grasp the will of Heaven, until his instincts were also transformed, and who learned to appreciate the things of the spirit. Still, the mention of Heaven is discreet. Confucius' words do not vibrate with a passionate longing for union with Heaven, or God, as do the words of many Western mystics.

The Development of Confucian Spirituality

In the centuries immediately following Confucius and Mencius, Confucian spirituality is represented by the emphasis on *li* (ritual) and *yüeh* (music), while the religious belief in a supreme god as the Lord on High or Heaven continued to diminish in importance. During this period Hsün-tzu interprets rites to mean such practices as the sacrifice to Heaven offered by the sovereign. He himself professes a disbelief in Heaven as a supernatural being or power. In speaking of the sacrifices to ancestors, of weddings and funerals, he pays some attention to the aesthetics of rituals,

to details of rubrics as well as to a sense of balance and
beauty:

> Rites trim what is long and stretch out what is too
> short, eliminate surplus and repair deficiency, extend
> the forms of love and reverence, and step by step bring
> to fulfillment the beauties of proper conduct. Beauty
> and ugliness, music and weeping, joy and sorrow are
> opposites, and yet rites make use of them all, bringing
> forth and employing each in its turn.[3]

For Hsün-tzu, music serves the same functions as rituals,
usually in conjunction with rituals. By music the ancient
Chinese meant a union of instrumental and vocal music and
rhythm with verse and dancing. The Confucian school was
especially fond of the formal music performed at ancestral
and other religious sacrifices.[4] In Hsün-tzu's words, "Music
(*yüeh*) is joy (*lo;* a variant pronunciation of the same character), an emotion which man cannot help but feel at times.
Since man cannot help feeling joy, his joy must find an outlet
in voice and an expression in movement."[5] In the *Book of
Rites*, a text which manifests the undeniable influence of
Hsün-tzu, the chapter on music also extolls it as a help in
gaining inner equilibrium and tranquillity—the equilibrium is
the reflection of the harmony of elegant music. According
to this chapter, "it belongs to man's nature, as from Heaven,
to be still at birth." In the process of growth, man is acted
upon by external influences, and he responds by showing
"likes and dislikes." Unless these are properly regulated by
an interior principle, he runs the risk of self-alienation, of
becoming a stranger to his original, deeper self, and thus of
losing his "Heavenly principle" (*t'ien-li*). But music and rituals
serve to maintain or restore this inner harmony, which is, or
ought to be, a reflection of the harmony between Heaven
and earth.

> Harmony is the thing principally sought in music: it
> therein follows Heaven, and manifests the spirit-like
> expansive influence characteristic of it. Distinction is
> the thing principally sought in ceremonies: they therein
> follow earth, and manifest the spirit-like retroactive

influence characteristic of it. Hence the sages made
music in response to Heaven, and framed ceremonies
in correspondence with Earth. In the wisdom and
completeness of their ceremonies and music, we see
the directing power of Heaven and Earth.[6]

Doctrine of Equilibrium and Harmony

Emotional harmony and psychic equilibrium—the harmony of
due proportion rather than the absence of passions—is to
become in Sung times the cornerstone of Confucian spirituality and the essence of Confucian meditation itself. Here,
the *Chung-yung,* or *Doctrine of the Mean,* another chapter
of the *Book of Rites,* is especially helpful. It speaks of two
states of mind or heart, the "pre-stirred" state, before the
rise of emotions, and the "post-stirred" state. According to this
doctrine, the mean lies in the harmony of emotions which have
arisen and which resembles the equilibrium of the earlier state.
It goes on to say that this harmony puts a person in touch with
the processes of life and creativity in the universe:

> While there are no stirrings of pleasure, anger, sorrow
> or joy, the mind may be said to be in the state of
> equilibrium (*chung*). When these emotions have been
> stirred, and act in their due degree, there ensues what
> may be called the state of harmony (*ho*). This equi-
> librium is the great root of all-under-Heaven, and this
> harmony is the universal path of all-under-Heaven.
> Let the states of equilibrium and harmony exist in
> perfection, and a happy order will prevail throughout
> Heaven and Earth, and all things will be nourished
> and will flourish.[7]

The philosophical assumption behind such speculation is
the traditional correlation between the microcosm and the
macrocosm, between the inner workings of man's mind and
heart and the creative processes of the universe. The mystical
dimension is obvious. And while the meaning of the word

Heaven mentioned in the above passages is ambiguous, there is a clear expression of a belief that emotional harmony opens man to something greater than himself. What this is, and how emotional harmony is to be acquired, remain unclear. But it is no surprise that such a text should provide impetus to the development of a form of meditation that may be called specifically Confucian.

The Neo-Confucian Contributions

A long time passed before Confucian spirituality became finally crystallized. This came about through the work of the Neo-Confucian philosophers of the Sung and Ming dynasties. Their contributions were made partly as responses to the philosophy and spirituality of Buddhism. The responses themselves, however, were articulated in Confucian terms, even if the new world view reflects Buddhist as well as Taoist influences. In place of the early belief in a supreme and personal deity, we tend to find a pantheistic, or should we say, panentheistic universe, with Heaven as impersonal or transpersonal force.[8] We also find a mature doctrine of spiritual cultivation, oriented to the achievement of sagehood. The nature of the spirituality of the Neo-Confucian response is well revealed in the language of spirituality which was developed. Largely derived from Confucian texts, the words used by Neo-Confucians were now invested with technical meanings. Taken together, they form a language of specifically Confucian inspiration, even though some of the resonances may be Buddhistic. The dynamic quality of the language of spirituality makes it hard to analyze and classify, but we shall attempt to examine it under the two categories of "diminution" and "growth" in order to understand more clearly the specificity of Neo-Confucian spirituality. The distinction drawn is mainly heuristic, since, in spiritual terms, the two categories are paradoxically convergent, for spiritual growth is possible only when accompanied functionally by a certain degree of self-denial.

The Language of Diminution or Self-denial

In *Analects* XII.1, Confucius defines the virtue of *jen* in terms of "self-conquest" (*k'o-chi*), undertaken for the sake of "restoring propriety" (*fu li*). This is an example of the language of diminution or "abnegation." It is what naturally follows self-examination—a purgative effort. In the same passage, when asked what are the steps of such self-mastery, Confucius gives the "guard or custody" over one's senses:

> Look not at what is contrary to propriety; listen not to what is contrary to propriety; speak not what is contrary to propriety; make no movement which is contrary to propriety.

The Neo-Confucians did not forget this lesson. They recognized the need of "preserving the Heavenly principle and eliminating human passions" (*ts'un t'ien-li, ch'ü jen-yü*). They also practiced the art of "self-examination" (*hsing-ch'a*), literally, of looking into, and of watching over, themselves, even frequently keeping a "spiritual account" of themselves. From biographies, we also know the discipline they followed, including in some instances such practices as keeping a detailed spiritual journal with precise accounts of faults detected and resolutions made.

Such developments brought with them a corollary: the practice of reading back into the Classics a doctrine of asceticism, of attributing to the ancients the virtues of such asceticism. In T'ang Shun-chih's biography in the *Ming-ju hsüeh-an*, for example, Huang Tsung-hsi refers to King T'ang, the dynastic founder of Shang, who is said to have "sat up waiting for dawn,"[9] to Wu-ting, or King Kao-tsung, one of his successors, who "kept silence for three years," allegedly during a mourning period,[10] and to Confucius, who "did not know the taste of meat for three months" (*Analects* VII.13), as examples of reverence and self-discipline. Huang was, of course, following an interpretation established by a long line of exegetes. And yet, if we read the classical *Book of Documents* more carefully, we might not be so sure that these were such good historical examples of asceticism. The contexts seem to suggest that King T'ang rose early in order to profit from the light of day, that Wu-ting's silence was remarked *after* the mourning period was over[11] and might even be the result of sickness, and, certainly, that Confucius lost his taste for meat because he was so enthralled with *shao* music while visiting the state of Ch'i, and so was hardly practicing any act of mortification.[12] The tradition, however, of reading the classics ascetically, and the language of diminution it produces, is witness to the importance of asceticism itself in the Confucian and, even more, the Neo-Confucian tradition.

We should nevertheless remember that Confucian—and Neo-Confucian—asceticism remained a discipline of moderation, which did not inspire any flight into deserts or produce any monastic movement. The Confucian teaching was to control one's passions, not to live as if one were without them. Besides, Confucian asceticism was always practiced for the sake of a higher goal, that of rendering the individual more humane for others, in the service of a larger group, namely, the family and the society.

The Language of Growth

The school of Confucius has always considered *becoming humane* (*jen*) as a process of spiritual growth. This view took on special significance when, under Buddhist influence, the word *jen*, assumed the meaning of a "seed," with potential for growth and maturation.[13] With the Neo-Confucians, the word *jen* became interchangeable with the term "Heavenly principle" (*t'ien-li*). To become humane—that is, a perfect human being—one must "preserve" (*ts'un*) and "nurture" (*yang*) the Heavenly principle within one's mind and heart. Its growth enables one to participate in the cosmic processes of life and growth—again the microcosm–macrocosm parallel. But how is this growth to be cultivated? On this point, the various philosophers do not always have the same answers. Chu Hsi, responsible for the synthesis of Sung Neo-Confucian thought, offers the dual formula of *chu-ching ch'iung-li*, of abiding in a disposition to reverence and pursuing exhaustively the principles (*li*) of things. His is a formula which combines spiritual and intellectual cultivation.

The Doctrine of Reverence

The fact that scholars have translated the term *ching* in Chu Hsi's phrase as reverence, seriousness, or composure shows the difficulty of explaining its usage in general and Chu's intended meaning in particular. The use of the word can be traced to various Confucian texts, including the *Book of Documents*, where the ancient sage kings are frequently described as being "reverentially obedient" to the Lord on High, while their descendants are exhorted to imitate such reverence. With Confucius, the word is used more with regard to oneself than to a higher being: "In retirement, to be sedately gracious, in doing things, to be reverently attentive (*ching*), in contact with others, to be very sincere" (*Analects* XII.19).[14] The *Book of Changes* continues in the same vein, when it says: "The gentleman practices reverence to maintain inner rectitude, and righteousness to assure exterior correctness."[15]

Chu Hsi, in speaking of "abiding in reverence," defines it in terms of single-mindedness and freedom from distraction (*chu-i wu-shih*), and compares it to the Buddhist practice of mindful alertness (*hsing-hsing*). He also associates it specifically with the teaching of *shen-tu* ("vigilance in solitude" or being watchful over oneself when alone) in the *Doctrine of the Mean*. But he is careful to guard his disciples against a *dead* reverence which merely keeps the mind alert without also attending to moral practice. For Chu Hsi, "reverence" points to the process by which the original unity of mind is preserved and made manifest in one's activity. Thus he gives the meaning of the word a dimension of depth which transforms it from the earlier, occasional usage in Confucian thought to a doctrine of personal and spiritual cultivation. In his words:

Reverence does not mean one has to sit stiffly in solitude, the ears hearing nothing, the eyes seeing nothing, and the mind thinking of nothing. . . . It means rather keeping a sense of caution and vigilance, and not daring to become permissive.[16]

The practice of reverence is very like that of "recollection" in Christian spirituality. The English word recollection is usually understood in terms of "remembrance." However, as a technical term in spirituality, it refers to the "collecting" or "gathering" of one's interior faculties, keeping them silent and "recollected" in an atmosphere of peace and calm, in preparation for formal prayer or in an effort to prolong the effects of such prayer. In a work on Christian spirituality, Canon Jacques Leclerq says:

The word recollection has no meaning for many worldly people. . . . Yet recollection is the chief disposition required for the interior life. It is not itself interior life but it is so much a condition for it and prepares us for it to such an extent that it almost necessarily develops it. . . . It is simply the calm which is born into the soul through solitude and silence, interior calm. Man has need of it to find himself as well as to find God.[17]

The closest Chinese term to recollection is *shou-lien* (literally, "collecting together"). While it also has a practical meaning ("gathering" a harvest), its usage in Neo-Confucian spirituality has made it too a technical term. Chu Hsi writes about the need for scholars to "keep always recollected (*shou-lien*) without allowing oneself to become dispersed."[18]

Chu Hsi's predecessor, Ch'eng I (1033–1107), who articulated the doctrine of reverence before him, said that "Cultivation (*han-yang*) requires the practice of reverence." The term *han-yang* includes the meaning of nurturing. The aspirant to sagehood needs to nurture the seeds of goodness in his mind and heart, and reverence refers to this process of nurturing as well as to the goal of emotional harmony characteristic of the sage.

The Role of Meditation

The Confucian term for meditation is "quiet-sitting" (*ching-tso*). This term suggests strong Taoist and Buddhist influences, calling to mind Chuang-tzu's "sitting and forgetting" (*tso-wang*) and the Buddhist practice of *dhyāna* (meditation), from which the term *Ch'an* or Zen is derived. Chu Hsi had experience of both Taoist and Buddhist practices of meditation. But he also made a special effort to show the distinctiveness of Confucian meditation and its difference from Taoist and Buddhist meditation. For the Taoist or Buddhist, meditation is an exercise by which the mind concentrates on an object, including itself, to the exclusion of all distracting thoughts and for the sake of attaining inner unity. Especially in the case of the Taoist, the motive was to preserve health and prolong life. For the Confucian, unity and harmony are the goal, together with knowledge of the *moral* self, of one's own strengths and weaknesses. The Confucian sought through meditation to achieve self-improvement in the practice of virtues and elimination of vices.

Chu Hsi gives some importance to quiet-sitting, especially with the view of making possible a fuller manifestation of the Heavenly principle within. What is implied is a reversion: a return to one's original nature; a recapture of the springs of one's being; and the permeation of one's daily living by this state of psychic unity and harmony. Chu Hsi sees quiet-sitting as different from the Buddhist practice of "introspection," which has reference only to oneself and not to the larger world:

> According to the Buddhist teaching, one is to seek the mind with the mind, deploy the mind with the mind. This is like the mouth gnawing the mouth or the eye looking into the eye. Such a course of action is precarious and oppressive, such a path is dangerous and obstructive, such a practice is empty of principle and frustrating. They may sound like us [Confucians]; they are in reality quite different.[19]

Confucian meditation as it developed assumed a character more and more different from Taoist and Buddhist meditation. It entails not just an examination of conscience, but is definitely oriented toward a higher consciousness through the emptying of the self and of desires. As a form of inner concentration, Confucian meditation stands somewhere between two other forms: the intellectual effort of discursive thought and the moral effort of assuring that there is no thought. Confucian meditation seeks peace without doing violence to human nature. It does not require the attainment of a state of intellectual and emotional impassivity. Thoughts may come and go; they need not become distractions except when one pays attention to them.

The Extension of Knowledge

A problem which frequently arises in the different spiritual traditions is the place assigned to intellectual cultivation. In Western Christian spirituality, it is formulated in terms of the primacy of the intellect or of the will in the soul's union with God, with the Dominican order, for example, preferring the intellect and the Franciscan order the will. Dominican spirituality is therefore more intellectually oriented, while Franciscan spirituality is more action-oriented, and can even be described as anti-intellectual.

The word *hsüeh* (literally, learning) has a broader meaning than the solely intellectual in Confucianism, for it refers especially to "learning to become a sage." There is on the other hand an intellectual dimension to Confucian spirituality which is remarkable and distinctive. This is the tenet expressed in the *Great Learning*, that knowledge may be extended through the investigation of things (*ko-wu chih-chih*). It is a tenet especially fully developed in the philosophy of Chu Hsi, in which it is explained in terms of the "pursuit of principles" (*ch'iung-li*). The focus is on the search for knowledge, especially for intellectual comprehension of the essences of all things, with the word "things" understood as including not only the objective world outside of the mind, but also the subjective world of the mind itself and the intersubjective world of human relationships and human affairs. As Chu Hsi writes:

If we wish to extend our knowledge to the utmost, we must investigate the principles of all things with which we come into contact. For the mind and spirit of man are formed to know, and the things of the world all contain principles. So long as principles are not exhausted, knowledge is not yet complete.[20]

According to Chu Hsi, the student is to proceed from the known to the unknown, moving from the knowledge he already possesses to the principles of things, and continuing his investigation until the task is finished. The end is reached as a sudden breakthrough, an experience of inner enlightenment occurring at the end of a long and arduous process of search and exertion:

After exerting himself in this way for a long time, he will suddenly find himself possessed of a wide and far-reaching penetration. The qualities of all things, both internal and external, subtle and coarse, will all then be apprehended, and the mind, in its entire substance (t'i) and in its relation to things (yung), will become completely manifest. This is called the investigation of things; this is called the perfection of knowledge.[21]

If the mind is ordained to know the truth of principles, truth itself also modifies the mind, making it manifest and radiant. Here we observe a circular movement, from the mind to things and back to the mind, but note that it is not just a movement from the mind to the mind. This is because knowledge is desired not for its own sake, but in order to act properly, to know moral behavior.

A problem therefore arises in Neo-Confucian spirituality as to how important book learning or intellectual pursuits are to the quest for sagehood. Chu Hsi's contemporary and rival Lu Chiu-yüan (1139–1193) and, in the Ming dynasty, Wang Yang-ming pointed out the problem inherent in any doctrine which gives too much priority to intellectual striving: that it necessarily makes intellectuals of all sages, rendering those deprived of the opportunities of study underprivileged in the quest for sagehood as well. Lu and Wang by contrast emphasize the moral and existential aspects of spirituality, regarding book learning almost as a distraction from the quest itself. While their influences have had an important impact, Confucian spirituality has still become mainly the spirituality of the intellectual, and the reading of the classics is itself interpreted as a spiritual exercise.

Mysticism

Spirituality is concerned with experiences of the inner man, and these may include mystical experiences. In Judaism, Islam, and Christianity, these are usually defined in terms of the soul's consciousness of its union with God, a union in which the two remain distinct, even if the experience of union is very intense and ineffable. The Confucian classics give evidence of a deep spirituality which suggests mysticism. Both the *Book of Poetry* and the *Book of Documents* represent the ancient Sage-Kings as partners in dialogue with the Lord on High or Heaven, indeed as reverential *sons* of Heaven, receiving from it instructions and commandments, and asking of it blessing and protection. This appears closer to the tradition of the Jewish kings and prophets than to that of mystical individuals lost in the contemplation of the divine. But the distinctively Confucian mystical tradition is better discovered in the *Mencius* and in those chapters in the ritual texts which speak less of the rites as such and more of the interior dispositions of the mind and heart.[22] Mencius alludes to the presence in the heart of an actuality greater than itself. According to him, knowledge and fulfillment of one's own mind and heart lead to knowledge and fulfillment of one's nature and to the service of Heaven:

> For a man to give full realization to his heart is for him to understand his own nature, and a man who understands his own nature understands Heaven. By preserving his heart and nurturing his nature he is serving Heaven (VII A.1).

Mencius' serene philosophy gave way to an intense quest for the ultimate on the part of various Neo-Confucians, probably under some influence from Buddhism. We possess one description of the experience of a mystical enlightenment (1593), by Kao P'an-lung during a journey to South China, first by boat and then on land. He wrote about his strict daily order, maintained even while on the boat, how he practiced meditation half of the day and read books the other half. He described how, for about two months,

> Whenever I felt ill at ease during meditation, I would just follow all the instructions of Ch'eng I and Chu Hsi—in all that concerns sincerity, reverence, concentrating on tranquility, observing joy, anger, sorrow and pleasure before they arise, sitting in silence to purify the mind, realizing in myself the heavenly principle. . . . Whether I was standing or sitting, eating or resting, I would not forget these thoughts. At night I did not undress, and only fell asleep when dead tired. Upon waking I returned to meditating, repeating and alternating these various practices. When the *ch'i* of the mind was clear and peaceful, it seemed to fill all Heaven and Earth. But such consciousness did not last.[23]

The ineffable experience of enlightenment came during his contemplation of nature, while he was staying in an inn, probably in Fukien.

> [The inn] had a small loft which faced the mountains, with a rushing stream behind. I climbed up there and was very pleased. Quite by chance I saw a saying by Ch'eng Hao [1032–1085]. "Amid a hundred officials, myriad affairs and a hundred thousand weapons, with water as drink and a bent arm as pillow, I can still be joyful [*Analects* VII.15]. The myriad things are all man-made; in reality there is not a thing."[24] Suddenly I realized the sense of these words and said, "This is it. In reality there is not a thing!" And as this one thought lingered, all entanglements were broken off. It was suddenly as if a load of one hundred pounds had instantly dropped off, as if a flash of lightning had penetrated the body and pierced the intelligence, and I merged in harmony with the Great Transformation

till there was no differentiation between Heaven and
Man, the outer and the inner.[25]

This is a testimonial of personal fulfillment, achieved not
without earnest striving, but serenely simple as an experience.
It is an experience of self-transcendence, of the consciousness
of merging with nature. The inscription by Ch'eng Hao which
became the occasion for this awakening is notable since it
grounds the Confucian mystical experience in a life of full
activity while expressing the central insight itself in a language
of negation evocative of Buddhist philosophy. Confucian
meditation developed in a tradition that did not know monastic life. It represents essentially a lay spirituality. And Confucian mysticism is the portion of the man who knows how
to unite contemplation and action, the inner and the outer,
for external activity is the expression of interior attitudes and
of the fountainhead of one's intentions. Confucian mysticism
enables the person to perceive the profoundly dynamic
character of the Heavenly principle within, the principle by
which birds fly, fishes swim and human beings love virtue.
He recognizes that this is the true meaning of man's oneness
with Heaven and Earth and all things.

Confucian Spirituality

In conclusion, we return to the question posed at the outset:
what is Confucian spirituality? The burden of this paper has
been to offer an answer to this question by arguing that the
quest for sagehood, which constitutes the heart of Confucianism, can only be understood with reference to the
"interior life," to the life of the spirit, to personal discipline,
and sometimes to mystical experience. This is tantamount to
saying that Confucianism itself cannot be understood unless
we have some sympathy for, and appreciation of, its doctrines
and methods of spiritual cultivation. I have therefore attempted to show how the secular character of the Confucian
tradition, which historically precluded the development of
monastic movements usually associated with ascetic and
mystical disciplines, has nevertheless permitted the develop-

ment of a horizon of spirituality such as that found in the world's other great religious traditions. Indeed, I hope I have shown that this horizon is central to Confucianism, just as belief in God is central to Judaism and Christianity. Assuredly, it is a spirituality peculiarly Confucian, not dependent on belief in God, as is Christian or Jewish spirituality. And yet it does not deny God's existence. It is a spirituality which unites "inner sageliness and outer kingliness," a life of contemplation and a life of activity.

It would not be possible to say that Confucianism has an answer to every problem, or that Confucianism does not also have its own inherent limitations. On the contrary, I believe that Confucianism has all the limitations that human systems possess—even those constructed by the best of us. The limitations of Confucianism are, however, the subject for another study, while this one has sought merely to suggest the horizon of the spirituality we can discover in Confucianism, and the horizon of meaning this spirituality can help us find. Even for the most spiritual Confucian, life may continue to pose problems. In fact, Confucianism cannot resolve the problems of human existence; it can only help us find the wisdom and strength to cope with them, including those problems that we shall never understand. Yet, the person who determines to follow the spiritual path that Confucianism outlines, a path committed to moral values and social responsibility, to culture and to life, may become a better human being; not necessarily a sage, but perhaps a more humane person. For that person will have discovered transcendence in immanence, the absolute in the relative, the constant in the transient, and meaning in every moment of time.

CHAPTER 5

On Confucian, European, and Universal Aesthetics

BEN-AMI SCHARFSTEIN

The essay that follows is part of an attempt to discover what is common to the art of every time and place. It is also an attempt to evoke the principle in art that expresses the individual's desire to overcome and transcend his condition of isolation. It is not, properly speaking, an essay in Sinology, but in the use of Sinological materials for the sake of a generalized aesthetics. Although it argues for the recognition of what I call "the aesthetic universal," my examples will be drawn from the Chinese and the European aesthetic traditions only. To recognize this aesthetic universal is, in a way, to solve the most pressing general problem of aesthetics. I say "to recognize" rather than "to discover" because I lay no claim to be a discoverer and because I aim to do no more than to bring to clearer light what everyone apprehends at least vaguely.

In the course of my discussion it will be necessary to take up several issues germane to this topic. The first concerns artistic creation and tradition, and the problem that will be explored deals with the extent to which art expresses constant values, or is traditionless and perpetually self-renewing. The second issue is that of artistic interaction, as a result of which both European and Chinese art have been subject to mutual influences. The third is the notion of fusion, an idea central to my understanding of the aesthetic universal, which I shall explore in its various aspects. Fusion as a concept in art will, in turn, lead me to the question of mysticism in both the European and the Chinese traditions.

"The aesthetic universal" should not be taken in too Platonic a sense. It is not a kind of constitutive "idea" the quantity of which in a work of art makes that art more or less good, as the quantity of sugar in food makes it more or less sweet. Nor does the aesthetic universal, as I mean it, give any direct measure of the aesthetic value or importance of a work of art. It is the particular quality of the human condition that makes art both universal and indispensable. It is both a need and a power, and it can be grasped, according to the intellectual preferences of the grasper, as biological, sociological, psychological, metaphysical, or aesthetic. It can be seen in the light of any or all of these ways because it is so general and basic, because it is rooted in our biological nature and, rooted there, makes possible our most human achievements, for it joins the animal in us with the human in its most imaginative, concentrated, powerful, and subtle expressions.

To speak of the importance of such an aesthetic universal is not at all to belittle that which is simply local in art. I fully believe that an accurate, more or less intuitive grasp of the nuances of art must be based on intimate acquaintance, just as an accurate, more or less intuitive grasp of the nuances of emotion must be based on the type of intimate acquaintance that develops within the family. What I am saying about the essentially local nature of the nuances of art holds true of art theory and aesthetics as well. Their life, too, resides as much in their detail, their historical and emotional coloration, as in the need or emotion that animates them and the neutral abstractions into which they can be translated. Works of art and aesthetic theories alike live and have their being in determinate places at determinate times—it is there and then that they are most fully themselves. Yet that which is universal in art and which I am now trying to clarify, the animating need or emotion, or the neutral abstraction by which this can be characterized, allows us to see art everywhere as an extensive series of variations of the same theme, and therefore as having a deep genuine likeness.

Let me suggest an analogy. Nutritional customs and preferences obviously vary in different parts of the world. These differences are based on all sorts of factors, geographic, economic, aesthetic, historical, and perhaps physiological. An aesthetics of gastronomy might deal, intelligibly enough, with food preferences alone. Surely, however, these preferences would be more fully understood if the geographic and economic and other factors influencing them were explained. Yet even such enriched history does not explain everything. To know more deeply we should also have to know, as far as possible, all that was relevant of human physiology and nutrition in general, and even, if we take the psychological point of view, how and why human beings enjoy food and try to vary it in order to enjoy it more. All eaters, gastronomically sophisticated or not, are individual human beings, with individual but probably generalizable predilections. All diets are local, and all nuances of diet must be understood locally; but local understanding is by nature restricted to a narrow angle of vision, and its detail is so accurate and so intuitively grasped exactly because of the myopia of its local judges.

Artistic Creation and Tradition

Contemporary art is what we ourselves have created either directly as artists or indirectly by means of our preferences or our acquiescence in the preferences of others. Yet I, like many others, find much of contemporary art uncomfortable, especially when it becomes extreme in its primitivism or primitive in its extremism. The weakening or breaking down of our tradition, particularly in the visual arts, has had many causes; but I have been struck in particular by the sheer quantity of knowledge now at our command. This knowledge, which has been the unmitigated joy of the scholar, has been the joy and the confusion of the spectator and both the joy and the bane of the artist, who has been swamped by the simultaneous presence of the art of every time and place. Such wisdom as is taught by art history has enabled us to live more comfortably in art's past than in its present. Aware above all of change, we applaud each new success in turn, take refuge in a sociable but perhaps thoughtless hedonism, and wait for the historian (who is better at description and classification than judgment) to sort things out.

Yet, although much of our loss of a common Western tradition in art stems, as I see it, from the increase in our knowledge, it is possible that if we become more attentive to this knowledge, more analytical and sensitive, we can regain something almost equivalent to a tradition. I believe that beneath the chaos of different artists, different periods, different countries, and different cultures, we can find analogous sensitivities that, grasped as alike and different, will allow us to understand art in general in a deeper and more comprehensive way. This should be the more true if we concern ourselves seriously with non-Western cultures.

A comparison of our own period with the Ming dynasty, for example, reveals that in China, too, knowledge of precedents became minutely available to the artist, whose response was sometimes one of some strain or doubt. The answer of Tung Ch'i-ch'ang (1555–1636), artist, critic and historian, was to classify the history of Chinese art into a good and an evil lineage, in this way guiding Chinese literati into a quasieclecticism in which each artist, or style, or substyle was dogmatically approved or disapproved, but in which the ideal was a "great synthesis."[1] Late in his career, his painted "imitations" sometimes bore a relation so distant from their "originals" that they might be compared in distance to that between certain Picassos and the paintings of David, Delacroix, Velasquez, or Manet, of which they were variations. While I do not want to express any particular opinion of Tung's paintings, and although his dogmatic views are hard to sustain now, he did show himself able to remain sensitive to his artistic past and yet to arrive at a developed individuality of his own. His comprehensive knowledge did not maim his creative ability.

However, I do not assume that a more comprehensive understanding will enable us to settle aesthetic disputes by appealing either to facts or to sensitivities. Aesthetic disputes, no less than others, are a quite indispensable expression of life. Yet it is possible to make them an occasion for learning as well as for self-assertion. To live in the aesthetic present is essential to art; but to live there alone, cut off from the past, is seriously dehumanizing. When fashion shuts one of the artist's eyes and rebellion or arrogance the other, he becomes blind; and although a blind artist can surely be an interesting one, his art, like his person, expresses the fact that he is maimed by being too imprisoned within himself. It would help us if we could adopt something of the Chinese attitude that required the rebel in art, no less than the conformist, to have a discriminating knowledge of his predecessors, whose brush compositions he performed on silk or paper rather like classical music. For the rebel, too, used his skill and temperament to repeat the great artists of the past, that is, to internalize their particular kinds of vitality, and so to keep their accomplishments alive in himself and in his time.

Perhaps, instead of pursuing the volatile present alone or, in its place, the will-o'-the-wisp of an absolute, more-than-traditional power of judgment, we should try to take part in the creation of a new tradition whose locale is the face of the earth and whose memory assimilates the previously separate memories of all the old traditions. Then all the histories of art could become a single, enormously rich history, a record that could lend our present art a context wide and deep enough to stabilize it to a degree. Perhaps, absorbed into what we shall one day recognize as the unqualifiedly human tradition, we shall succeed in building on the past again, even if only loosely, and in grasping nuances against a background whose variation will make them even more clearly individual.

In abstract terms, my position is that we have created a false and damaging antithesis between an objective and a subjective attitude towards art. The old view that art should by nature express objective, eternal, traditional values has had a number of recent learned advocates, among them René Guénon and Ananda Coomaraswamy; but they have not impressed the far more numerous advocates of a subjective, perpetually self-renewing, practically traditionless art. These two extremes are better for argument than for understanding. If the kind of analysis I am undertaking is even approximately correct, art is neither objective alone or subjective alone, but both. Its objective character results from the biological and psychological likeness between individuals, and from the basically analogous methods by which all communities, unique though each one is, have tried to preserve their individual unity. The subjectivity of art lies, of course, in its ability to give direct expression to the nature of individuals and to arouse their equally subjective reaction. It should be clear, however, that objective and subjective, or, as I understand them, traditional and individualistic, require one another for their existence. This is so because the function of art to unite the individuals who make up a community is also its function to distinguish them from one another. In its formally emotive language, art also says, "I belong to this that I now exhibit, just as this that I now exhibit belongs to me, to my particular role, talent, or style."

The Interaction of Chinese and European Art

This suggestion of a unifying of artistic traditions and sensitivities is generalized from already numerous episodes of cross-cultural contact, some of which have been destructive to one tradition or another, but others of which have proved to be enriching. Let me recall a few of the more outstanding of these contacts. The Buddhist art of India was surely influenced by Hellenistic or Roman art. Such influence is quite evident in the art of ancient Gandhara (parts of contemporary Pakistan and Afghanistan) from the first to fourth centuries A.D., as well as in sculpture of the Amaravati style. Although it is difficult to disentangle the detailed history of Greek or Roman influence on Buddhist sculpture, there is no doubt that it was considerable, especially in the establishment of the image of the Buddha itself. Here there seems to have been a fruitful fusion. Much later, at the court of the Mughal emperors, artists were influenced first by European Renaissance art and later by contemporary Italian,

Dutch, and Flemish painting. To the purist lover of Persian flatness and decorativeness, the Mughal perspective, three-dimensionality, and realism are nothing less than an aesthetic betrayal; but Mughal art has its own intensity and kind of greatness. Persian painting itself was obviously influenced in its motifs, spatial arrangements, and drawing techniques by Chinese painting.[2] To go on with a very incomplete list, there was also the fruitful influence of Chinese on European ceramics, decoration, furniture, and, in a particularly diffuse way, gardening.[3] The reciprocal influence of Japanese printmakers and European artists is very well known by now, as is the general influence of Japanese on European style.

Let me concentrate on China, and give some examples of the interaction within China of European and Chinese painting.[4] European engravings came in the late sixteenth century with the missionaries, who then and in the seventeenth century used religious paintings for purposes of conversion. A number of the missionaries were painters, and some even served in the Emperor's studio. Some of the converts were capable painters themselves, and it was natural that they were somewhat influenced by Western painting. It is not unlikely that it was just this influence that explains why portraiture, which had been consigned for so long to artisan-painters, was taken up again by serious artists.

One such artist was Tseng Ching (1568–1650).[5] A contemporary source describes Tseng's portraits as looking like "images reflected in a mirror," the spirit and feelings of the subjects captured with skill and rich coloring. The pupils of the eyes in the pictures, we are told, were dotted to endow them with life, and the faces "would glare and gaze, knit their brows or smile, in a manner alarmingly like real people. . . . When one stood looking at such a face one forgot both the man and oneself in a moment of spiritual comprehension."[6] Tseng would never tire, we are told, of "adding washes and shades, often tens of times, until he had achieved real artistry,"[7] a method distinctly different from any of the simply Chinese styles. Nor was Tseng Ching alone in his approach. He is said to have had many followers. Unfortunately only his works in a lighter, a predominantly Chinese, style have survived.

In the early Ch'ing Dynasty, more purely European

portraits began to appear. The following is a contemporary Chinese description of the art of Chiao Ping-chen (active towards the end of the seventeenth century), who served in the imperial studio during the time when the Emperor favored missionaries as court painters and astronomical observers:

> Chiao Ping-chen as a painter is unique. As he has long been versed in the measurement of the latitudes of the heavenly bodies and the topographical differences of the earth, he can show, within the space of a single foot in his paintings, layer upon layer of mountains and high peaks which represent distances as far as ten thousands of *li*. . . . In my humble opinion, the Western method excels in painting shades. It dissects the picture into minute parts to distinguish *yin* and *yang*, front and back, slanting and upstanding, long and short, and applies colors either heavy or light, bright or dark, according to the distribution of shades. Therefore, viewed at a distance, figures, animals, plants and houses all seem to stand out and look rounded. In addition, the casting of daylight, the spread of mist and cloud, and every depth and extremity [in nature] are represented distinctly on a small piece of paper.[8]

Acting on the Emperor's command, another eighteenth-century court painter, Men Ying-chao, used light and shade in the European style to make realistic pictures of the Imperial collection of ink-slabs. Western painting as a total or near-total method depended on Imperial patronage and therefore simply vanished when this patronage was withdrawn.

The best known of the Western missionary painters in China was, of course, Guiseppe Castiglione (1698–1768).[9] The Emperor urged him to adopt a relatively Chinese, that is unshaded, water-color technique, but also to create with the whole a fusion of the European (which predominated) and the Chinese styles. The Emperor particularly admired Castiglione as a painter of horses, considering him the equal of the greatest Chinese painters of the past in this specialty. Few of the literati had much enthusiasm for Castiglione's work. Yet a Chinese connoisseur of the time wrote in praise of one of Castiglione's horse scrolls: "His method opens up new horizons. The use of color is particularly noteworthy, for it enables relief to be represented in a satisfactory manner. Mountains, rivers, plants and trees are admirably rendered and absolutely realistic. Furthermore, in this painting *shen* (spirit) is present."[10]

The usual Chinese criticism of Western painting was that it was no more than craftsmanship and lacked genuine style. Wu Li (1632–1718), known as one of the Six Masters of early Ch'ing painting, was a convert to Christianity, but he remained devoted to traditional Chinese standards. As he explained: "Our painting does not seek formal resemblance. It does not restrict itself to the beaten paths of tradition. It is inspired and untrammeled. The Europeans work according to certain rules concerning light and shade in order to represent what is near and far. They strive by painstaking labor to obtain a formal resemblance. They do not utilize the brush in the same manner as we do."[11]

For the most part, Europeans were as critical of Chinese painting as the Chinese were of European painting. The Europeans emphasized the Chinese lack of perspective, shadows, and knowledge of human anatomy. Nonetheless, one Jesuit wrote that the painting in the imperial palace "has a great deal to teach our painters as to the way to treat a landscape, to paint flowers, to render a dream palpable, to express passions, etc."[12] European and Chinese methods and attitudes generally clashed. In China the European gave way, no doubt because of the disfavor into which Christianity fell, but also because the missionary painters, who had to adopt a compromise, did so very reluctantly. The resultant mixed style was ridiculed by Europeans and thought foreign and vulgar by Chinese connoisseurs.

We should not, however, overlook the fruitful European influence on certain Chinese painters who, although innovative, remained distinctively Chinese. These painters were active in the early seventeenth century and lived in or near Nanking. One of them, Wu Pin (active 1576–1626), became a court artist and is likely to have seen the European paintings and illustrated books presented to the Emperor in 1601.[13] While his practices as a painter may have been basically derived from Chinese sources, European influence seems suggested as well. A near-contemporary wrote that "in his compositions he never followed old models, but always depicted real scenery."[14] Those who saw Wu's paintings were said to have been struck with amazement, and the extraordinary claim was made that he painted directly from nature. The angles from which he viewed his landscapes, the way he cut off structures and trees, his use of reflections in water, his skies with rainstorms, clouds, and sunsets, and his pronounced *chiaroscuro*, all suggest European influence.[15]

Other painters of about the same time also show characteristics likely to have been accentuated by the European pictures they encountered. The best known of these is Kung Hsien (1620–1689), whose somber, dense landscapes, which stand out in Chinese painting as something new and extraordinarily expressive, make an acquaintance with European engravings easy to conjecture.[16] A similar acquaintance is likely to have helped Chang Hung (1577–ca. 1652) render landscape paintings that appear to be more visually accurate or empirical than previous ones, and so like natural hills and valleys "that they were reputed to be mysterious."[17] In Chang's case, European inspiration is suggested by "a more consistent application of the principle of the distant, elevated point of view, an attempt to represent objects as if seen from a single viewpoint, a new spaciousness with suggestions of light and shadow, an interest in rendering architecture from different angles, new ways of dotting, stippling, etc., to represent forms."[18] Chang's departure from Chinese tradition caused Chinese critics to rate him low; however, the European historian of Chinese art, thinking in terms of a European modification of the Chinese standards, asserts that his paintings are excellent works of art.[19]

The Idea of Fusion

The interaction of art and artist in technique, attitude, and innovation is certainly significant, but the idea and ideal of fusion are more relevant to the understanding of the aesthetic universal. This ideal claims the fullness of or denies the conventional separation between the different arts, for it is often careless of or denies the separation between art and nonart, and between one person and another. In terms of this ideal, a poem is equally a picture, a statue, or a musical composition, for it is an emotion or a complex of emotions, the truth, the cosmos reflected in a microcosm. In Europe, the artist who expressed himself equally in different media was a well-known phenomenon. In the fourteenth century there was Guillaume de Machaut, poet, musician, and story-teller (as well as churchman and diplomat); in the Renaissance there were men such as Ghiberti and the fabulously many-sided Alberti; and in the Romantic period, when the mental climate was favorable, there were multiply talented men such as Blake, E.T.A. Hoffman, composer, critic, and storyteller (and for years, like the ideal Chinese scholar-artist, a government official), and the poet-painter Rossetti. In China the man who was calligrapher, painter, and poet was a widely accepted ideal, and was embodied by Wang Wei (ca. 699–ca. 761); by Su Shih (Tung-p'o; 1036–1101); and by the trio of Shen Chou (1427–1509), his pupil Wen Cheng-ming (1470–1559), and Wen's friend T'ang Yin (1470–ca. 1523).

Su Tung-p'o was the central figure in the first circle of literati poet-painters. The spirit that prevailed among the members of the circle is suggested by a poem written by Huang T'ing-chien (1045–1105) on a painting, done jointly by Su and Li Kung-lin (Lung-mien; 1049–1106) and entitled *Herd-boy with Bamboo and Rock.*[20] The poem is preceded by a short preface in prose:

> Su Tung-p'o painted a clump of bamboo and a fantastic rock. Li Kung-lin added a slope in the foreground and a herdboy riding a water-buffalo. The picture, full of life, has inspired these playful verses:
>
> Here's a little craggy rock in a wild place, shadowed
> 　　　　by green bamboo.
>
> A herdboy, wielding a three-foot stick, drives his lum-
> 　　　　bering old water-buffalo.
>
> I love the rock! Don't let the buffalo rub his horns on it!
> Well, all right—let him rub his horns—but if he gets too
> 　　　　rough he'll break the bamboo!

Painted by two friends and expressed in poetry by a third, the literal subject is love for a rock, modified by sympathy for a buffalo, modified by sympathy for the bamboo. The metaphorical subject is the hardness, the resistance to time and weather, of the rock, the more flexible resistance of the bamboo, and the interdependence of natural things. The basic subject is the union in act and feeling of three friends, the union of each with the others and with nature and all with those who might see the picture and read the poem. In other words, the basic subject is fusion—of art with art, friend with friend, and art with reality.

The desire for fusion is analogous to the desire for love. In an often less direct but no less real way, painting, like poetry, very often (and perhaps, taken deeply, always) deals with love: the love of the painter for his subject, for things in general, for his fellow men (which he may not be able to express adequately in any other way), and for the activity of painting, which is the sum of the other loves that painting, like the other arts, makes accessible. In different ways, this idea of love finds expression in the work of Michelangelo, Bernini, Van Gogh and Kirchner.

In Condivi's biography of Michelangelo, Michelangelo, who is plausibly taken to have been responsible for its tone and content, is described in the following words, strongly tinged with Neo-Platonism:

> He has . . . loved the beauty of the human body as one who knows it extremely well, and loved it in such a way as to inspire certain carnal men, who are incapable of understanding the love of beauty except as lascivious and indecent, to think and speak ill of him. . . . And that no foul thought could have arisen in his mind is evident from the fact that he has loved not only human beauty but everything beautiful in general; a beautiful horse, a beautiful dog, a beautiful landscape, a beautiful mountain, a beautiful forest, and every place and thing which is beautiful and rare of its kind, admiring them all with marveling love and selecting beauty from nature as the bees gather honey from flowers, to use it later in his works. All those who have achieved some fame in painting have always done the same.[21]

These are Michelangelo's own sentiments, in words that he might essentially have dictated; but they match the emotion he invested in his sculptures. In the words of an eloquent commentator:

Stone was Michelangelo's life. It was his friend, his enemy, and his enduring love. In poem after poem, many times quoted, he tells us how the statue is there inside the stone, and how it grows as the stone shrinks. He sought out perfect stone in the wildest mountains, only to abandon it in St. Peter's Square. He cut it, beat it, loved it, hated it, finished it with infinite care down to the most minutely calculated tensions, hesitations, and curves, left it in rugged masses. It was his triumph and his defeat. He carved it for seventy-five years. He was born with it and died with it. In the very process of bringing shapes out of the "hard and Alpine stone" he could find metaphors of life, love, and death, discern the will of God, and foresee redemption.[22]

Something similar is said of the great sculptor and architect Bernini:

Baldinucci describes how Bernini in his old age, whenever he was not engaged in architectural projects, would work tirelessly till seven in the morning on his marble sculptures, with a bag beside him to ensure that in a moment of abstraction he did not tumble off the scaffolding. "Let me be, I am in love," he would reply when he was asked to rest, and such was his concentration that he seemed to be in ecstasy. It appeared, says Baldinucci, that the force to animate the marble was projected from his eyes. Before the angels in Sant'Andrea delle Fratte all this is credible.[23]

Van Gogh's love is more openly directed at the human beings with whom he longed to be joined by means of his painting. Although he had been repeatedly rejected, he reassured himself in the language of his art that he was not cast off and said, in effect, "I, Vincent, have not been rejected and cast off but am beloved by and united with those I love."[24] His work made him feel alive, excited him, and made him forget his loneliness. "The worse I get along with people," he said, "the more I learn to have faith in nature and concentrate on her."[25] Like the Chinese who translated resistance into painted or poetic rocks, resilience into bamboos, and old age into twisted old trees, Van Gogh translated tree trunks and limbs into strength and dependence, beauty and ugliness, loneliness and company. He paired sun and moon like people, and complementary colors like couples "which complete each other like man and woman."[26] He loved, in a unifying way, others, himself, the world, and his work. "How rich in beauty art is," he wrote. "If one can only remember what one has seen, one is never empty or truly lonely, never alone."[27] Even if it were true, he said, that he was nothing, an eccentric disagreeable man, he wanted to show what there was in the heart of such an eccentric man; for his ambition was founded less on anger than on love, more on serenity and less on passion. In spite of his frequent misery, he felt a calm pure harmony and a music within himself.[28]

In much the same vein, Ernst Ludwig Kirchner, the German Expressionist wrote, "My work comes out of the longing for loneliness. I was always alone, the more I ventured among men, the more I felt my loneliness. . . . I did not have the art of becoming warm in people's company. That is fate, and perhaps one of the major reasons for my becoming a painter. Art is a good way to show one's love for men without inconveniencing them."[29]

Fusion as a Cosmic and Social Principle

Art tends to be expansive, to approximate in its tendency what is generally and inadequately known in the West as pantheism, but which is essentially the desire to go, feel, and even be beyond one's own limited self. This desire for fusion can be expressed in cosmic or in social terms, or, in an amalgam of both.

Two essays—the first written by the most famous of Chinese calligraphers, the fourth-century Wang Hsi-chih (307–365), and the second by the seventeenth-century "individualistic" painter Shih-t'ao (Tao-chi; 1641–c.1710)—illustrate the idea of fusion as a cosmic and social principle.

Wang's essay is a preface to thirty-seven poems written by a select and influential group of men who had met for a traditional purification ceremony. His preface recalls the ceremony as a time of perfect communion: "What with drinking and the composing of verses, we conversed in wholehearted freedom, entering fully into one another's feelings. The day was fine, the air clear, and a gentle breeze regaled us, so that on looking up we responded to the vastness of the universe, and on bending down were struck by the manifold riches of the earth. . . . What perfect bliss!"[30] What made the situation ideal, at least in memory, was the fact that·the companions were attuned not only to one another— and this in the concentrated expressiveness of poetry—but to the universe as well. Hence the perfect bliss. Wang explains that there are persons who are unreflective and insensitive to art, but not in that group, "for in men's association with one another in their journey through life, some draw upon their inner resources and find satisfaction in a closeted conversation with a friend." Then Wang grows melancholy. "It is idle," he writes, "to pretend that life and breath are equal states, and foolish to claim that a youth cut off in his prime has led the protracted life of a centenarian." Having expressed the melancholy so widespread in Chinese literature, Wang then finds consolation in the sharing of even melancholy sentiments: "Even when circumstances have changed and men inhabit a different world, it will still be the same causes that induce the mood of melancholy attendant on poetical composition." He concludes with the hope of all authors of every time and place: "Perhaps some reader of the future will be moved by the sentiments expressed in this preface."[31]

The cosmic implication is stronger in Shih-t'ao's discussion than in Wang's. It is based upon the very fundamental of Chinese painting: the single stroke. His term for what we may call his ontology of art is the "one-stroke" (or "oneness of stroke," or "one-strokedness"). He uses this term to express the inherent fusion of things—their common source and their overwhelming affinity—within nature and (if the difference need be marked) between nature and true art.[32] He says, using, not the common speech of the Ch'an Buddhists with whom he had once cast his lot, but the elliptical language of the literati: "To have method, one must have transformations. Transformations, then, yield the method of no-method. Painting is the great way of the transformation of the world."[33]

To Shih-t'ao this transformation is equivalent to self-realization. What he wants in his theory and in his painting is something that is both general and particular, both vague and definite, both easy and difficult, both humble and universal. The very simplicity of his thought is meant to have its own richness and dynamism, showing that the single stroke, the stroke with which the child is first taught to write, remains, in all its nuances and power, the ultimate test of the mastery of an accomplished calligrapher or painter—that which distinguishes weak from strong, genuine from false. The simple, fundamental stroke is also the stroke (the horizontal line) of the *Book of Changes*. Shih-t'ao implies that, like the trigrams and hexagrams of the *Changes*, the brushstroke in painting is a version of the creation of the universe. By implication, it is the same as that of Confucius (*Analects* IV.15) when he said that his way is that of the One and embraces the universal, or that "There is one single thread binding my way together."[34]

Shih-t'ao boldly says, "A single stroke which identifies with universality can clearly reveal the idea of man and fully penetrate all things. Thus the wrist seizes reality, it moves the brush with a revolving movement, enriches the strokes by rolling the brush hairs, and leaves them unbounded by any limitations."[35] The wrist, to which the universe is attached as cause and as effect of the activity of true painting, is apt to seize the otherwise so elusive reality-in-itself.

This bold ontology of art must have been Shih-t'ao's answer to the confusion of styles and methods and the profusion of historical knowledge, which puzzled or intimidated students. His solution, the methodless method that engenders method, and the method that, so obtained, embraces all methods, recalls the "non-being" that in the *Tao-te ching* (chapter 40) engenders being, which engenders heaven and earth and all they contain. His effort to return to an elemental, all-encompassing simplicity is seen by a recent historian to be related to his greatness as a painter, but also, perhaps, to a finally destructive renunciation of the disciplines of Chinese painting.[36] However, Shih-t'ao's ontology may also be regarded as a particularly apposite restatement of the need for creative fusion, in which individual and nature and past and present are joined.

The idea of fusion as a cosmic and/or social principle finds expression in Europe as well. For example, in a letter to his father, Mozart wrote that if the audience does not feel with him what he was playing, he ceases to feel any pleasure.[37] Whitman begins his "Song of Myself" with the lines, "I celebrate myself, and sing myself, / And what I assume you shall assume, / For every atom belonging to me as good belongs to you." To show the variety of ways in which this fusion is expressed, I shall cite several eloquent examples, by the Norwegian painter Edvard Munch, the German painter Emil Nolde, the American poet William Carlos Williams, and the Austrian composer Arnold Schoenberg.

Munch, for the most part a tortured person whose life, as he himself said, had been spent "walking by the side of a bottomless chasm, jumping from stone to stone," wrote plainly:

> All in all, art results from man's desire to communicate with his fellows. All methods are equally effective. Both in literature and in painting the technique varies according to the aims of the artist. . . . A landscape will alter according to the mood of the person who sees it, and in order to produce a picture that expresses his own personal feelings. It is these feelings which are crucial: nature is merely the means of conveying them. Whether the picture resembles nature or not is irrelevant, as a picture cannot be explained; the reason for its being painted in the first place was that the artist could find no other means of expressing what he saw.[38]

Although Munch, like Shih-t'ao and innumerable others, said that nature in art is merely the means of conveying the artist's personal feelings, he came to believe in a hidden force of life whose existence is manifested in the cyclical renewal of nature. To express this belief, he painted a dead woman passing life on to the new generation by means of a tree of life.[39]

Nolde was equally preoccupied with the precarious sanity

of artists, albeit from a different standpoint. He was friendly with and provided material for the psychiatrist Hans Prinzhorn, who wrote pioneering studies of the art of psychotics and prisoners. Nolde the painter felt the attraction as well as the danger of painting, which erased perhaps necessary boundaries. Lying on his back and gazing for hours at a successful picture, merging with the picture as if he had no existence separate from it, he felt an "incomparable joy." He also felt that this joy brought him close to the danger of annihilation. He fused with the things he contemplated and those that he made. In a letter, he wrote "When I am painting with the utmost intensity, I find that I have lost my voice. . . . As soon as I slack off, my voice comes back."[40] Strangely—or perhaps not at all strangely—he tended to dislike the people closest to him, and therefore to love, along with the whole of creation, unknown human beings. In his words:

> Human beings are, nearly all of them, the artist's enemies, and his friends and near relations are the worst. He is like a man shunning the light, and they are like policemen with a lantern. He is a man with the devil in his bones and God in his heart. Who can conceive the enmity and conflict of such powers? The artist lives behind walls, in a time-less state, seldom on the wing, often withdrawn into his shell. He loves to watch strange things that go on in the depths of nature, but he also loves bright, clear reality, moving clouds, flowers that bloom and glow, the whole of creation. Unknown human beings are his friends, people he has never met, gypsies and Papuans—such people carry no lanterns.[41]

Of William Carlos Williams I want to capture only a brief, touching description of his last days, when a stroke had paralyzed his right arm and deprived him of the ability to speak. He continued, however, to write. Sickness and age drove him to create. As Williams said, "When you're through with sex, with ambition, what can an old man create?" Art, of course, a piece of art that will go beyond him into the lives of young people, the people who haven't the time to create. The old man meets the young people and lives on."[42]

There is also, of course, creation that attempts to arrive at fusion or, more simply, at sympathy, by means of a complaint or confession of failure. Consequently, in the successful work of art the complaint or confession is incorporated into a state of ambivalence resembling a logical self-contradiction, or, psychologically speaking, a contradiction of self. The music of Arnold Schoenberg exemplifies this type of creation. As an artist he was rejected for his radicalism. His wife left him for a friend, rejecting him as a person. Thus Schoenberg's theme was, equally, the isolated, unrecognized artist and the failed self. Art and artist become the tragic clown in "Pierrot Lunaire," while in the cantata "Jacob's Ladder," technique and the text both say, "Redeem us from our isolation!"[43]

Stated generally, without reference to a particular art, artist, or culture, art is the attempt to remain separate and individual in expression, but also to merge or fuse with what is beyond the individual, to be, in theological terms, both transcendent and immanent. Art insists on both separateness and symbiosis. It demonstrates the individual's uniqueness, just as it demonstrates his separateness from the rest of nature. It is his form of participation in local humanity and perhaps in humanity at large, and it makes him, as he often feels himself to be, the creative collaborator of nature.

Tendencies Toward Mysticism in Aesthetic Traditions

As stated earlier, the aim of this paper is to discover that which is common to the art of every time and every place. Toward this end I shall now turn to the beginnings and the development of the aesthetic traditions in Europe and in China, in order to show some of the principles held in common by both traditions.

In Europe, the dominant impulse in aesthetics, which issued from Plato or Plotinus, is one I shall call, for short, the Neo-Platonic. In the case of Plato, I am not referring, of course, to his polemic against the making images of images, with which Plotinus agreed when he refused to allow anyone to make his portrait. Rather, I refer to Plato's belief that love of the beauties of the body leads to love of those of the soul, and that love of those of the soul leads to the vision of everlasting beauty. As for Plotinus, not only was he vitally concerned with beauty and art, but he also believed that the artist could grasp a sublime archetype. Hence, for example, his statement that "the arts do not simply imitate what they see; they go back to the *logoi* from which nature derives; and . . . they do a great deal in themselves: since they possess beauty they make up what is defective in things. Phidias did not make his Zeus from any model perceived by the senses; he understood what Zeus would look like if he wanted to make himself visible."[44]

It is clear that, to Plotinus, the mind of the artist shares the nature of the creative *Nous*, which he took to be the actualized form of the One or Good that could simply not be grasped in and for itself. Again and again Plotinus writes eloquent praises in favor of the beauty which is Form, and, even more than form, is Life; and so he declares that badly proportioned but living faces have more beauty than symmetrical but lifeless ones.[45] To him, true beauty is the radiance cast upon the world by the Good that is the One; it is the source of the world's existence and beauty, or, rather, the source of its beautiful existence, because existence is beautiful as such, in exact proportion to its intensity, its closeness to the One. Therefore beauty in itself is without form. "The experience of lovers is evidence of this; as long as the lover is on the level of the impression made on his senses, he is not yet in love. It is only when he produces from this, by his own outward action, an impression which is not on his sense, but in his undivided soul, that love is born . . . His first experience was love of a great light from a dim gleam of it. For shape is a trace of Something without shape, which produces shape, not shape itself."[46] Non-being which produces being, the Taoist would say; and the Neo-Confucian, too, has his analogue.

Medieval aesthetics was closely related to Neo-Platonic themes, and so, naturally, was the aesthetics of the succeeding Renaissance, though the Renaissance also required anatomy, perspective, and an idealized nature, as the Middle Ages, until its last phase, did not.[47] According to Alberti, the artist who paints all the parts of the body should "not only render a true likeness but also add beauty to them; for in painting, loveliness is not so much pleasing as it is required." As Alberti was hardly a transcendentalist, he, like other theorists of the early Renaissance, emphasized harmony and proportion. Whereas, Ficino, Neo-Platonist that he was, defined beauty as a "victory of divine reason over matter" and as "radiance from the face of God."[48] Neo-Platonic theories such as Ficino's became prominent in art theory in the second half of the sixteenth century, when the artist was taken to be the person who could give nature a perfection and beauty that nature alone could not attain.[49] Michelangelo accepted Plotinus' idea that the artist revealed the beauty inherent in the stone.[50] In this manner, the medieval comparison of the artist with God was extended to the point where the artist himself was considered to be in some measure divine.

It would be pointless to continue with an abbreviated history of European aesthetics, most of which can be classified as a set of variants of Neo-Platonism. This is surely true, as well, of Romanticism and Symbolism. From the late nineteenth century, variants of the Neo-Platonic ideal were often merged with ideas imported from India, for example, by Schopenhauer and, later, by the Theosophists. Because of this synthesis, it is perhaps wiser to speak of mysticism rather than Neo-Platonism. Certainly mysticism remained widespread among artists. The German Expressionists voiced mystical opinions, as, in their fashion, did the Surrealists and the pioneering abstract artists: Kupka in the name of Orphism, Malevich in the name of Suprematism, Kandinsky at first in the name of the Blue Riders, Mondrian in the name of De Stijl or Neo-Plasticism, Ozenfant and Jeanneret in the name of Purism, and so on. Doctrines that can reasonably be called mysticism were characteristic of many members of the New York School. Reinhardt studied and was affected by Chinese philosophy, Pollock had Taoist leanings, and Rothko, Still, and Newman, too, had mystical leanings. The desire of the New York group, wrote Newman, was to transcend the particular, reaching beyond the known world and familiar art to create an abstract art of the sublime.[51]

Karel Appel described this kind of mysticism when he

wrote, in 1978, that past and future disappear when he paints. "The canvas is ready to be beyond consciousness. Just be. Beyond the human dualities." He says, "Only in this non-dual work together with my painting I lose myself, my body also. In my painting the form becomes vibrations, it enters the formless form, formless existence that I paint—vibrations of color."[52]

The conclusion to be drawn from such evidence is very simple: The thought of European aestheticians and artists has been strongly tinged with mysticism and has, in some cases, been predominantly mystical.

This tendency toward mysticism may be seen in Chinese aesthetics as well. The chief underlying idea is the all-important concept of *ch'i*. Its early meanings include "vapor," "breath," "exhalation," and "life-spirit." *Ch'i* is not at all abstract because it is, among other things, the very air we breathe. It is the source of our life; it disperses when we die; in anger we swell with it; in old age we shrink as it diminishes. As universal energy, present everywhere in different concentrations, *ch'i* came in time to be regarded as not only the life in things, but as that into which solid things condense and dissolve. Thus matter was regarded as impure or congealed *ch'i*. The Greeks might have called it "ether."[53]

The concept of *ch'i* plays an important role in the theory of every Chinese art. In literature, for example, its chief function is "to impel and buoy up, to maintain the connection between the parts, to give unity, to vary the pace."[54] Elusive though *ch'i* is, it can be captured if one shares the tension-creating twists and turns by which words are related. A piece of literature is, as Herder and other Europeans also took it to be, a "living" organism—perhaps with the quotation marks around living omitted. For calligraphy and painting, the concept of *ch'i* was most used in combination with *yün*, meaning "reverberation," or "resonance." The ubiquitous combination *ch'i-yün* may therefore be translated, as it often is, as "reverberation of the life-breath." In the first of the famous canons of Chinese art, set out by Hsieh Ho in the late fifth century, this phrase was coupled with another, *sheng-tung*.

The whole may be translated as "reverberation of the life-breath, that is, the creation of movement," or as "the reverberation of the life of breath creates life-movement."[55]

It seems that in the early development of Chinese art-theory *ch'i-yün* was applied to the life-force of the natural objects being depicted, the force the painter aimed to capture. But the phrase could take on moral overtones, and it came to mean the vital creative force of the universe, in which everything partook. The presence of *ch'i* in art was then equivalent to the presence of Tao, that is, of the vital spirit of the universe.[56] The concept of *liang-chih*, which posits the identity of mind and nature and the principle of life and consciousness, is permeated by the *ch'i* that permeates everything and makes nonduality possible.[57]

Chinese aesthetics, based on this idea of the vital spirit, tended to specify its subprinciples in terms of pairs of polar opposites. Tung Ch'i-ch'ang emphasized such compositional principles as "opening and closing" (*k'ai-ho*), "void and solidity" (*hsü-shih*), "guest and host" (*pin-chu*) and "frontality and reverse" (*hsiang-pei*).[58] Such ideas, real or ostensible clarifications of earlier ones, continued to be elaborated. In China, the work of art is always regarded as organismic; there is always the sense of opposing, vivifying forces, lines of force that unify the parts, which in turn have a forceful unity of their own. The feeling is always one of breathing, expansion and contraction, of the alternation of the dense and the rare, of the closed and the open, of the opposition and harmony of all forces, of excessiveness restrained and want supplied, and of the individual and the universe as parallel to and even, if one sees sharply enough, contained within one another. As Shen Tsung-hsien said in the eighteenth century, everything everywhere both expands and contracts "from the revolution of the world to our breathing."[59]

The critic Wang Fu-chih, who believed more in spontaneity than in the possibility of conscious control of poetic expression,[60] summarized the conceptualization of duality-unity. Poetry, he insisted, is more concerned with life than with literature as such, for it is a continuation of the eternal processes of the universe as human consciousness interacts with it, and it helps to re-create the human–universal bond that too many persons have broken.[61]

The Potential for Self-Transcendence in Art

I want to suggest that the various European aesthetic concepts or attidues, Neo-Platonic or otherwise mystical, share elements that go even further in justifying the assumption of an aesthetic universal. The aesthetic universal thus conceived is related to the modern German theory of *Einfühlung*, usually translated "empathy", with mystical sources in Herder, Novalis, and others. However, the modern German theory differs radically from its sources in that it exchanges their pan-psychism for something more prosaic—the outward projection of individual consciousness, allowing the other person or the outward object to be experienced psychophysically as if he or it were oneself.[62] Theodor Lipps (1851–1914), an exponent of empathy in this sense, .regarded it as "the objectified enjoyment of the self,"[63] a view perhaps related to Indian attitudes. Lipps' use of empathy is also similar to the Neo-Confucian *jen*, which, though more moral in intention, is characterized by a psychophysical dynamism related to the function of *ch'i.* Among European artists, the Expressionists were particularly influenced by the theory of empathy; it gave them a justification for assimilating the objects of their art to their own emotions.

Together with the emphasis on empathy, art, on all levels, also expresses the need of the individual to live beyond himself. At every level, art carries the message, "This is what I am like," the "I" in this case pertaining less to external than to internal characteristics, to those that in human beings we are inclined to call spiritual. This message has a natural extension, which can be put as an appeal or demand, and which can be made with varying degrees of insistence. The extension of the message is, "Sympathize with me, empathize with me, identify with me, resemble me, join me, or at least pay attention to me, as I really am, as I may play some role, sexual or otherwise emotional, in your life." Art can appear to be ethically neutral; but it issues an incessant moral invitation, or makes an incessant moral demand. This demand is individual, on the one hand, and has social implications, on the other.

The moral demand, in turn, is related to what may be termed a subtle emotion, which provides the impetus for fusion. This emotion underlies the philosophy of Plato and Plotinus, both of whom express it as the desire to participate and be participated in. Variations of this idea characterize most of Western aesthetics. It also underlies mystically oriented Indian aesthetics, according to which art creates a state of identification with what has been depicted that is so powerful that the ego is pierced and a unique calm pervades the spectator, auditor, or reader. It also underlies the Chinese aesthetic principle, that art is a tonic pulsation by which individual and universal life are joined. The moral demand together with its motivating emotion is the Neo-Confucian principle of *liang-chih*, the identity of mind and nature, a doctrine that can be attributed to Confucius' statement, "There is one single thread binding my way together." Mencius describes it as the emphasis on inborn sympathy and the ability to know the good. It is also the Chinese virtue of *jen*, "compassion" or "humanity," which is defined in Neo-Confucianism as "to regard oneself and another as one and not two."[64] *Jen* is given cosmic connotations in Wang Yang-ming's famous essay of 1527, "Inquiry into the Great Learning":

> When a person sees a child about to fall into a well, he cannot help having a feeling of alarm and commiseration. This shows that his humanity (*jen*) forms one body with the child. It may be objected that the child belongs to the same species [as he]. Yet when he observes the pitiful cries and frightened appearance of birds and beasts [about to be slaughtered], he cannot help feeling an "inability" to bear their suffering. This shows that his humanity forms one body with birds and beasts. It may be objected that birds and beasts are sentient beings too. But when he sees plants broken and destroyed, he cannot help having a feeling of pity. This shows that his humanity forms one body with

plants. It may be said that plants are living things too. Yet even when he sees tiles and stones shattered and crushed he cannot help having a feeling of regret. This shows that his humanity forms one body with tiles and stones. This means that even the heart of the small man must have [in potentiality] this humanity which unites him to all things.[65]

There is then something in art, pertaining to its essence, that I think of as a subtle emotion, one perhaps of self-enlargement or self-transcendence, but also one, perhaps, of self-diminution or self-recession. In this emotion, bird and human being join. I am referring to whatever it is in a person, like singing in a bird, that connects him in emotion with another, and that thins the boundary between him and anyone and anything else. It is that which allows and encourages the individual to escape the threat of isolation and feel himself integrated into the society of others or the society of the universe. The whole purpose of the emotion, if it is merely that, is to give a deeply inward response that is directed outward—to go above, below, through, and beyond, the individual, in time, space, and nature. It is an emotional–intellectual bridging; and it is a sensuously apprehensible, non- but sub-mystical and quasi-moral hope or demand.

I think as I say this of a disorderly collection of responses in which all distinctions of time, place, and culture are forgotten. I think of the Chinese, who are always painting and writing that they need solitude and that they need friendship in order to escape solitude. I remember the fifteenth-century painter Shen Chou making a painting for a friend and writing on it in a poem that in the mountains above the river (the physical, the painted, the poetic river) they sensed their lasting friendship.[66] I remember Van Gogh, unable to live with human beings but painting in order to prove that, all the same, he could love them. I remember Thomas Mann writing to his future wife Katia that his existence had been cold and impoverished, organized purely to display art and only represent life, and pleading with her to affirm, justify, and fulfill him and be his wife and savior, the plea being put, like his art and as a specimen of it, in writing.[67] I remember Stephen Spender's idea that every writer is secretly writing for a parent, a childhood teacher, or the like, and explaining that to write is to have faith that in art one can be even more than oneself.[68] I remember the contemporary photographer Burk Uzzle saying of his pictures, "They are me, they are my pictures. My work is my visible love," and another photographer, Jill Freedman, saying, "A photograph is a shared experience. It's, 'Hey look at this.'"[69] I remember the painter Clyfford Still writing, "When I expose a painting I would have it say, 'Here I am: this is my presence, my feelings, myself!'"[70] I remember the painter Robert Mother-well saying that the experience of a work of art is, like making love, a contact "determined precisely by its form"; and I remember the painter Barnett Newmann saying that he hoped that his painting would give someone else, as it gave him, "the feeling of his own totality, of his own separateness, of his individuality, and at the same time of his connection to others, who are also separate."[71] I remember and summarize all these and all the other reactions that might be added, in two simple, anonymous lines from an anthology compiled in Japan in the tenth century:

> If I love and keep on loving,
> can we fail to meet?[72]

The emotion I am referring to runs through all expressive behavior, but is at its most concentrated in art, the object of which is to externalize internality in as effective a way as possible. With all the emphasis at my command, I say that this emotion, though essential to art, is not sufficient for it. Art in the full sense can be characterized but cannot be given a very useful definition because it is implicated in too many things and too hard to separate from them, because it is present in every form we give our acts. Art is by nature inexhaustibly local and variable, and not at all as bare as an abstraction or as the obscure emotion that I have spoken of and almost tried to name. Yet though this emotion, which I have called the universal of art, is inexhaustibly far from explaining all of art, little of importance in art can be understood unless it is kept in mind. The reason is that art in all its forms is always the instinctive and willed antithesis of loneliness.

CHAPTER 6

Human Rites—An Essay on Confucianism and Human Rights

WM. THEODORE DE BARY

Foreword

On this special occasion which evokes the memory of Vitaly Rubin, I hope I may be allowed to indulge in a few personal reminiscences which may help to explain his connection to the subject of this essay. From the beginning of my friendship with Vitaly, Confucianism and human rights were both deeply implicated in our relationship. When he first wrote me from Moscow about my work and later sent me some of his own, I learned that his interest in Confucianism paralleled my own, but on a level of personal involvement even deeper than mine, if that is possible, since it was inseparable from his personal struggle for human freedom and dignity. Not long thereafter this developed into a struggle for his release from the Soviet Union and, as it unexpectedly turned out, into an issue which would greatly occupy the Columbia campus during my years as Provost. In the early 1970s the campaign to free Vitaly Rubin rose to one kind of climax, in the protest meeting held at the Collège de France in connection with the 1974 Congress of Orientalists in Paris, over which I had the honor to preside, and to another peak in the publication of Vitaly's book, *Individual and State in Ancient China*, by the Columbia University Press in 1976.

When Vitaly was released in 1976, his friends, who had been prepared for a long struggle, were almost taken aback by the sudden success of our efforts (though to this day I cannot be sure how much it was due to our vociferous protests and how much to the quiet diplomacy of people like Marshall Shulman at the State Department in Washington). In any case, the culmination of our activities came with a memorable university convocation at Columbia in September of 1976, at which we welcomed Vitaly and Inessa Rubin. At that time Vitaly spoke most movingly of his experiences and his convictions concerning the struggle for human rights in the Soviet Union. It seemed important to me then that we should not lose the moral momentum gained from such a rare success, but should seek to transform it into a continuing intellectual and scholarly movement for human rights at Columbia. The first step taken was to hold a series of public symposia on human rights—we called them General Education Seminars—and the second was to establish a permanent center, the Center for the Study of Human Rights. Under the leadership of Louis Henkin, Mitchell Ginsberg, and Arthur Danto, the latter has since become a major center for promoting research, instruction, and scholarly exchange in the field of human rights.

Human rights are admittedly a new field of study and even, as a form of public advocacy, a comparatively young one. Most people think of human rights as a product of modern Western civilization, which is true enough as regards its present form and its most advanced stage of development. Unfortunately the usual corollary of this for most people is that human rights are and have been a peculiarly Western concern. Even those well informed about the current struggle for human rights in China and intensely committed to it, think of such rights as a wholly modern conception for which there was no precedent before Western liberal thought reached China in the early years of this century. To some extent this involves a disagreement over terms and definitions which I shall not try to sort out here, but to an even greater extent it is a matter of long-standing preconceptions about China. Such views are held even by relatively well-educated persons, many of whom had thought that Mao's revolution would liberate China from a despotic past, only to find that new repressions, collectively stigmatized today as work of the "Gang of Four" or the "Cultural Revolution," outdid even past tyrannies. They now resignedly accept this as somehow inevitable, concluding that since time immemorial the Chinese had become inured to, and were perhaps even prone to, inhuman behavior. From this the view arises of the Chinese tradition as inherently repressive and incapable of sharing or expressing the sentiments which underlie human rights in the West. In that vein, Confucianism, the ethical core of that tradition, is often spoken of as conservative and authoritarian, as fundamentally indisposed to value human rights.

This is not a new idea, however understandable it may be as a reaction to recent events. It was a view of Confucianism widely prevalent in the nineteenth-century West, and one form of it became a mental fixture of the Marxism–Leninism with which Vitaly Rubin had to contend as a young scholar. This is why I found it altogether refreshing to discover how free Vitaly's own work was from the preconceptions one expected to encounter in Soviet scholarship on China. As I wrote in the foreword to his *Individual and State:*

> What strikes one immediately in Rubin's work is its freedom from ideological preconceptions and sterile typologies. That such an independent standpoint could emerge in an atmosphere heavy with dogmatic definitions and befogged by partisan polemics, takes us quite by surprise—less expectable even than Solzhenitsyn's volcanic eruption from the Gulag Archipelago. Through all the doctrinaire stereotypes of good guys and bad guys in ancient China, and in the face of the modern anti-Confucian campaign, Rubin has come to his own

appreciation of Confucius' unassuming greatness and capacity to inspire even a brutalized generation of men.

To let Vitaly speak for himself, I cite this representative passage from the book, which tries to dispel the conventional view of Confucius and Confucianism:

> Sometimes the existing literature ignores the ideal of the *chün-tzu*, and characterizes Confucianism entirely on the basis of the ideal of the obedient subject. From this premise Confucianism is defined as a conservative ideology of feudal aristocracy, bureaucracy, or despotism. But on the basis of the ideal of the *chün-tzu* we are compelled to considerably modify such appraisals. As a harmonious and self-sufficient person, the *chün-tzu* must not carry out the ruler's every command. On the contrary, he must resist when he deems the ruler's conduct immoral. If the remonstrances of the *chün-tzu* are ineffective, and unscrupulousness and profit-hunting are reigning in the state, then the *chün-tzu* must refuse to serve, because honor and wealth dishonorably gained are not for him. It is shameful to think of enrichment in a state constructed on injustice. . . .
>
> Confucius particularly stressed the *chün-tzu*'s nonconformism by asserting that the *chün-tzu* aims at harmony, not uniformity. Cheng Hsüan, a Chinese commentator of the second century A.D., in explaining this passage, wrote, "A *chün-tzu*'s heart is in harmony with others, but his views are distinguished from theirs." This theme of autonomy, of the independence of the worthy and learned man, was continued in a number of later Confucian works. One of these, a small treatise entitled "The Conduct of a Confucian," is part of the *Li-chi*. It waxes enthusiastic about the self-sufficiency of the gentleman—saying, for example, that the Confucian does not deem gold and jasper precious, but faithfulness and justice alone. If one should try to tempt him with riches and corrupt him with pleasures, despite everything set out before him, he would still not turn away even an inch from justice. "Even when

power is in the hands of a tyrant he will not change his position."[1]

For the most part Vitaly's scholarly work was confined to the early period, but he always worked with an eye to its modern parallels. Had he lived to this day I am sure Vitaly would have wanted to contribute further to the clarification of human rights issues in China both past and present. This he would no doubt have done with the same combination of humane sympathy and critical acuity shown in his earlier work, but above all he would have been as firm in opposing current abuses of human rights as he had asked us to be in his own behalf.

In that same spirit I offer the following initial exploration of human rights conceptions as found in the later, more developed, tradition of Confucian thought. To fully evaluate that tradition as a working system, or to assess its virtues and defects on any comparative scale, is a task which seems beyond our present scholarly capability. Nevertheless, it is not too early to suggest, if only in a sketchy way, how the matter might be viewed in a less prejudicial manner than in the past.

Some Modern Perspectives

As a matter of conscious advocacy the concept of "human rights" is a relatively recent Western invention, yet it is also understood to be the product of a long evolution in Western thought, having its own distinctive features. From this the conclusion is often reached that "human rights" are peculiarly Western. Whether this is so or not, however, depends on how one interprets "human rights." In the nineteenth century Chinese and Japanese intellectuals had to face this problem when, by means of commonly used Chinese characters, they formed new compounds and expressed "human rights" with such terms as the Japanese *jinken* and the Chinese *jen-ch'üan*, and "peoples' rights" with the Japanese *minken* and the Chinese *min-ch'üan*. The same applied to the assimilation of such concepts as "liberty" or "freedom" (Jap. *jiyu*/Ch. *tzu-yu*), or liberalism (Jap. *jiyu shugi*/Ch. *tzu-yu chu-i*), where the translation emphasized the importance of the individual and the principle of voluntarism. Though neologisms formed in order to convey the special quality of Western ideas, these new terms also had, for Chinese, Japanese, and Koreans, traditional associations attached to their component parts. Old coins were being recast into new currency. Thus the component for "human" (*jin/jen*) had strong associations with the central value of "humaneness" or "humanity" in Confucian culture. The term for "rights," *ken-ch'üan* in this compound, while expressing the idea of authority or discretionary power, also had some connotations of "subject to discretion or qualification," hence "provisional," "accommodative," and even "expedient," rather than "constant" or "unvarying" as one might think of "inalienable human rights."

In this respect the assimilation of modern Western concepts bears some resemblance to the Chinese adoption of Buddhist concepts in the early Middle Ages. At that time the Chinese readily converted certain new ideas into familiar terms, even though the equation might not be exact. This was true of such a key concept as the *dharma*, "law" or "truth," which was rendered by the Chinese *fa*, "law," "system," and "method." On the other hand the equally important concept of meditation (*dhyāna*) was rendered phonetically, as "*ch'an*," apparently in the belief that nothing quite like it existed in Chinese. In both cases, however, these terms developed their own hybrid uses. Along with its other meanings, *fa* acquired its own Chinese Buddhist significance, and *ch'an*, though originally seen as a foreign term and practice, evolved into perhaps the most distinctly Chinese form of Buddhism. All this, too, in the face of resistance from some traditionalists who continued to view Buddhism as essentially foreign and incompatible with the native way of life.

Something similar to this has been going on in the past century with the assimilation of such concepts as "liberty," "freedom," and "human rights," but with at least one significant difference. This is the element of force or duress which accompanied the opening of China and Japan. On the one hand it added a sense of urgency to the need for accommodation with the West; on the other it left a sense of resentment and resistance. The aftereffects of this on the perceptions of some Asians of human rights as alien intrusions were perhaps predictable. Nevertheless strange incongruities appear. Some supposedly revolutionary elements regard "human rights" as mere pretexts of the imperialistic West for intervening in Asian affairs. Yet others of a more traditional, often Confucian, orientation, today talk about human rights or individual freedoms as if they were natural rights or had become second nature even to the Chinese. In prewar Japan liberalism and human rights were stigmatized by rightists and leftists alike as too individualistic, too bourgeois, too Western; yet in postwar Japan the rights guaranteed by a constitution adopted under U.S. occupation have come to be accepted almost unquestioningly, without any sense of their representing foreign imposition, and left-wing elements have been among their most vocal defenders. Ironically, however, in the People's Republic today human rights are spoken of again, officially, in much the same negative tone as prewar Japanese nationalists had taken.

In my view nothing is to be gained by arguing for the distinctively Western character of human rights. If you win the argument, you lose the battle. That is, if one claims some special distinction for the West in this respect or asserts some inherent lack on the part of Asians, one is probably defining human rights in such narrow terms as to render them unrecognizable or inoperable for others. If, however, one views human rights as an evolving conception, expressing imperfectly the aspirations of many peoples, East and West, it may be that, learning from the experience of others, one can arrive at a deeper understanding of human-rights problems in different cultural settings.

There is one other aspect of our theme which requires some clarification at the outset—this is the fact that Confucianism has served a function which in other cultures has been identified with religion. Aside from its importance in Chinese traditional culture, religion has quite recently acquired a somewhat enhanced status in the People's Republic. This is so even in the absence of any explicit official approval, if only because of the increased attention being paid to religion for both political and scholarly reasons. Everyone knows that both of these—religion and Confucianism—have been subjects of intense controversy in twentieth-century China, with both often involved in the same controversies. Today in East and Southeast Asia one hears of Confucianism making something of a comeback after years of repudiation or neglect. In the People's Republic, where this revival is perhaps less clearly in evidence, there is undeniably both a renewed scholarly interest in the study of Confucianism and a popular interest in religion, reported first among the young and disillusioned and then among authorities who feel that such a trend cannot go unwatched or unexamined. No doubt there are other reasons for this renewal too. Among them is official recognition that religion is an important factor in international politics (especially in relation with China's Asian neighbors), and that since both Asian religions and Confucianism have become major subjects of scholarly study abroad, the People's Republic can no longer afford to go unrepresented.

Today Confucianism has definitely become a major focus of study in the new Institute of World Religions of the Academy of Social Sciences in Beijing, as well as in the Institute's regional branches. The director, Professor Ren Jiyu, has attacked Confucianism as a religion and as a reactionary force in Chinese history. Opposing this view is the world-renowned philosopher, Fung Yu-lan, professor of philosophy at Beijing University, who argues that Confucianism is not a religion. This was so even though, in his characterization of the essential doctrines of Neo-Confucianism at a recent meeting in Hangchow (October 1981), he included many points which would be usually assigned to the sphere of religion. I do not propose here to sort out the issues in that debate. For my purposes it should suffice to say that I do not consider Confucianism a religion by conventional Western standards, but the religious dimensions of human experience have always held great importance for Confucians. Moreover, because religious attitudes and practices have tended to find expression in this as in other established teachings or ideologies, there is much to be learned about religion from the study of the historical development of Confucianism.

Religious Dimensions of Classical Humanism

These reflections pertain in particular to those religious attitudes often thought to underlie human rights questions in other traditions. I have in mind such concepts as the "inherent dignity of man or of the individual," "human equality," the "natural rights of man," and so forth. One can point to the central importance in Confucianism of the concept of "humaneness" or "humanity," and one can see this as constituting the essential basis of Confucian humanism. One can even argue that, given its primary attention to the study of man and the present needs of man, Confucianism is the most distinctly "humanistic" of the world's major traditions. But since so much of what Confucius has to say about being truly human also involves a deeply reverential attitude, expressed in the term *ching* ("reverence"), one might well call this a religious humanism.

Much of the Confucian *Analects* is concerned with the virtue of "reverence" and with the practice of ritual, both religious and civil. Respect for life in the present, to which Confucius gave a high priority, was linked to a reverence for life and for the sources of life, often identified with Heaven or one's ancestors. So thoroughly integrated were these two spheres, the Heavenly and the human, that one often has difficulty in judging whether the Chinese word *ching* should be translated as "reverence" or "respect." Two things are clear, however: First, that this attitude is not concerned with an afterlife, and second, that to render *ching* as "worship" (as for instance in the expression "ancestor worship") has no warrant in the Confucian context since Confucius explicitly disavowed any need for placating the spirits of the dead or for abasing oneself before Heaven.

Many of the religious traditions Confucius respected were rooted in a clan and family system undergoing change even in his time. In the *Analects* there is an increasing focus on the individual, as compared to the more social character of earlier classics. But for Confucius it was important to reaffirm these earlier roots, even while recognizing that the natural processes of growth led upward from the individual and outward from the family toward participation in a larger

community and wider world. Much of Confucius' discussion
of the nature of the individual, as represented by the ideal
of the "gentleman" or "noble man" (*chün-tzu*), stresses this
organic rootedness, this essential particularism, while also
drawing out its implications for a universal ethic. Thus:

> Tzu-lu asked about the noble man. The Master said,
> "He cultivates himself with reverence." Tzu-lu then
> asked, "Is that all?" The Master replied "He cultivates
> himself so as to make others feel secure and at ease."
> Tzu-lu then asked again, "Is that all?" To which Con-
> fucius responded "He cultivates himself so as to make
> all people feel secure and at ease." (*Analects* XXIV.45).

This same order of priorities, in which the reverent
attitude begins in the individual and reaches out to others,
is also expressed in the following passage:

> Let the noble man never fail reverently to order his own
> conduct, let him be respectful to others and observant of
> rites (decorum); then all within the four seas will be his
> brothers (*Analects* XII.5).

The saying "all men are brothers" truly expresses the
Confucian sense that family relations and a spirit of intimacy
or kinship should provide the basis for the conduct of social
relations at large. "Brotherhood" is not, of course, a peculiarly
Chinese notion. The French Revolution, heralding the modern
age, proclaimed *fraternité* as a universal ideal, but in a quite
different context. In ancient China the early development of
agriculture, its overwhelming dominance in the economic life
of the Chinese, and the continuing importance of the family
as a basic economic unit probably account for the enduring
strength of the family system and its special role in the
formation of Chinese social and cultural traditions. Trade,
with its emphasis on contractual relations, which functioned
so importantly in the multicultural, interstate world of the
ancient Mediterranean civilization, played less of a part in
China's more self-contained, homogeneous and settled agricul-
tural communities. In China, instead of explicit contractual
obligations, implicit customary practices, of a kind understood
within the clan or family, were preponderant. This, at least,

would seem a plausible, if only partial, explanation for the power and durability of a pattern of social and religious relations which survived, albeit in modified form, the transition from the archaic, clan-centered, "auguristic–sacrificial" order of the Shang to the formation in the late Chou of the more humanistic, rationalistic but family-centered outlook of traditional Confucianism. Confucians enshrined these familial relations in their new humanistic traditions, emphasizing filiality as the source of all virtue and reciprocity or mutuality as the key to the conduct of all social relations.

A distinctive feature of this value system was that it linked a reverential attitude toward human life with forms of respect for others which were expressed in concrete relationships. The treatment one was entitled to was not guaranteed by some contractual arrangement or enforced by some legal sanction, but instead was defined in relation to the whole network of responsibilities which the members of a family or community owed to one another. The emphasis was on loving, affective relations, not on impersonal, legalistic ones. These obligations had a certain objective, formal definition, for example, in the rules of decorum or of ceremonials. In contrast, however, to a strict contractual quid pro quo or legal requirement, they were considered to depend for their fulfillment on a spirit of good will and mutual regard that could not be measured in quantitative terms alone. Being grounded in natural human affections, this system had a dynamic of its own and did not require external intervention or the threat of force to make it operative.

Another distinctive feature of the system was its emphasis on equity rather than on equality in social relations. Confucians accepted social distinctions as an inevitable fact of life, and believed that differences in age, sex, social status, and political position had to be taken into account if equity were to be achieved in relations among unequals. In such cases reciprocity would not be won through the exchange of identical goods. A child, for instance, could not, in his infancy or youth, be expected to render to his parents the same kind of care and guidance which they, as adults, were obliged to provide for him. Hence the virtue appropriate to the parent–child relation was defined not in terms of obedience or service, but of loving care on the part of each, differentiable according to their respective capabilities and sometimes returnable at a later stage of life. Likewise the virtue appropriate to the relation of ruler and minister was not unconditional loyalty or unquestioning obedience, but *i*, moral propriety in the performance of the shared duties of rulership, again differentiable according to their respective functions.

In this way the underlying principles of reciprocity (*shu*) and equity or propriety (*i*) were blended to serve a moral equality among men understood to derive from Heaven, the common source both of human life and of the order among men which fostered that life. This, in turn, represented an order of values to which Mencius gave priority over the social and political order in the following memorable passage:

> Heaven confers titles of nobility as well as man. Man's titles of nobility are duke, chancellor, great officer. Those of Heaven are humaneness, righteousness, true-heartedness and good faith. . . . Men of old cultivated the nobility of Heaven and the nobility of man followed naturally from this. Men today cultivate the nobility of Heaven only with an eye to achieving the nobility of man, and when that has been gained, they cast away the other. But this is the height of delusion, for in the end they must surely lose the nobility of man as well (*Mencius* 6A.16).

Such at least was the Confucian way of thinking, which tended to express "human rights" in terms of "rites" and reciprocal relations, not in terms of "laws." Recourse to the law in cases of conflict was, for Confucians, only a last resort, something identified with official interference in the normal processes of community life and associated with the violence or coercion of externally imposed rule. The sanctions of law might indeed be invoked against recalcitrant members of a community who by their own violent actions put themselves beyond the pale of familial or neighborly sympathy; thus in a very limited sphere Confucians accepted the need for something like our criminal law. But in the conduct of human relations generally they looked on litigation or recourse to the courts as something to be avoided if at all possible. Chinese "courts," indeed, were not independent bodies entrusted with the impartial exercise of judicial functions, but simply another aspect of administration from above, rarely kept separate from the political and fiscal interests of the state. Similarly "law," in Confucian eyes, served as an instrument of state power, indeed frequently of exploitation. It was therefore most often viewed as a hostile force, rather than as a covenant or contract among consenting persons or as a body of principles and precedents expressing a consensus among the people as to how their common interests and rights might be protected.

It was however not the Confucian but the opposing Legalist view of law as an instrumentality of state control that won out in the establishment of the imperial dynastic system. The Confucians were left in a permanent state of estrangement from, or what we might call loyal opposition to, the new autocracy. In the Han period, Confucian ministers like Tung Chung-shu (177–104 B.C.) made grudging accommodations to the new system, linking "laws and punishments" to the *yin* aspect of life, which restored some kind of balance to the human order whenever things got out of hand. For the most part, however, Confucians continued to believe that the revival of some authentic ritual order would yield the only satisfactory basis for a positive (*yang*) social order, in which the individual might expect his "rights" to be insured by "rite," that is, he might expect the respectful treatment of himself and others according to the norms of civilized behavior. It was out of such a conviction that Confucians in the Han period devoted themselves to the painstaking scholarly efforts of reclaiming and codifying the body of traditional ritual. By contrast, there was no comparable body of legal literature preserved by Han Confucians (though later scholars, of course, have done much to reconstruct Han law).

Neo-Confucian Reformulations

This same state of affairs by and large continued through most of the first millennium A.D., a period in which marked political disunity both preceded and followed the unification achieved by the Sui and T'ang dynasties. In these centuries the intellectual and spiritual life of China were dominated by Neo-Taoism and Buddhism. Law underwent a considerable development, especially in the codes of the T'ang dynasty, which became models for all East Asia. As the term "T'ang Codes" implies, these were articulations of dynastic law and administrative regulations. Though reflecting at times certain perennial Confucian values, they could not be considered to express any consistent Confucian philosophy, much less a "humaneness" that actively asserts the Confucian respect for human life. Nor, on the other hand, could one see in these great dynastic codes any influence of the Buddhist concept of law. The latter, though deeply concerned with the spiritual liberation of the individual, did not contribute any substantial philosophical basis for the assertion of human rights or their protection under these codes.

After the long ascendancy of Buddhism, the Confucian revival in the Sung from the tenth century on brought forth several developments in Chinese thought which were of potential significance for human rights. Reform movements in the eleventh century drew attention to political and social needs which, it was alleged, Buddhism and Taoism had ignored. In reaffirming Confucian ethical principles as a basis for reform, Sung philosophers also elaborated new theories of human nature. Many of these doctrines were drawn from classical Confucianism, especially from the book of *Mencius*, but they also took into account Buddhist views concerning "nature" (*hsing*, understood by Neo-Confucians primarily as "human nature" or "the moral nature"). In the Ch'eng-Chu school this "nature" was seen as one aspect of a larger cosmic infrastructure of natural or heavenly principles (*t'ien-li*) inherent in all things. Innate in man's mind-and-heart were all the principles needed to understand and deal with affairs of the world; these principles were manifested above all through man's value judgments and empathetic responses in human relations. Neo-Confucians called these principles "real," "substantial," or "solid" (*shih*), in contrast to the Buddhist view of things as "empty" (*k'ung*), that is, insubstantial, having no nature of their own, no "own-nature." Neo-Confucian principles were constant and enduring; they could be conceptualized in rational and moral terms so as to be of service in dealing with practical problems of everyday life. The nature in Buddhism, on the other hand, as expressed in the prevailing form of Ch'an Buddhism, could only be "pointed to" and intuited within one's own mind-and-heart; it could not be expressed in words (*pu-li wen-tzu*). Neo-Confucians, denying that universal change could only be accounted for in terms of impermanence, evanescence, and unpredictability, characterized reality as a process of growth, governed by constant norms or patterns. Among these the most essential for Neo-Confucians was the ineradicable moral sense in all men which Mencius had characterized as "the goodness of human nature."

It is this concept of the inherent goodness of man's moral nature which provided Neo-Confucian thought with a premise for social doctrines somewhat akin to the "inherent dignity of man" or the "intrinsic worth of the individual." In the *Doctrine of the Mean* (*Chung-yung*), one of the favorite texts of the Neo-Confucians, the opening lines speak of the nature as having been ordained by Heaven. Chu Hsi's explanation of this text emphasizes the reality of the nature as differentiated in each individual.[2] "Honoring the moral nature" was indeed the starting point of all learning and the foundation for all political and social action. Moreover, Mencius saw what was ordained by Heaven as written in the consciences of men so that they were impelled to right injustices and were even justified in overthrowing rulers who violated the ordinances of Heaven.[3] Writers today often refer to this doctrine as the "right of revolution." Admittedly this is putting it in modern terms; revolution is not exactly what Mencius had in mind. But if the Mandate of Heaven is seen to confer on man an authority or justification for acting in accordance with his moral nature, we may be entitled to ask whether this Neo-Confucian doctrine of the innate moral imperative does not provide a basis for asserting certain human rights.

Much of Neo-Confucian teaching is directed at members of an educated class who also bear leadership responsibilities in society. Quintessentially this teaching is addressed to the ruler and those who act as his ministers. In my Ch'ien Mu

Lectures at the Chinese University of Hong Kong, I discussed the importance in Neo-Confucianism of the concepts of "learning for oneself," "getting it oneself" (that is, finding the Way in oneself), and "taking responsibility [for the Way] oneself."[4] In each of these notions the autonomy of the individual is stressed, but there is greater emphasis on the responsibility of each individual than on his rights. Today we often hear it said that for every right there is a correlative responsibility. The Neo-Confucians did not say it in so many words, but they implied that with every responsibility goes a correlative right.

This view appears especially in the Neo-Confucian reaffirmation of the responsibilities to each other of persons in the paradigmatic human relations: parent and child, ruler and minister, husband and wife, elder and junior, and friend and friend. In these reciprocal relations a person was entitled to a certain kind of treatment attaching to these constant human relationships. Chu Hsi, in discussions with his friends and students, tended to speak of these reciprocal obligations and correlative responsibilities in the context of Confucian "rites," not of legal rights. Throughout his life he devoted much study to the traditional rites or rules of decorum appropriate for members of the political and cultural elite, believing like the ancients that these social forms set the norm for all and thus were the key to social harmony. His approach reveals that he was deeply conscious of the special responsibilities of the educated man. It is significant, however, that this concern did not extend to the study of laws, still a comparatively neglected subject among Confucian scholars, but rather focused attention on developing the individual's capability in responsible leadership, to be accomplished through self-cultivation within the context of "rites."

As Chu explained in his commentary on the *Great Learning* (*Ta-hsüeh*), the noble man had a responsibility first to cultivate his own person, his own moral nature, and then to assist all men in fulfilling their own natures.[5] Chu's preface to the same text holds up as an ideal the system of universal education which he believed had obtained under the Sage-Kings. He strongly implied that the innate moral nature in each man entitles him to whatever help the ruler can give in developing his natural capabilities.[6]

This ideal, and the corresponding responsibility to try to fulfill it, led Chu Hsi to give particular attention to education among the common people. Chu's experience of civil administration was mainly at the local level, and he saw education as properly woven into the fabric of institutional life at that level—not only in local schools, to which he gave great personal attention, but also in the organization and conduct of community affairs. He built libraries and had shrines erected to honor distinguished men of the locality who had exemplified qualities worthy of general emulation; for his students and subordinates he provided guidance in the performance of rituals long neglected in popular practice; he prepared proclamations for the moral edification of common people who might receive no other education. A representative example of the last is the ten-point proclamation which he issued in Chang-chou (1190–1191).[7] The most notable general feature of the proclamation is its emphasis on mutuality and reciprocity, rather than on the imposition of superior authority or law, as the basis for the proper conduct of public affairs. The appeal here is to a combination of self-respect and mutual regard among persons as the natural means of upholding a voluntaristic social order, for this is seen as preferable to the enforcement of state control.

This same approach is built into the community compact (*hsiang-yüeh*) which Chu Hsi, adapting the ideas of one of the followers of Ch'eng I, Lu Ta-chün (1031–1082), proposed as the basic "constitution" of a self-governing community. The ideal of voluntary cooperation which inspired this system is expressed in the term *yüeh*, a compact or contract entered into by members of a community for their mutual benefit. Most notable is the personalistic character of the contract, which places a stronger emphasis on mutual respect for the needs and aspirations of persons than on respect for property rights or an exact quid pro quo in the exchange of goods. The main provisions of this compact call for mutual encouragement in the performance of worthy deeds, mutual admonition in the correction of errors and failings, reciprocal engagement in rites and customs, and mutual aid in times of distress and misfortune. Under each of these headings there are detailed specifications of the kinds of actions for which members of the compact were to take personal responsibility. There is also provision for the rotation of leadership within the group for carrying out the terms of the compact.[8]

Here was a model for a popular education that bore a direct relation to the daily life of the community, a practical way of implementing basic Neo-Confucian principles in a context wider than kinship or personal relations. In a time which witnessed the steady extension and aggrandizement of state power, Chu was not content simply to let public morality depend on the discipline of family life alone, or even on the five-family (wu-pao) units of local organization, but sought to incorporate the principle of voluntarism and mutual respect into community structures which might mediate between state power and family interests. In the community compact, he recommended a social program on the basis of which one might limit the intervention of the state in local affairs, share authority among more autonomous local units, and rely on popular education and ritual observance as an alternative to punitive law. Underlying this program was the idea of personal self-transformation and communal coopera- tion as the basis of the polity. Other expressions of this attitude are to be found in the type of local instruction based on Chu Hsi's own proclamations, in the community granaries to which Chu devoted much attention as district official, and in the so-called Family Ritual of Chu Hsi (Chu-tzu chia-li).

Chu's treatment of these programs was extraordinarily detailed, showing a fine grasp of practical administration. It is not surprising that they should have become models for the implementation of his teachings in later times. Because it was on the local level that these most authentic of Neo-Confucian institutions had their importance, they often escape the attention of modern scholars preoccupied with affairs of the imperial court and the state. Their significance has not always been appreciated. Some scholars in Chinese social history, however, are aware of the long but uneven history of the community compact in later dynasties.[9] It had great appeal not only because of the prestige of Chu Hsi's endorsement, but also because its voluntaristic and coopera- tive character accorded well with the emphasis on local autonomy and self-government in the Neo-Confucian doctrine.

Hsü Heng (1209–1281) referred to it as "governing men through self-discipline."

The community compact experienced many vicissitudes, owing to the difficulty of sustaining a spirit of both personal initiative and collective responsibility. Successive reformers, however, including Wang Yang-ming in the Ming dynasty, saw the revival and reinvigoration of the community compact as the key to local self-government. In Wang's case the voluntaristic character of the community compact accorded well with his own voluntarist and activist philosophy, and it is not unnatural that there should have been such a meeting of minds between him and Chu Hsi on an institution of local self-governance which embodied so well their common principles. Outside of China there was an even more impressive development of the community-compact system in its widespread adoption in Yi dynasty Korea, in the importance attached to it by leading Korean Neo-Confucians, and in its continuation down into the twentieth century as a key institution for the exercise of local autonomy on the principle of "governing men through self-discipline."[10]

Inadequate though the preceding is as an account of Chu Hsi's view on ritual and popular education, it may at least offset the tendency to think of Chu as addressing himself exclusively to the needs of the educated elite or as concerned only with the elite's control over the uneducated. In fact even among his writings addressed to the uneducated, few fail to stress ritual and popular education as the base on which higher culture rests. It is probably only the greater difficulty of dealing with the historical details of times remote from our own which has made us slow to study and evaluate adequately the influence of Chu's views on ritual and education at the grass roots level.

Rites, Principles, and Laws

Some observations are in order concerning the significance of the foregoing for our understanding of human rights in the Neo-Confucian context. Chu Hsi thought of the ritual order as the embodiment in human society of principles inherent in the universe, principles which had both a static and dynamic aspect—that is, they represented both a basic structure or pattern in the universe (*li*) and a vital process of change and renewal (*sheng-sheng*). In addressing the problems of twelfth-century China, Chu felt a need to restructure society on a humane basis, avoiding, on the one hand, the moral relativism and pragmatism fostered by Ch'an Buddhism and Taoism and, on the other, the absolutism identified with an increasingly autocratic state. Ritual could provide a flexible structure for a humane social order, but to accomplish this the traditional ritual had. to be adapted to the changed conditions of Sung China. In both the *Family Ritual* and the community compact Chu Hsi took as his models earlier Sung examples or experiments adumbrated by the Ch'eng brothers, Chang Tsai (1020–1077), Ssu-ma Kuang (1019–1086), and the aforementioned Lü Ta-chun. These he then amended to incorporate elements from the classic rituals. In so doing Chu recognized that the economic, social, and political circumstances of the Sung literati differed greatly from those of the old Chou aristocracy. He himself, as a poor scholar, could not dream of performing the elaborate and costly rituals prescribed for the elite of an earlier time.[11] Without being a social leveller, he wanted to adjust the ritual to the level of the condition of the common man.

Another approach to what we call human rights is illustrated by a follower of Chu Hsi in the Ming period, Ch'iu Chün (1420–1495). In his *Supplement to the Extended Meaning of the Great Learning* (*Ta-hsüeh yen-i pu*), Ch'iu discussed the institutional reforms needed to provide for the people's physical well-being and moral health. He reiterated the ruler's responsibility to protect and sustain human life as a duty ordained by Heaven. The conditions for achieving self-fulfillment are something to which men are in principle entitled by their very nature—the moral nature which Heaven has ordained to be cultivated and perfected in every man. In this light the ruler was obliged to serve the common good of all men (*kung*) and not any private or selfish interest (*ssu*). (This distinction did not preclude one's legitimate personal interests and entitlements as long as they were not pursued at the expense of others.) On this basis, then, Ch'iu proceeded to anathematize all edicts of the ruler which violated such principles. He called such edicts both "contrary to rites" (*fei li*) and "contrary to law" (*fei fa*).[12] One can see from this that Ch'iu ascribed to rite all the validity of law—without the force—and indeed even claimed a higher authority in that, in his eyes, rites should be the first resort and law the last. Here one could say that Ch'iu was making a case for "human rites" in terms that came close to what we call "human rights."

In the thirteenth to fifteenth centuries, with the rapid spread of Neo-Confucian education, a distinct intellectual and moral uplift was felt in one region after another as new schools and academies became centers of a learning inspired by Chu Hsi's emphasis on lecturing and discussion (i.e., dialogue between teachers and students) as a means of arriving at truth. This educational method became widespread in the sixteenth century and was not confined to any one school. Chan Jo-shui (1466–1560), an independent thinker and friendly critic of Wang Yang-ming, greatly stimulated lecturing and discussion and the building of schools and academies. The ideal of learning was especially popular within the Wang Yang-ming school, even among less educated folk in villages and towns. Both the academies of the educated elite and the meetings of the community compact groups became settings for "learning by discussion" (*chiang hsüeh*) which encouraged the exchange of ideas concerning moral issues and social problems in the conduct of daily affairs. Such a social and cultural climate in turn tended to promote a certain humanitarianism and egalitarianism in education, reflected especially in the reformist thought of the T'ai-chou school. Thus the voluntarist approach of both Chu Hsi and Wang Yang-ming bore some fruit in a social movement which contributed to the individual's self-fulfillment as well as to the edification of the group.

If these developments seem promising from a modern point of view, they nevertheless fell short of producing anything like the advocacy of human rights by significant numbers of people. There was a certain organizational weakness in the schools, the scholarly associations, and the community groups which supported such discussion; and they proved unable to sustain themselves under the pressures

of official repressions, economic difficulties, and civil disturbances at the end of the Ming. Another, perhaps more
fundamental, reason was that the heavy emphasis on self-
cultivation and self-fulfillment often led more in the direction
of individual spiritual liberation than of institutional or social
reform. It led more often to a reliance on converting individual
rulers to the Way of the Sages than on establishing laws and
institutions protective of peoples' rights.

A proper assessment of these issues awaits more detailed
comparative study of Neo-Confucian education in China,
Korea, and Japan. Among the important questions which
remain to be addressed is the ambiguity which attaches to
the idealistic aims of the Neo-Confucians. In one sense they
were elitist, attempting to uphold a high and strict standard
of personal accountability among members of the political,
social, and cultural leadership. In both traditional and modern
times these standards have been criticized as too severe and
repressive. In other words, the life of austerity and self-denial
which Chu Hsi and his colleagues thought appropriate and
necessary self-discipline for members of the ruling class
entailed difficulties when extended to the people at large.
Without a commensurate effort at participatory general education, the attainment of such extremely rigoristic standards
would perhaps rely too heavily on social controls and not
enough on the voluntary acceptance Chu Hsi had envisioned.
At this point the natural principles which might have been
construed as protective of human rights and values would,
on the contrary, be perceived as cruel impositions of an
exploitative, authoritarian system. This, of course, was not a
problem peculiar to Neo-Confucianism. The Chinese reacted
similarly to the extreme, rigoristic demands of the revolutionary morality imposed by the Cultural Revolution, considering
these to infringe on basic human rights even when they were
put forward in the name of equality.

Another question about Neo-Confucian goals has to do
with the adequacy of a method which relies too heavily on
individualized approaches to the solution of political and
social problems or, alternatively, which tends to rely on "rites"
as a substitute for laws. The later development of Neo-Confucian studies in the field of rites has not received much

scholarly attention, and a great deal may yet be learned from it of interest to the social sciences. But it seems safe to say that these studies became increasingly archaistic and ir- relevant. The real Neo-Confucian "rites" were not to be found in reconstructions of classical ritual texts but in practical efforts like the community compacts, local granaries, schools, and academies for which Chu Hsi had sought to develop new rituals. It was the relative health and continuing vitality of such institutions, not the excellence of classical research, which would decide the fate of Confucianism.

After the collapse of the Ming dynasty, Neo-Confucian scholars who had experienced the Manchu conquest as a crisis for Chinese civilization, reexamined many of the fun- damental assumptions of the Confucian faith. One such scholar was Huang Tsung-hsi (1610–1695), who abandoned the traditional Confucian hostility to law and reliance on ritual. While rejecting dynastic law as truly unlawful, he insisted that the people's welfare could only be guaranteed by legitimate laws and institutions. Huang was not alone among seventeenth-century scholars in recognizing the crucial importance of institutions in an increasingly complex society, but he was certainly the most outspoken in attacking the despotic state and in asserting a new concept of law as essential to the protection of the people against arbitrary rule.

In so doing Huang Tsung-hsi minimized the power of the individual to effect political and social reform simply by his personal example or by his practice of rites. In place of the earlier Neo-Confucian slogan "self-cultivation (or self-dis- cipline) for the governance of men" (*hsiu-shen chih-jen*),[13] he held that "only when the laws are well ordered can men be well governed" (*yu chih-fa erh hou yu chih-jen*). Only when good laws are in place can individual efforts and the power of personal example be effective.

Huang was careful, however, not to go to the other extreme of subordinating the individual to the state. Nor did he deprecate the earlier contributions of Sung and Ming philosophers to the understanding of human nature, their espousal of the inherent worth of the individual, or the essential voluntarism they felt was necessary in the political and social order. Indeed, unable to pursue actively his reformist goals, he made it his life's work to preserve the record of Neo-Confucian thought in the Sung, Yüan, and Ming periods. Under the Manchus his anti-authoritarian views were politically inexpressible and philosophically out of style, and were only resurrected in the late nineteenth century. But his works still bear witness to the fact that an authentic Confucian, speaking for his tradition after surveying the long experience of the Chinese people, could conceive of a better human state in which the rights of all men are protected by an adequate system of laws.

PART III

Confucian Protest and Moral Responsibility

CHAPTER 7

Scholarship and Autobiography: A Review of Vitaly Rubin's Work on Confucianism

IRENE EBER

The quest for meaning in life, which reflects the search for new or different ways of confronting existence, is always unique to the individual and inseparable from his circumstances. One form of such a quest is autobiography, in which the development of a life is traced, where events and relations are selected, ordered, interpreted, and thus given meaning. There are, however, still other forms, such as poetry, fiction, or philosophy, all of which are in some degree autobiography in the sense that their authors seek meaning and understanding within the confines of their own lives.

Indeed, what one person considers history, psychology, or poetry may be autobiography to another; in the same way, the subject of a scholar's research, his sources, and the work he eventually writes may be autobiography as much as scholarship.[1]

These reflections express thoughts that are self-evident. Yet they should be stated because any review of Vitaly Rubin's work on Confucianism clearly reveals how much his scholarly research is intertwined with his quest for the meaning of his life, first in Soviet Russia and later in Israel. Both the subject of Rubin's research and the manner in which he pursued it were shaped by events in the last twenty-odd years of his life; as such, these events must be taken into account when appraising Rubin's published books and articles, as well as his unpublished notes and manuscripts.

The events are, briefly, as follows. After Stalin's death in 1953 and Khrushchev's denunciation of Stalin during the Twentieth Party Congress in 1956, a programmed de-Staliniza-tion began which included the much-publicized "thaw" in intellectual life. At first it was primarily the younger generation of writers and artists who demanded an end to the cultural strangulation of the Stalin period. After 1960 a second phase of opposition began with the support of scholars and the technological intelligentsia. Khruschev's political demise in 1964 and the emergence of new political constellations did not stop the surge toward intellectual liberalization. Cracks had appeared in the structure of the authoritarian state which could no longer be cemented over. The brief Prague "spring" of 1968 gave further encouragement to those searching for new ways of scholarly, artistic, or literary expression. De-Stalinization was not, however, universally accepted. The "sudden smashing of the idols," as David K. Shipler terms this crucial event in Soviet life, unleashed complex reactions that transcended mere political pro- and anti-Stalin attitudes.[2] For many, de-Stalinization posed a profound dilemma, for it threatened a world view that had been constructed over the lifetime of a generation.

The 1960s in Soviet Russia were, therefore, important years. In the new climate, private if not public criticism could be voiced, and a certain freedom prevailed in intellectual and cultural life. The same period saw the emergence of other movements, among them the Jewish "resistance," whose goals crystallized after Israel's Six-Day War in 1967. The newly awakened Jews in this movement called for bettering their cultural and political position in the Soviet Union and allowing those Jews who wanted to leave the Soviet Union to emigrate.[3]

Vitaly Rubin began his scholarly career against a background of de-Stalinization and political change which promised intellectual change but saw as well constant attempts at frustrating this promise. That his scholarly interests became closely intertwined with a personal search for meaning comes, therefore, as no surprise. In the following pages I shall first trace the content and direction of Rubin's studies in Chinese history and thought, as well as his growing determination, as expressed in his diary and in articles, to put forth critical views independent of Marxist categories of analysis. Secondly, I shall attempt to determine the changes that occurred in his scholarly work after 1976, when he reached a safe and congenial haven in Israel.

Despotism, the Individual, and the State

Rubin's "Kandidat" dissertation, which he wrote between 1955 and 1957, dealt with the *Tso chuan* as a source of history. Prior to his defense in 1959 he had published some studies on Chinese archeology and early Chinese history. Later he published several articles based on his *Tso chuan* studies, the most significant of which is his article on Kung-sun Ch'iao, usually known by his *tzu, Tzu-ch'an*, a statesman of the sixth century B.C. in the state of Cheng. Rubin apparently had trouble with this article, and diary notations from the early sixties indicate that his scholarly interests were already beginning to take a new direction. He was no longer concerned with the impersonal social and institutional issues which he had explored in the *Tso chuan* but had begun to address the more specific question of personality and conduct and of the ideological and philosophical framework on which conduct is based. This new interest did not easily translate into words, and in the summer of 1962 he agonized repeatedly over revising the Tzu-ch'an article, feeling that a Marxist framework concerned with class analysis and productive forces provided a sterile approach to the subject. Tzu-ch'an had been a live person, and Rubin wanted to portray him as such. But, he remarks in his diary, the analysis of personality is a new method which might prove unacceptable to Soviet scholarly circles.

While working on the Tzu-ch'an article Rubin dutifully continued to translate the *Tso chuan*. But new ideas, especially on the origin of despotism in China, were beginning to occupy his attention. Hence, in spite of encouragement from other scholars to make the study of this text his "life work," Rubin began to have second thoughts. A study of despotism, rather than of the *Tso chuan*, reads a diary note of December 1962, would at last enable him to use his own, individual approach, without having to employ prescribed analytical criteria.[4]

By the beginning of 1963 Rubin had taken two significant steps. A growing urge to develop an independent scholarly approach to the study of Chinese history had led him to reject Marxist categories of analysis. And a growing interest in personalities rather than in institutions persuaded him to focus on men and ideas. Chinese intellectual history of the Warring States period, with its issues of morality and politics, the authoritarian state, and personal conduct, had come to hold for him a profound message which touched on his own existence in the Soviet Union. Rubin recognized only much later that 1963 had been a turning point in his scholarly development.[5]

Rubin's work on Tzu-ch'an convinced him that Confucians and Legalists held diametrically opposed political theories. When, in the next few years, he set himself the task of exploring the differences between the two schools, he seemed to find the ideas of Confucius personally satisfying and developed a deep revulsion against Legalism. The "stifling atmosphere" of Han Fei-tzu's theories disgusted him. He granted that the Legalists contributed a mechanism for governing the state but said that a state must also have a "sense of life" which can only be expressed by Confucian humanism. To him Confucian moral ideas provide a "spiritualization" of the Legalist mechanism.[6] Although Rubin did not draw an explicit parallel with the Soviet Union at this time, the comparison was implicit and would be made with increasing frequency as he continued his research.

Meanwhile he worried a great deal that his views on Confucian humanism might not prove acceptable and that his research might not, in fact, be publishable.[7] His anxiety was certainly justified. The entrenched scholarly establishment was as yet not prepared to admit new points of view. A lecture which Rubin delivered at Moscow University in May 1964 was harshly criticized by colleagues who accused him of using unorthodox methodologies: His focus on Confucian humanism was inadmissable; he should have identified progressive versus reactionary thinkers and their class backgrounds.[8] Two articles which he had written on Confucius and Confucianism earlier in spring for an encyclopedia were similarly criticized.[9]

A period of indecision and doubt ensued after these unpleasant confrontations. Although Rubin continued to participate in scholarly meetings and symposia, he questioned the wisdom of engaging in a line of research that was obviously vulnerable to destructive attacks. Again he turned to translating, considering even translating the *Analects*, but his heart was not in it. He felt completely misunderstood. While he was in this frame of mind a colleague suggested that he submit his article on Tzu-ch'an (completed two years earlier) to *T'oung Pao*, thereby avoiding the Russian censor. Rubin eagerly accepted the idea, and the article appeared in print the following year.[10]

Rubin no doubt felt encouraged by the publication of his work in an international journal. Still, becoming known abroad did not compensate for the stifling scholarly atmosphere in which he worked. Nor did it relieve his acute sense of isolation. David Shipler has remarked that the dissenters' decision to make a break did not come in "a moment of fiery rebellion," but grew imperceptibly over years of accumulating dissatisfaction until compromise was no longer possible.[11] Although this moment was still some years off for Rubin, it had its beginnings in 1965 and 1966, when he began to experience the intense sense of rejection that followed his Moscow University lecture.

From 1965 on Rubin's diary notes frequently return to the parallel between Soviet Russia and the Confucian struggle against Legalist authoritarianism. He had been asked to write a review article on Soviet studies of Oriental despotism. He decided he would not discuss economic determinism, which "everybody was tired of anyway," he noted in his diary in September 1965. Instead, he would discuss the origins of despotism and the content of the despotic system. In this way he would be able to relate the subject to the present situation in Russia. With a touch of sarcasm he remarked, the following month, that "the personal dictatorship of the tyrant" has apparently no place in Soviet scholarship; for the theory of class struggle eliminated the role of personality once and for all.

Apparently Rubin became less concerned with publishing his research. Perhaps he was more confident that, within the changing intellectual climate, there was room not only for his own brand of non-Marxist analysis of Chinese thought, but also for his implied criticism of the Soviet authoritarian system. A book dealing with morality and politics, the individual and the state, was slowly taking shape in his mind. In September 1966 he noted in the diary that he had begun writing his first book.

In the course of writing the different portions of *Ideology and Culture in Ancient China* Rubin increasingly identified in Chinese thought the problems of his own existence in the Soviet Union. By clarifying and describing these problems he came to assume a point of view which resulted in the fateful decision to apply for an exit visa.[12] But before turning to the content of the book, it will be useful to review some of the changes in Rubin's life in the second half of the sixties, as they quite certainly had an impact on the outspoken content and often thinly disguised message of the book.

By 1966 the scholarly climate had begun to catch up with liberalization in other areas of cultural life. A certain flexibility began to be felt which encouraged Rubin to take another look at his 1964 lecture with a view toward revising and enlarging it into an article. He completed this article, "Two

Sources of Chinese Political Thought," in October 1966, and was jubilant when it appeared in the prestigous *Voprosy Istorii* in March 1967.[13] Still, as he was to remark some time later, he knew that his work was now being recognized not because it was in the mainstream of research on China, but precisely because it was outside the mainstream.[14] Rubin evaluated the new flexibility that had finally reached the scholarly establishment with considerable caution. "My research", he wrote in September 1967, "takes place on the only recently established outer perimeter of the permissible. Whether I will continue to work depends on the stability and continued existence of this boundary."

Within Soviet Sinology the article was indeed a defiant challenge to the orthodox Marxist interpretation of early Chinese history and thought. There was no mention of class background, economic change, or productive forces. Rubin concentrated entirely on the ideological struggle between Legalists and Confucians and its implications. He defined this struggle as a universal conflict between those who champion a political state based on moral and humane principles and those who insist that only a despotic and authoritarian government can be orderly. Rubin went on to point out that the Confucians did not always advocate conservative tenets, as has been generally asserted; rather, they were nonconformists "who went against the stream." When the Legalist Ch'in state was established in 221 B.C. the nonconformists were executed. Thus the First Ch'in Emperor's infamous book-burning in 213 B.C. signified more than a mere silencing of Confucian opposition. It was part of the Legalist program to destroy all culture and tradition.

The article's double meaning was obvious to those who knew how to read it. In the book, which he was writing at the same time, Rubin similarly pursued his argument on two levels. He knew, of course, what he was doing. In January 1968 he noted in the diary, "My analysis of the spiritual situation in China . . . is marked by 'presentism' [the term is in red ink]. . . . I took the road of arbitrarily transposing to ancient China the contemporary spiritual situation. . . ." The scholarly establishment apparently ignored both Rubin's technique and its message. In September 1967 the book was approved for publication; in January 1969 he began working at the Institute for Oriental Studies, where his subject for the next three years was to be "The Development of Political Thought in Ancient China."

Ideology and Culture in Ancient China, which appeared in 1970,[15] contained ideas that Rubin had expressed earlier either in print or in lectures. Now, however, they were fitted into a larger context, and his discussion of the Legalist–Confucian confrontation was presented in conjunction with Mohist and Taoist theories. Rubin focused on specific personalities and their views. He praised Confucius, who enunciated the principle of personal morality. And he condemned Mo-tzu, who first conceived of the state as an impersonal machine; Shang Yang, who believed that the people exist for the sake of the state; and Chuang-tzu, who rejected all ethical norms and morality. However, as is indicated by its English title, in a larger sense the book is about the fact that certain individuals find it impossible to live in an oppressive and authoritarian state. Or, to rephrase this, the despotic state denies the individual autonomous existence.

Confucius' *chün-tzu* exemplified for Rubin the true individual, whose nonconformity, autonomy, independence, firmness of point of view, and courage made him what he was. Rubin also stressed that the question of personality was the crucial element in Confucius' thought, and that for Confucius individual morality, culture, and tradition were inseparably intertwined. Culture creates morality.[16]

The implications of this formulation are clear: Rubin proposed an idealist analysis of action. The autonomous personality with firm convictions prevails on the stage of history. Personal morality may be a function of culture, but culture is meaningless without personal morality. History, far from being the unfolding of impersonal events, is the record of autonomous human beings and their moral actions.

Chuang-tzu, who is generally considered the nonconformist among the ancients, a free spirit who preferred withdrawal to enslaving obligations, was criticized by Rubin for amorality. Chuang-tzu, Rubin argued, rejected ethical norms and opposed all forms of civilization; he upheld self-preservation and negated the importance of differentiating "between good and evil, tyrants and benefactors." Rubin's insistence on ethical action and moral responsibility led him to look askance at what he came to regard as Chuang-tzu's indifference to human suffering[17] and his negation of morality and culture. To Rubin nonconformity and morality were personality traits that led to an autonomous position.

It must be mentioned here that Rubin's antagonistic attitude toward Taoism changed considerably after he had finished the book. Between 1969 and 1972 he worked energetically on his doctoral dissertation. Although he never completed it, a sizeable section on Chuang-tzu and the *Tao-te ching* indicates that he was retreating from his earlier, negative position. Rubin emphasized in this section that, even though Chuang-tzu criticized Confucius, he often sided with Confucians who criticized Mohism and Legalism. On the question of withdrawal and the refusal to assume political office, Rubin believed that Confucians and Taoists held kindred views. He noted in particular Chuang-tzu's examples of men who refused wealth, power, and honor, and who preferred suicide to the shame of sharing power and participating in injustice and oppression.[18] In his comments on the *Tao-te ching*, too, he mentioned the rejection of Legalist militarism, pointing out that the notion of *wu-wei*, with its emphasis on noninterference and nonviolence, is analogous to Mencius' ideas of humane government.[19]

Shortly after the appearance of *Individual and State in Ancient China* in 1970, Rubin became persona non grata in the Soviet Union, and, as far as is known, the book was never reviewed there. However, even if it had been, it is inconceivable that Soviet scholars would have accorded it a favorable reception. In claiming priority for personality and moral action, Rubin neglected class analysis, and he neglected as well the central tenet of Soviet scholarship, that objective material conditions determine personality. In addition, Rubin's negative assessment of Chuang-tzu contradicted the views of Soviet scholars who considered the Taoist thinkers progressive materialists.[20]

The Problem of Withdrawal
and Participation

The issues of despotism and the negation of personal morality and culture, as well as the denial of individual autonomy, continued to occupy Rubin during his prolonged struggle with the Soviet authorities.[21] However, he was no longer able to devote much time to his research, and, once his position in the Institute of Oriental Studies was terminated in 1972, sustained research and writing became very difficult and at times impossible. Even after he and Inessa left Soviet Russia and settled in Jerusalem, he had little or no time for serious work during their initial period of adjustment. Meanwhile the focus of his interests in Confucianism had undergone a subtle change. In Israel, where his work was neither subject to bureaucratic supervision nor to censorship, Rubin began to inquire into the meaning of protest and dissent within the larger context of personal predisposition and appropriate action. Opposition to despotism and nonconformity was no longer his major concern. Reflecting his changed circumstances, he now questioned why men choose to withdraw from society and under what kinds of conditions they decide to participate. Possibly he was attempting to understand his own "withdrawal," that is emigration to Israel, as a continuing form of protest rather than as retirement from the scene of conflict.[22]

The autonomous individual remained at the center of his inquiries, and he concluded that only such an individual can engage in autonomous action, for his actions are the result of free choice. According to Rubin, freedom of choice in classical Confucianism comprised "loyalty (*chung*) to personal principles and . . . harmony with the moral situation."[23] Therefore, Rubin did not define freedom of choice as choosing from among a number of given alternatives nor as the result of an inner will. Instead he proposed that it involves acting in accordance with personal proclivities without considerations of the external social or political conditions which prevent or are conducive to freedom of choice.[24]

Rubin saw the precedent for freely choosing to participate or to withdraw in the figures of Po-i and Shu-ch'i, whose conduct Confucius had held up as exemplary. Po-i and Shu-ch'i were brothers who opposed the unfilial conduct of Wu-wang and, rather than support the Chou conquest, they retired to the mountains where they starved to death. When Rubin first began to pay attention to the brothers he was undoubtedly attracted by their uncompromising attitude, their willingness to make sacrifices for the sake of principle, and their certainty that when a person acts righteously his name, even if obscure in his lifetime, will be made known after death. To Rubin the brothers represented the ideal of the just.[25]

But freedom of choice was not the central issue for Rubin, who was far more concerned with the motives for and effect of the individual's participation. Mencius, he argued, introduced the notion of responsibility as a natural prerequisite for action and political involvement. However, while responsibility was a necessary motive, acting in an impure world endangered personal purity. Thus Rubin was led to ask how a person can retain his integrity while cooperating with an unworthy political system. The answer was again suggested by Mencius, who had said that a person can retain his purity (*ch'ing*) despite involvement, because purity is as important as humanity (*jen*). Rubin argued that, if purity is equal in importance to humanity, then the decision to either participate or withdraw must be interpreted as an act of courage. Therefore, Po-i's withdrawal and subsequent death meant not the mere readiness to sacrifice a career; the choice held mortal danger. While still in the Soviet Union Rubin had maintained that suicide was preferable to living in shame. Now, however, the act of suicide had larger implications. Not the suicide, but that which preceded it, was truly important. Prior to death is the courage of dissent, or "the courage of civil disobedience."

Although the argument is not clearly developed, the shift in Rubin's thinking is obvious. Participation need not necessarily lead to being coopted; withdrawal is not a passive act. No matter what form it takes, "the struggle for justice and truth demands an unlimited amount of courage," he noted in the diary in 1968.[26]

Po-i became to Rubin the prototype of a dissident whose

courage and humanity impelled him to choose a certain way of acting and a certain way of dying. Rubin did not relate this choice to an inner will but traced it to the courageous choice of inner purity and humanity. To him the two concepts had a concrete meaning. He wrote, in the notes for his lecture to "The Profound Person," that, since Hsün-tzu is not concerned with purity, he did not understand that a person coopted by the establishment is in danger of losing the ability to act courageously.

Rubin's analysis of Mencius' attitudes toward action illustrates as well his emphasis on the inner imperative of action. "Loyalty to personal principle" (we might say truthfulness to oneself) moved to the center of his concern in this restatement of Mencius. Mencius described four personalities, wrote Rubin, and attributed to each one a different attitude toward action. To Confucius Mencius attributed timeliness (*shih*), meaning that all situations have their appropriate attitudes. Confucius possessed the highest possible knowledge, for he understood that the sage can choose the attitude proper to the situation. This insight is not given to all, and those who cannot follow Confucius in timeliness must examine themselves to find their dominant attitude and then act in accordance with it. Engagement or withdrawal, Rubin argued, are ultimately dependent on just this inner attitude.[27] And the decision to engage in action need not mean that the inner imperative had been ignored.

Po-i and the Quest for New Meaning

In the unfinished manuscript tentatively entitled "A Chinese Don Quixote: Changing Attitudes to Po-i's Image," on which he began work in 1979, Vitaly Rubin again raised, and also amplified, questions regarding participation and withdrawal, purity and responsibility. Although the first half of this manuscript is more consistent than the later half, where his arguments are not yet clearly worked out, he would undoubtedly have continued to revise the first part. Still, it is possible to follow the development of Rubin's ideas since he apparently sought to create here a more subtly reasoned framework for ideas that had occupied him since 1978.

The Don Quixote image had already appeared in his *Individual and State*, in a passing reference to Confucius.[28] In the manuscript Rubin defined Don Quixote as "an idealist whose dream fails to correspond to reality" and one who can be compared to Po-i. Rubin, however, did not go on to develop this parallel (he might have eventually decided to drop the comparison altogether), but instead raised the intriguing question of Po-i's changing image in Chinese intellectual history. A sheaf of notes written in April 1981 indicate that he may have planned to carry his investigations past Han thought to include Sung Neo-Confucianists.

Rubin was less concerned with establishing the historicity of either Po-i or Shu-ch'i than with explaining the development of their attributes in selected literary texts. According to his introduction, Rubin intended to determine in addition what were Po-i's and Shu-ch'i's motives for refusing to serve Wu-wang and to show that the brothers' withdrawal was the first instance in Chinese history of a nonconformist position of protest. The main thrust of this essay was, however, and probably would have remained, an examination of various interpretations of Po-i's and Shu-ch'i's characters and actions.

Rubin began by arguing his case along the same general lines that he had used in "The Profound Person." Confucius praised the brothers' conduct (in spite of the criticism this implied of the Chou dynasty) because they preferred to remain obscure rather than serve an unjust ruler who offended standards of morality. According to Rubin, "withdrawal is the most eloquent practical expression of the autonomy of the *chün-tzu* and of his right to dissent." (see below, p. 162). Rubin suggested that Confucius did not consider other forms of protest as effective as withdrawal because withdrawal, unlike escape or unconditional self-sacrifice, derives from an inner position. In this connection, he again raised the issue of inner purity and outward responsibility, now assigning the same significance to both. Since, according to Confucius, one is no less important than the other, Rubin felt that Po-i and Shu-ch'i did accomplish their goal: to achieve moral purity is as important as the moral reform of society. Rubin concluded that in Confucius' view fame after death is preferable to honor and wealth in life if the latter are obtained by unprincipled means.

Rubin again discussed Mencius' ideas at length, pointing out that Mencius ignored Shu-ch'i's role and concentrated only on Po-i. In discussing Po-i's flight from the last Shang ruler, Mencius transformed Po-i "into an emigré political figure," stressing his "fastidiousness" (or rigid adherence to norms). According to Rubin, Mencius thereby shows Po-i not as the *chün-tzu* of Confucius' description, but as a person whose high ideas of moral purity imposed limitations on his conduct. Po-i was an extremist. Rubin not only pointed out the difference in interpretation between Confucius and Mencius, he also acknowledged for the first time that Po-i might be a less than ideal figure. For, he said, Mencius suggested the possibility of moving from a rigid, purity-preserving stand to the assumption of responsibility. Active involvement need not taint the man who is intent on preserving his moral purity. Here Rubin's interpretation of Mencius again led him to imply that withdrawal is not the only means for remaining pure.

Rubin seems to have been developing a more critical view of the Po-i figure, one consonant with his shifting focus from outward dissent to inner attitude. In sorting out the differences between Confucius' and Mencius' attitudes toward withdrawal, Rubin set aside the question of nonconformity and protest to address an issue that has been paramount in Chinese thought ever since Mencius, that of how a person can engage in action and still retain his integrity. We cannot know whether Rubin would have returned to withdrawal as a positive act of protest and dissent in a later revision of this manuscript. The fact is that he did not raise the question again, and the first part of his essay as it stands ends with evident approval of Mencius' views on the positive value of assuming responsibility.

In the second part of this essay Rubin addresses the act of sacrificing one's life and dying for the sake of principle. Here, too, his views have apparently changed and he seems more hesitant to view death as the only positive solution. Although he still did not consider survival—the patient waiting for a new dawn—as a truly positive goal, Rubin was willing to examine the importance of remaining alive. In this portion of the essay he also explored discussions of Po-i and Shu-ch'i in two non-Confucian texts, the *Spring and Autumn Annals* of Lü Pu-wei (*Lü-shih ch'un-ch'iu*) and the *Chuang-tzu*. Unfortunately, his major ideas were only loosely connected, and he would undoubtedly have subjected the text to repeated revisions.

Rubin noted at the start that, whereas neither Confucius nor Mencius emphasizes the brothers' deaths, the non-Confucian texts take precisely this as the major issue. The *Lü-shih* text specifically underscores the "satisfaction of strivings" (*yü-ch'üan*) and the renunciation of life to establish the will, both of which were attempted by Po-i and Shu-ch'i. "Satisfaction of strivings" led Rubin to speculate on Yang Chu and on the nature of hedonism and to conclude that a person should strive to fulfill a "whole life." Rubin did not consider such a conclusion an expression of hedonism because the fulfillment of desires is not the major issue: The point is to live life fully and intensely. Any restrictions placed on personal experience and freedom make life less desirable. Establishing one's will, meaning in this case asserting one's will in order to engage in a certain kind of action, does not receive the attention it deserves in Rubin's analysis. "Will" (*i*), moreover, is described as neutral, and Rubin does not explore the significance of this concept any further.

Rubin was as critical of Chuang-tzu in 1981 as he had been ten years earlier in *Individual and State*. He still maintained that Chuang-tzu negated the principle of morality and preached selfishness when he denied the purpose of Po-i's and Shu-ch'i's deaths. On the other hand, in 1981 he no longer considered Yang Chu the outright hedonist that he had in his 1973 essay, "The End of Confucianism?"[29] Whereas in that essay Rubin had condemned both Yang Chu and Mo-tzu for their utilitarian and profit-seeking motives, now he questioned the content of Yang Chu's hedonism.

Rubin apparently intended to conclude this portion of the manuscript with an evaluation of writers who considered Po-i's self-sacrifice a futile act. His main source was to be poetry, and he suggested that the poets' attitudes were due to the influence of Taoist philosophy. Rubin no longer dismissed out of hand the Taoist dilemma which held accepting the world as it is was impossible and that dying for one's principle was undesirable.

Two additional sections, which he planned to entitle "The

Injustice of Heaven" and "Loyalty," remained unwritten. Some indication of their general direction can be gleaned from the rough notes which he made in the spring of 1981. The issues of nonconformity and protest are not raised in these notes, a fact that provides further substantiation that, unless he planned to return to this theme in the section on loyalty, Rubin's search for meaning in life had undergone a decisive change.

In the section "The Injustice of Heaven" Rubin intended to deal with Po-i's image in Ssu-ma Ch'ien's *Shih chi,* in Wang Ch'ung's *Lun-heng,* and in Han Ying's *Han shih wai-chuan.* The major difference between Confucius and Ssu-ma Ch'ien, Rubin noted, was that Confucius believed that the *chün-tzu* would be recognized at some time in the future, when the Tao prevailed, whereas Ssu-ma Ch'ien sought vindication by history. For that reason, Ssu-ma stressed the injustice of a fate that denied recognition to Po-i and brought about his subsequent suffering. Wang Ch'ung took the view that whether a person was recognized depended on the times. In his notes Rubin paid special attention to the political implications of the Po-i story, a topic only briefly alluded to in the body of the paper. Were the brothers, by refusing to serve Wu-wang, professing loyalty to the vanquished Shang dynasty? Rubin acknowledged Wang Ch'ung's approval of the criticism Po-i made of Wu-wang: A minister to the Shang king, Wu was in fact a subordinate who had turned against his superior. Other rebellions, such as Kao-tzu's overthrow of the Ch'in dynasty and Kuang Wu-ti's rising up against Wang Mang, cannot be compared to Wu-wang's overthrow of Shang. Rubin finally turned to Han Ying, noting Han's Taoist view of the importance of preserving life even while acknowledging that life is not worth living under all circumstances.

I would hazard a guess that nonconformity and protest, which Rubin viewed as a major issue when he began work on this paper, might have become subordinate to his goal of analyzing the various interpretations of the Po-i image over a given period. He might thus have been led to conclude that Ssu-ma Ch'ien's personal tragedy—"the suffering of a righteous man"—was reflected in his handling of the Po-i story;

that Wang Ch'ung, the critical Han skeptic, was inclined to view Po-i's action in terms of political morality; that not all Taoists were as uncompromising as Chuang-tzu on the question of life and death. Perhaps Rubin would have been led to search for a closer correlation between the changing concerns of the period and the handling of ideas. His mention, at the end of his notes, of Chia I's "Lament for Ch'ü Yüan" and his reference to Laurence A. Schneider's *A Madman of Ch'u* indicate that he planned a comparison between the divergent interpretations accorded Po-i and Ch'ü Yüan and the uses such interpretations serve. I am even tempted to conjecture that this exercise in intellectual history might have led Rubin to a closer examination of his own ideas in this area.[30]

The choice of "The Injustice of Heaven" as the title of this section is in many ways troublesome. Perhaps Rubin intended to deal with the Confucian themes of not being born at the right time, or of not having met one's time, or of the way true worth remains obscure and is only recognized with the passage of time. Perhaps the juxtaposition of Heaven's injustice with freedom of choice and exercise of will would have provided him with the opportunity to follow through on ideas raised earlier. He might have wanted to suggest that "loyalty and dissent," to borrow Schneider's phrase, and subsequent suicide, as in the case of Ch'ü Yüan, demonstrate the injustice of Heaven. Here he may have wanted to show that Ch'ü Yüan's act of withdrawal and suicide are different from the withdrawal and death of Po-i and Shu-ch'i. Ssu-ma Ch'ien's view that it is Heaven's injustice which results in the righteous man being made to suffer might have become too limiting once Rubin explored Taoist and other views.

Rubin's very incomplete notes for the last section, "Loyalty," are almost all based on Julia Ching's article "Neo-Confucian Utopian Theories and Political Ethics."[31] This article apparently provided the point of departure that he needed to counter Wang Ch'ung's political interpretation: loyalty to the Shang dynasty. Julia Ching's exploration of the dilemma raised by the principles of responsibility to oneself and responsibility to serve corresponded to Rubin's reflections on this topic. Hence he welcomed Ching's dual application of the concept of loyalty (*chung*): The individual must be loyal (or true) to his own mind and, in the case of a ruler or minister, he must be loyal to the people as well. Julia Ching also argued that the concept of loyalty was redefined when the Sung government successfully concentrated political power and when the Ming emperors developed an increasingly despotic government. In his notes, Rubin reiterated Ching's conclusion that after the Sung dynasty the people were increasingly thought to exist for the ruler who governed them and the ruler increasingly thought to serve the spiritual powers of the universe and his ancestors. The minister consequently had to be absolutely faithful to the ruler.[32] Had Rubin planned to consult Neo-Confucian sources for this section? Although he stated in his introduction that he intended to confine himself to Chou and Han texts, it seems that, as he thought and wrote about the various issues, he began to see the larger dimensions of his task.[33]

Rubin was excited by the challenge of his inquiry. Readers of this unfinished manuscript cannot escape the conclusion that in writing this essay Rubin was venturing outside classical Chinese thought, that he was charting new paths by combining philosophical inquiry and intellectual history. His quest had not only carried him a long way from the stifling limitations of Soviet scholarship, it had also led him toward new definitions regarding his own life.

Conclusion

Vitaly Rubin's interest in personality and in the moral individual initially led him to the conviction that culture cannot exist without personal morality and that the absence of morality in the despotic state therefore signifies the absence of culture. Under such conditions, he then concluded, the only stand that the moral and autonomous individual can choose is that of nonconformity and dissent.

After coming to Israel these issues were no longer in the forefront of Rubin's concerns, and he began to explore the question of the individual's inner state and his involvement in the outer world. Rubin did not pose the problem as one of simple correspondence between motive and action. Rather, he was interested in defining the inner imperative that leads to moral conduct and action and then explaining how individuals choose to engage in action.

The questions which Vitaly Rubin chose to address in Chinese philosophy were clearly related to what was happening to him as a human being, both in the Soviet Union and thereafter in Israel. The content of his research did not change radically after he was permitted to leave the USSR. The changes are subtle, and must be looked for in his method, in the way in which he distanced himself from his previous role as dissident, and in the strong sense of belonging to and being part of Israeli society which he experienced after settling in Israel. Rubin had moved from the position of outsider and stranger in the Soviet Union to a new position of identification with Israeli society and the future of the State of Israel. The effects of this change on his self-perception are reflected in his published works, but they are even more evident in his uncompleted essay on Po-i and Shu-ch'i and, especially, in his notes for the unfinished portions.

Rubin's work between 1978 and 1980 reflects in some ways an attempt to explain his departure from the Soviet Union. He chose the figures of Po-i and Shu-ch'i to illustrate moral conduct, dissent, and withdrawal, and he viewed leaving Russia as a similar act of protest and withdrawal. However, the analogy to Po-i and Shu-ch'i was only a partial one. As the Rubins were, after all, withdrawing in order to begin a new life, self-sacrifice was hardly the issue.

It was for this reason that in 1980 and 1981 the manuscript took a rather different direction than Rubin had initially intended. Although he ascribed protest and nonconformity to Po-i and Shu-ch'i in the earlier portion, he soon turned to the question of how to assume responsibility and act on behalf of society without sacrificing personal integrity. Whereas he had initially tended to accept Confucius' view that Po-i and Shu-ch'i exemplified the conduct of the *chün-tzu*, Rubin now inclined toward Mencius' view that Po-i's concern with personal integrity (or purity) was extreme and inimical to action. He also showed a readiness to reconsider the views of Yang Chu, not only in regard to hedonism, but also in regard to the personal freedom allowed the individual to experience life.

None of these ideas was fully developed. Nonetheless it is obvious that in writing this unfinished essay Rubin set aside those questions asked by the outsider and stranger and turned instead to topics that concern the individual who wants to act in the society of which he is a part. I suggest that by the time Rubin wrote the notes for the last two sections of the manuscript he no longer felt the need to work out the philosophical position of protest and dissent. Responsibility and action had moved to the center of his inquiry, perhaps motivated in part by the political views which he had come to hold. Rubin's work suggests that Confucian teachings had contemporary relevance for him as a twentieth-century Western individual. One is tempted to speculate that new political commitments might eventually have led Vitaly Rubin to reevaluate early Confucian thinkers in this light rather than in juxtaposition to Legalist opponents. Rubin was becoming increasingly attracted to the methods of the intellectual historian, and he might have discovered different dimensions in Confucian humanism through their use. What he seems to be saying is that, even within the context of present political realities, humanism continues to be heard.

CHAPTER 8

A Chinese Don Quixote: Changing Attitudes to Po-i's Image

VITALY RUBIN

Introduction

There is an image in Chinese literature that can be compared with Don Quixote in European literature. This is the image of Po-i. Like Don Quixote, Po-i was inspired by noble ideals, and like him, he tried to realize them and failed.

Just as in European literature Don Quixote represents the image of an idealist whose dreams fail to correspond to reality, the image of Po-i in ancient Chinese literature symbolized a type of pure man who preferred to die rather than betray his noble ideals. But there are clear differences between these two images. Whereas Don Quixote belongs to fiction, the legend of Po-i lays claim to a historic origin. Whereas Don Quixote is guided by principles of chivalry, the priority of which is love and devotion to the lady, the main principles

155

of Po-i are filial piety and devotion to the lord. Finally, whereas Cervantes often depicts Don Quixote ironically, the sources relating to Po-i betray no irony whatsoever.

The European attitudes to Don Quixote help us to understand certain important features of the intellectual history of Europe during the last few centuries. Similarly, in order to understand Chinese intellectual history, it is necessary to ascertain how the image of Po-i was both initiated and interpreted. Although the interpretation changed in the course of Chinese history, I intend to limit myself herein to interpretations in ancient Chinese literature, including those of the Han dynasty.

Po-i's Story

Po-i lived at a time when the Yin dynasty was overcome by Chou conquerors, that is in about the eleventh century B.C. However, the first comprehensive account of his story was prepared by Ssu-ma Ch'ien in his *Records of the Historian (Shih-chi)*. Po-i's biography begins the longest section of the *Records*, "Biographies" *(lieh-chuan)*. This chapter *(chüan 61)* is of outstanding interest with regard to both Po-i's life story and the interpretation of his image. It therefore seems useful to give a full translation:[1]

> Although in the world of learning there exist a large number and variety of books and records, yet their reliability must be examined in the light of the Six Classics. In spite of deficiencies in the *Book of Poetry* and *Book of Documents*, we can nevertheless know something about the culture *(wen)* of the times of Yü and the Hsia dynasty. When Yao wished to retire from his position he yielded the throne to Shun of Yü. When Shun in turn yielded to Yü, all his relatives and court officials recommended Yü, and he was given the throne for a period of trial. After he discharged these duties for some tens of years and his attainments and ability were already manifest, the rule finally was ceded to him. This shows that the world under Heaven is a

heavy vessel,[2] the great heritage of the ruler, and that its transmission is a matter of extreme difficulty. Yet there are some people who say that Yao tried to yield the empire to Hsü Yu and that Hsü Yu was ashamed, would not accept it and fled into retirement (*yin*).[3] In the time of the Hsia dynasty there are similar stories of Pien Sui and Wu Kuang. Why are these people praised?

The Grand Historian says: "When I ascended Mount Ch'i I found at the top what is said to be the grave of Hsü Yu. Confucius eulogized the ancient men of humanity, wisdom and virtue, and especially mentions T'ai-po of Wu[4] and Po-i. Now I heard that Hsü Yu and Wu Kuang were the men of highest righteousness, and yet in classical books there appears not the slightest reference to them. Why would this be?"

Confucius said: "Po-i and Shu-ch'i never bore old ills in mind and had but the faintest feeling of rancor.[5] They sought humanity and got it; why should they repent?"[6]

I am greatly moved by the spirit of Po-i, but when I examine the song that has been attributed to him, I find it strange.[7]

The tale (*chuan*) of these men states that Po-i and Shu-ch'i were two sons of the ruler of Ku-chu. Their father wished to set up Shu-ch'i as his heir, but when he died, Shu-ch'i yielded in favor of Po-i. Po-i replied that it had been their father's wish [that Shu-ch'i should inherit the throne], and departed from the kingdom. Shu-ch'i likewise, being unwilling to become a ruler, went away, and the people of the kingdom set up his second son as a ruler. At this time Po-i and Shu-ch'i heard that Ch'ang, the Chief of the West, knew well how to look after the old, and they decided to go and to follow him.[8] But when they had gone they found that the Chief of the West was dead and his son Wu-wang had taken up the ancestral tablets of his father honored with the title Wen-wang and was marching east to attack Chou [of the Yin]. Po-i and Shu-ch'i clutched the reins of [Wu-wang's] horse and reprimanded him saying, 'The mourning for your father is not yet completed, and you take up shield and spear. Can this conduct be called filial (*hsiao*)? You, a subject, seek to assassinate a lord. Is this what is called humanity (*jen*)?' The people around wished to strike them down, but T'ai-kung said, "These are just men," and he sent them away unharmed.

After this Wu-wang pacified Yin's disturbances, and the world under Heaven accepted Chou as the ruling dynasty. But Po-i and Shu-ch'i were filled with outrage and considered it unrighteous to eat the grain of Chou. They hid on Shou-yang Mountain where they tried to live by gathering ferns to eat. When they were on the point of starvation, they composed a song:

> We ascend this western mountain
> And pluck its ferns.
> He replaces tyranny (*pao*) with tyranny
> And knows not his own fault.
> Shen Nung, Yü, Hsia,[9]
> If only they did not perish.
> Whom now should we follow?
> Alas, let us die
> For our fate has run out.

They died of starvation on Shou-yang Mountain. When we observe this, do we find rancor or not?

Thus ends the story of the two brothers. In addition, Ssu-ma Ch'ien gives his own interpretation, one that transcends the content of this particular story and takes up a problem best described as the suffering of a righteous man. Ssu-ma Ch'ien's views will be discussed below in the section "The Injustice of Heaven." Here I would merely like to pose the question which, though not of central importance to this discussion, is nevertheless of some interest: To what extent is the story told by Ssu-ma Ch'ien based on historical facts?

In a paper regarded as containing the most detailed analysis of the story of the two brothers in modern Sinology, Li Chi accepts as factual the general content of Po-i's biography. But he doubts the historical exactness of the information supplied by Ssu-ma Ch'ien.[10] Li Chi sees the two brothers as the earliest Chinese recluses, whose "choice of a mountain retreat was a gesture of non-conformity and defiance."[11] Can we accept this opinion?

It is necessary to draw attention to one significant fact: Although the overthrow of the Yin dynasty and the establishment of the Chou is the main content of the *Book of Documents* (*Shu-ching*)—indeed, all our information about the events and persons of this period is taken from this source—there is no mention of Po-i. Ssu-ma Ch'ien hints at this omission when he is astonished that "in classical books there appears not the slightest reference to such men of the highest righteousness as Hsü Yu and Wu Kuang." In spite of this awareness, and in spite of the fact that both men are mentioned in *Chuang-tzu*, Ssu-ma Ch'ien does not have a biography for either Hsü Yu or Wu Kuang. Thus it is significant that Po-i has a full biography in the *Records* and that the description of his life opens a new section in Ssu-ma Ch'ien's work. Here I must emphasize that this is one of the few cases where we have absolutely no knowledge of the sources for the ancient story told by Ssu-ma Ch'ien.

This consideration alone is, however, not sufficient for determining the historicity of Ssu-ma Ch'ien's information. When we ask whether Po-i and Shu-ch'i really existed at the time of the Chou conquest, we are led to give an affirmative answer because they are mentioned in other ancient Chinese works. Possibly Professor Kaizuka Shigeki is right when he writes that "The whole legend is anti-Chou in sentiment and reflects the resistance of the barbarian tribes who originally occupied the area of the state of Ch'i to the invasion from the West."[12]

However, from the point of view of intellectual history it is far more important to ascertain whether Po-i and Shu-ch'i are the first recluses for whom retreat was an expression of nonconformity. In other words, the problem is not so much a question of what really happened, as it is one of establishing the motivation of the heroes.

I assume that an answer to this latter question is possible. According to Ssu-ma Ch'ien's description, the protest of the two brothers against Wu-wang's behavior was connected with the fact that such behavior was incompatible with two basic virtues expected of a good ruler: filial piety (*hsiao*) and humanity (*jen*). Therefore, we need to ask whether the idea of these virtues existed during the lifetime of the two brothers.

The notion of *hsiao* was already known during the Yin epoch. Karlgren shows that this character occurs in the *Book of Poetry* (*Shih-ching*). It can be traced to its original form in the inscriptions of the Yin as well as on the bronze vessels of the Chou dynasty. "This graph has 'old' above and 'child' below."[13] The origin of the second character, *jen*, is different. It is absent in Yin inscriptions and appears for the first time in the *Poetry* with the meaning "kind, good."[14] It is generally known that this term was introduced into Chinese philosophy by Confucius to describe the highest and, at the same time, all inclusive, virtue. In his article entirely devoted to the development of this term, Wing-tsit Chan writes: "The word *jen* is not found in the oracle bones. It is mentioned only occasionally in pre-Confucian texts, and in all these cases it denotes the particular virtue of kindness, more especially the kindness of a ruler to his subject."[15]

The late appearance of *jen*, together with its circumscribed meaning, casts doubt on the main episode of Po-i's and Shu-ch'i's story. Leaving aside the inappropriateness of the character *jen* to the situation depicted by Ssu-ma Ch'ien, it seems highly unlikely that the brothers refused to serve Wu-wang because he did not conform to the ideal image of a ruler. In Wu-wang's time the concept of *jen* did not yet exist. Assuming that such a refusal did actually take place, the reasons for it may have been quite different: it may have been only during subsequent interpretations that it acquired the form typical of the nonconformist.

The Precedent of Confucian Protest

The fact that Po-i's and Shu-ch'i's names were preserved in history is undoubtedly the result of Confucius' admiration for them. Ssu-ma Ch'ien also stresses this fact when he mentions that Po-i "became through Confucius even more illustrious in fame."[16] How can we explain Confucius' preference for the brothers?

In the *Analects* Confucius mentions Po-i and Shu-ch'i four times, that is twice as often as Wen-wang, to whom he refers on one occasion as the embodiment of the element of *wen*.[17] The brothers occur as often as his beloved hero, the Duke of Chou.[18] Confucius' high regard for the brothers' behavior is even more meaningful when we consider that he identified himself with the Chou dynasty: "The Chou is resplendent in culture . . . I follow Chou (*wu ts'ung* Chou)."[19] He said also that "the virtue of the house of Chou may be said to have been the highest,"[20] and his pupil Tzu-Kung saw "the Way of Wen-wang and Wu-wang (*Wen Wu chih tao*)" as the beginning of Confucius' teaching.[21]

Confucius' identification with the Chou dynasty acquires additional significance when it is remembered that the overthrow of the Yin dynasty demonstrated the moral and historical principle of pre-Confucian ideology, namely the concept of the Mandate of Heaven (*t'ien ming*). According to this concept, the ruler who does not fulfill his religious and moral obligations and who neglects his duty towards the people loses his right to rule, and Heaven then transfers his rights to the next dynasty, which enjoys the admiration and support of the people. We find this concept in the speeches of the Duke of Chou preserved in the *Documents*,[22] and we can assume that Confucius admired the Duke not only for his immaculate conduct, but also for formulating the doctrine which Confucius considered himself to be continuing.

To what extent was Confucius a continuator? In answering this question we have to analyze the balance between conservative and innovative elements in his thought. A characteristic feature of Confucian doctrine is its basic conservatism: Confucius often refers to his time as an epoch of decay, "when Tao was lost in the Empire," the Son of Heaven (*t'ien-tzu*) lost his power, and the kings (*chu-hou*) or, what is worse, their officials (*ta-fu*), conduct the ceremonies, music, and the military campaigns.[23] This conservatism also appears in Confucius' perception of his own function as one who carries out the teaching of Wen-wang and the Duke of Chou. That is to say, he regarded himself as a transmitter rather than a creator.[24] Such self-appraisal may have contributed to the fact that the Chinese term for Confucianism (*ju chiao*) is not connected with Confucius' name.

Nonetheless, there is no doubt that, by using some traditional elements, Confucius introduced revolutionary changes in Chinese ideology.[25] One of the most important of these was the new interpretation of the term *chün-tzu*. Prior to Confucius it meant an aristocrat, or a king's son, but in the *Analects* it came to mean a noble person who harmoniously combines the knowledge of cultural traditions and moral perfection. The *chün-tzu* is an autonomous personality whose spiritual level gives him the right to choose his own way of behavior, and this decisive feature is formulated in Confucius' famous saying, "the *chün-tzu* is not a utensil (*ch'i*)."[26]

In the political realm the *chün-tzu* expresses his autonomous behavior by defining for himself the crucial question regarding the predominance of Tao in the world. Accordingly, he has to choose between participating in ruling the state or refusing to do so and disappearing into obscurity.[27] However, if as counsel to the ruler he discovers that his advice is not considered and that the ruler violates accepted traditions and moral standards, he must express his protest in withdrawal. He must prefer poverty and lowliness to serving an unjust ruler. Withdrawal is the most eloquent practical expression of the autonomy of the *chün-tzu* and of his right to dissent. Chapter 18 of the *Analects* contains references to numerous cases of withdrawal as an honorable form of protest against unjust rule.[28] The inclusion of Po-i and Shu-ch'i is, from our point of view, an interesting example of how Confucius himself tried to solve the contradiction between the traditional thinking that he had always proclaimed and the *chün-tzu*'s novel, ideal, and autonomous personality. In praising Po-i and Shu-ch'i, Confucius proclaimed that his "new" expression of moral right—protest by means of withdrawal—existed since the beginning of the Chou dynasty, and was embodied by Po-i and Shu-ch'i. At the same time Confucius completely ignored those views of the brothers that contradicted his own appraisal of events at the beginning of the Chou dynasty. How can we explain this? It seems to me that the explanation lies in the fact that Confucius, and to a great extent his followers too, preferred deeds to words. Moreover, in education as well as in practice, Confucians always stressed their desire to convince by personal example rather than by words. Answering the question about the just ruler, Confucius says: "If you set an example by being correct, who would dare to remain incorrect?"[29] Another reply to the same question consists in the prescription: "Let the ruler be a ruler, the subject a subject, the father a father, the son a son."[30] This preference of deeds to words is expressed even more clearly in those portions where Confucius writes about the behavior of the *chün-tzu:* "He acts before he speaks (*hsien hsing ch'i yen*) and then speaks according to his actions."[31] Confucius stressed that the *chün-tzu* "wants to be slow in words (*yen*) but diligent in action (*hsing*)"[32] and "is ashamed if his words exceed his deeds."[33] All such statements indicate that Confucius considered the brothers' behavior more important than their actual words, thereby revealing his general approach to the comparative value of deeds and words in the appreciation of personality.

The most meaningful explanation for Confucius' praise of Po-i and Shu-ch'i is contained in a passage where the following is ascribed to Confucius:

> When they see what is good, they grasp at it as though they feared it would elude them. When they see what is not good, they shrink from it as though putting a hand into boiling water—I have seen such men, I have heard this saying.
>
> It is by dwelling in seclusion that they seek the fulfillment of their noble aims, it is by deeds of righteousness that they extend the influence of their way (*yin chü i ch'iu ch'i chih, hsing i i ta ch'i tao*)—I have heard this saying, but I have never seen such men. Duke Ching of Ch'i had a thousand teams of horses, but on the day of his death people did not praise him for the single virtue.[34] Po-i and Shu-ch'i starved at the foot of Mount Shou-yang, and the people down to this very day praise them. Does not this saying illustrate the other?[35]

It is by now clear that Confucius admired Po-i and Shu-ch'i because they saw the fulfillment of their noble aims not by means of a career under an unprincipled ruler but by dwelling in seclusion. As a result, these men who remained devoted to their ideals vanished into obscurity. But, paradoxically, it is their very disappearance that allows for their permanent influence.[36] The last sentence of the passage leads us to conclude that the fame of the two brothers resulted from both their uncompromising refusal to serve a ruler who broke moral principles and the tragic outcome of their protest. Confucius' words show that he preferred posthumous fame to wealth and honors.

Closely related to the above passage is another in which Confucius said that the brothers "refused to surrender their noble aims or bring shame upon themselves" (*pu ju ch'i shen*).[37] The refusal "to bring shame upon themselves" through a compromise with an unjust ruler stresses the moral purity and dignity of the brothers.

Confucius' reply to the question of one of his pupils is also of great interest. The question was: "What sort of people were Po-i and Shu-ch'i?" The master said: "They were ancient worthies." "Did they have any complaints?" The master said: "They sought humanity and got it (*ch'iu jen erh te jen*). So why should they have any complaints?"[38] Confucius' words that "Po-i and Shu-ch'i never remembered old scores"[39] complement this passage.

A characteristic feature of this passage is Confucius' optimistic appraisal of the story of the brothers. As we see from the content of the story accepted by Ssu-ma Ch'ien, they expected to see a ruler who would be true to their ideal. But their meeting with Wu-wang was a great disappointment, which caused their withdrawal and subsequent death. How can we explain Confucius' proclaiming that they achieved their goal and also adding that they did not have any complaints? Here we are dealing with one of the most profound and essential features of Confucianism. The cited passage testifies beyond any doubt to Confucius' perception of the preservation of moral purity as both a method for "spreading out the Way" and a goal, no less essential than service to the public.[40] For if the preservation of inner integrity, honesty, and purity is no less important an achievement than the moral reformation of society, then the brothers did in fact achieve their goal, and Confucius' words that they "sought humanity and got it" are clear. As we have seen, Confucius denied that the brothers complained about their fate. This answer is characteristic of his determined denial of the tragic side of life. Here we must stress the deep contrast to the authors of the Old Testament, for whom, as is widely known, the suffering of the righteous man was a central problem and a riddle which constantly disturbed them. Clearly, for the monotheistic religion, with its insistent belief in a "just, creative God," the fact of suffering of the righteous was a far more acute problem than for a humanitarian doctrine. Confucianists considered the "lack of Tao in the world" as a fact of life to be taken into account. Primarily, the lack of Tao provides an opportunity for showing, in certain unfavorable circumstances, one's firmness, moral stability and inner strength. "The *chün-tzu* knows beforehand that the Way does not prevail" (*tao chih pu hsing*).[41]

There is still another question: Why did Confucius obviously prefer Po-i and Shu-ch'i to Pi-kan, Wei-tzu, and Chi-tzu, the three advisers of the last ruler of Yin Chou who protested against his crimes? Confucius only mentions them as the "three benevolent men of Yin."[42] In the story of Po-i and Shu-ch'i there was apparently something which attracted Confucius and that did not exist in the story of the three "benevolent men" of Yin. According to the *Documents*, the three protested against the measures of Chou Hsin, but their protest did not influence him. Finally Wei-tzu left; Chi-tzu simulated madness and was made a slave; and Pi-kan, who proclaimed that the subject has to fight without being afraid to die, was executed by Chou Hsin.[43]

No doubt, if one of these three "benevolent men" had corresponded to Confucius' ideal of the *chün-tzu*, he would not have needed to search for figures among small provincial dukes, whose names were not mentioned in the classic books. According to Confucius, the image of *chün-tzu* included the idea of self-respect; therefore, to withdraw was not to escape in order to survive, but to demonstrate protest. That is why the flight of Wei-tzu could not become a precedent for Confucian protest, and even less so, the madness of Chi-tzu.

But why did Confucius prefer Po-i and Shu-ch'i to Pi-kan, the courageous man who sacrificed himself? We can only hazard a guess. I think it is because the way of protest adopted by Pi-kan was not the typical form of protest of a *chün-tzu,* although Confucius would not openly express his disapproval of Pi-kan's action. At a later time Mencius formulated the rule whereby the man whose advice is not accepted has to resign, along with the man who cannot fulfill his office.[44] In the *Analects* this rule is not yet formulated, but Confucius' examples of withdrawal, and the fact that almost all of chapter 18 of the *Analects* consists of descriptions of such precedents of withdrawal, indicates that Confucius and his pupils regarded withdrawal as the most honorable way of demonstrating protest.

It is also possible that yet another consideration influenced Confucius to choose Po-i and Shu-ch'i as embodiments of behavior characteristic of the *chün-tzu.* According to the *Analects,* Confucius believed that the *chün-tzu* was chosen as an adviser to the ruler not because of his close relationship with the latter, but solely because of his moral and intellectual superiority. The three "benevolent men," however, were relatives of Chou Hsin, a fact which throws further light on all their relations with the tyrant that Confucius could not ignore.

Because there are no personages in the *Documents* whose behavior corresponds with the ideal of the *chün-tzu,* we have additional proof that this ideal image was created by Confucius. The nature of personal relationships that are described in the *Documents* shows that this image did not exist prior to Confucius. Therefore, in order to find a precedent of autonomous and honorable behavior typical of a *chün-tzu,* Confucius had to find figures who were not already mentioned in classical history. This made it easier for him to interpret their actions in a manner corresponding with his ideal of the *chün-tzu.* However, the behavior that he describes was not typical of the public consciousness of the time in which, according to the historical legend, the brothers lived.

The Embodiment of Purity: (Mencius)

Confucius' admiration for Po-i and Shu-ch'i derives from the fact that he saw in both examples of autonomous behavior typical of a *chün-tzu.* However, Mencius did not need to search for precedents of Confucian behavior because he had the example of Confucius himself, an example which overshadowed that of all other sages. Mencius' task was to defend Confucius' teaching against the critics as well as amplifying it on those points that were not elaborated by Confucius himself. Mencius' contribution to the problem of human nature in Confucianism is widely acknowledged. However, he also developed and systematized ideas regarding the relationship between the *chün-tzu* and power, a problem which is very important for Confucians. On this issue Mencius resorted to the personality of Po-i, who appears in his teachings as an embodiment of purity, one of the most important aspects of the Confucian personality. Mencius said:

> Po-i would neither look at an improper sight with his eyes nor listen to improper sound with his ears. He would not serve a prince whom he did not esteem, nor command a people of whom he did not approve. He would advance in a time of order and retire in a time of disorder (*chih tse chin, luan tse t'ui*). He could not bear to remain in a place of evil government and evil people. To be in company with a villager was for him like sitting in court cap and gown amid mud and ashes. During the time of Chou he retired to the shores of the North Sea waiting for the day when the world under Heaven would be clean again. Hence, hearing of the character (*feng*) of Po-i, the corrupt man becomes pure and the weak man becomes resolute (*wan fu lien, no fu yu li chih*).[45]

Further, Mencius mentions that in distinction to Po-i, I-yin was governed by the principle "Why should I not serve a prince or give orders to a people of whom I do not approve?" He would advance in a time of order as well as in a time of disorder (*chih i chin luan i chin*), because "he considered the world under Heaven his heavy responsibility." Liu-hsia Hui was also ready to serve any ruler if it would give him the possibility "to act in accordance with the Way." These different approaches to power are compared with that of Confucius, who was "the sort of man who departed quickly when it was proper to do so, delayed when it was proper to do so, retired when it was proper to do so, and took office when it was proper to do so." Mencius said:

> Po-i among the sages (*sheng*) was the pure (*ch'ing*) one; I Yin—the responsible (*jen*) one; Liu-hsia Hui—the accommodating (*ho*) one; Confucius—the timely (*shih*) one. Confucius was the one who gathered together all that was good.[46]

We have seen that Po-i is depicted as a sage, an embodiment of purity by Mencius. It is proper to say that the role which some Confucian thinkers attribute to Po-i may indicate a specific trend of thought within Confucianism. It is not by chance, therefore, that Hsün-tzu, who can be considered a forerunner in the establishment of Confucianism as the official state ideology, does not mention Po-i at all.

In Mencius' description of Po-i two features are evident: (1) the historical circumstances of Po-i's story are changed; (2) Mencius stresses Po-i's fastidiousness. In Mencius' story the figure of Shu-ch'i disappears completely; Po-i, who protested against the unjust behavior of Wu-wang, is transformed into an emigré political figure who fled from the tyranny of the last ruler of Yin. I mentioned above the anti-Chou tendency which was an obstacle for Confucius; Mencius' need to transform Po-i's image is thus obvious. Moreover, in distinction to Confucius, Mencius did not hesitate to adjust historical facts so they would coincide with his ideas.[47]

How can we explain the fact that Mencius stresses Po-i's fastidiousness? Aside from the passage cited, this fastidiousness is also mentioned in *Mencius* IIA.9: "He pushed his dislike for evil to the extent that, if a fellow-villager in his company had his cap awry, he would walk away even without a backward look as if afraid of being defiled." Why is it that, in passages generally favorable to Po-i, Mencius stresses this somewhat unattractive feature? Mencius personally sympathized with the plain people and was not inclined to fastidiousness. For example, he calls upon the king of Ch'i, Hsüan-wang, to share the enjoyment of music with the people.[48] He proclaims the people (*min*) to be the noblest element, in comparison with whom the altars of the earth and grain and even the ruler himself are secondary.[49] He quotes a text from the *Documents,* where the mystical connection between the people and Heaven is proclaimed: "Heaven sees as my people see, Heaven hears as my people hear."[50]

I think it is not by chance that Mencius stresses Po-i's fastidiousness; he depicts Po-i as an extremist and as a person with limitations, despite his high praise of Po-i's purity. He criticizes Po-i openly in one single passage: "Po-i was too straightlaced (*ai*); Liu-hsia Hui was not dignified enough. A *chün-tzu* would follow neither extreme."[51]

In the above description of the characteristics of various sages Mencius notes that Confucius "gathered together all that was good," but, at the same time, he does not explicitly indicate his preference for any one sage. However, certain facts allow us to conclude that Mencius was closer to I-yin's "position of responsibility" than to Po-i's position. Mencius stresses that I-yin understood his task as one of awakening people. "Heaven in creating the people has given to those who first attain understanding the duty of awakening those who are slow to understand. . . . I shall awaken this people by means of this Way."[52] We find a similar opinion in another passage, where Mencius says that the sage "is simply the man *first* to discover the common element in my heart."[53] Probably this conception reflects Mencius' approach to his own role.

Even more important is the fact that when Mencius describes I-yin's position, he indirectly expresses his own conviction that it is impossible to be indifferent to the suffering of other people. "He thought that if among the people of the world under Heaven, some common men and women did not enjoy the benefit of the rule of Yao and Shun, it is as if he himself had pushed them into a ditch."[54] In one of Mencius' most meaningful passages, which tells about a child falling into a well, he says: "No man is devoid of a heart sensitive to the suffering of others. Such a sensitive heart . . . manifested itself in compassionate government. . . . The heart of compassion is the germ of humanity."[55] Therefore we can say that I-yin's feeling of responsibility was an expression of compassion, one of the qualities most important in transforming men into real human beings.

The relation between the principle of responsibility and that of purity is established as polarization, a method typical of Chinese thinking; these principles, although they are opposed, are also complementary.[56] We find this confirmed in Mencius' characterization of I-yin in the passage just quoted, where he depicts I-yin as representative of the principle of responsibility. Mencius writes that at first I-yin

> ploughed the fields in the lands of Yü Hsin and delighted in the Way of Yao and Shun. If it was contrary to their righteousness and their Way, even were he given the world under Heaven, he would not have regarded it. . . . When T'ang sent a messenger with presents to invite him to court, he refused to move, and only after T'ang sent a messenger for the third time did he change his mind and say: "Instead of remaining in the fields, delighting in the Way of Yao and Shun, is it not better for me to make this ruler like Yao and Shun?"[57]

According to this passage I-yin moves from the position of "purity" to that of "responsibility"; this change takes place only after the third invitation by the ruler. However, it cannot be said that Mencius recommends this change without reservations. For we should remember how he describes the "great man" (ta-chang-fu): "A man dwells in the wide house of the world under Heaven, he stands in the correct position of the world and walks in the great path of the world. If he achieves his high purpose (te chih),[58] he practices his principles for the good of the people; if not, he walks in his path alone."[59] The attitude of a great man includes here both responsibility and purity.

Mencius is not satisfied with Po-i's position or with that of I-yin. He considers them too rigid and therefore unsuited to the complicated situations found in real life. Confucius' conduct was on a higher level, causing Mencius to say that he "retired when it was proper (k'o) to do so and took office when it was proper to do so."[60] This formula does not, however, offer a definition of what is "proper" and what is not. Without principal criteria, action can degenerate into opportunism under certain circumstances. Mencius apparently felt this danger; he therefore stressed that the feature which characterizes a wise man is his striving to preserve purity, untainted by any bad deeds, even those committed for the sake of gaining the Empire.[61]

In the long run the formula by which Mencius defines the behavior of Po-i ("he would advance in a time of order and retire in a time of disorder") became an integral part of Chinese political doctrine.[62] This saying expresses the polarities and hence reveals a certain discordance between the formula for retiring and participating and Po-i's actual behavior, since he did not want to take part in ruling. A polar situation is also contained in the formula which describes the behavior of I-yin: "he would advance in a time of order as well as in a time of disorder." Here only his participation in ruling is mentioned, although the description of his character indicates that at times he did not want to participate in ruling. The popularity of Po-i's formula was probably also related to its similarity to a "kind of moral science" in the *Book of Changes* (*I ching*), in which "conditions for 'advancing' and 'withdrawing,' engaging and disengaging were specified."[63]

Together with Po-i's image as an embodiment of purity, there is for the first time in *Mencius* the juxtaposition of Po-i as a "good man" with Bandit Chih as an embodiment of evil.[64] The beginning of such juxtapositions can be found in the *Analects*, where Po-i and Duke Ching are portrayed as opposites (XVI. 12). References occur also in Taoist and Legalist literature, where Po-i and the thief Chih are shown as opposites.[65] These juxtapositions of personality traits in some way complement the political contrast between the tyrants Chieh and Chou, on the one hand, and the good rulers Ch'eng T'ang and Wen-wang, on the other.

Death is Preferable to a Shameful Life

Whereas both Confucius and Mencius considered Po-i's decision to refrain from serving an unjust ruler as the most significant episode in his life, the non-Confucian literature attributes less importance to the question of whether "to serve or not to serve," stressing instead "to be or not to be." Neither Confucius nor Mencius regarded the death of Po-i as the central episode of the legend. According to them, although Po-i's death was indeed a consequence of his decision not to serve, Po-i did not really intend to die. The non-Confucian literature provides a completely different interpretation, turning the problem into a discussion of self-sacrifice in the *Spring and Autumn Annals of Lü Pu-wei* (*Lü-shih ch'un-ch'iu*).

A passage, bearing the title "Standing Alone" (*Chieh-li*) reports that:

> Just before the Chou dynasty came to power, there were two knights, named Po Yi and Shu Ch'i, who lived in Ku-chu. They said to one another: "We hear that in the Western region there unexpectedly appeared a chief, and it seems that he will possess the Way. Why not try to settle there?" They went westward and reached Chou. By the time they reached the sunny side of Mount Ch'i, Wen-wang was already dead and Wu-wang had assumed the throne. Here they observed the virtue of Chou. Wu-wang sent his younger brother Tan to Chiao Ko in Ssu Nei, and they concluded a pact (*meng*), saying: "You will be offered wealth of the third order and offices of the first rank." The pact was written in three copies and sealed in sacrificial blood; one copy was buried in Ssu Nei, and each party received a copy. Furthermore he [Wu-wang] sent a Guardian, Shao-kung to Wei-tzu K'ai, who lived at the mountain Kung T'ou, to conclude a pact saying: "Your rank of *hou* will be preserved for your descendants who will keep the sacrificial cult of Yin and the tradition of San-lin music. As an appanage you will receive Mong Chu." The pact was written in three copies and sealed in sacrificial blood. One copy was buried in the mountain Kung T'ou, and each party received his copy.
>
> Po Yi and Shu Ch'i, hearing about this, laughed, saying: "How peculiar! This is certainly not what *we*

would call the Way. In ancient times, when Shen-nung held possession of the world under Heaven, he performed the seasonal sacrifices with the utmost reverence, but he did not pray for happiness (*fu*). In his dealings with men he was loyal and trustworthy and observed perfect order, but he did not seek anything from them. He delighted in setting things right for the sake of setting things right; he delighted in bringing order for the sake of order. He did not use other men's failures to bring about his own success; he did not use other men's degradation to lift himself up. Now the Chou, observing that the Yin has fallen into disorder, suddenly makes a show of its ability of setting things right and to order, honoring those who know how to scheme (*shang mou*), handing out bribes (*hsing ho*), relying on weapons to maintain its might (*tsu ch'iu erh pao wei*), offering sacrifices and drawing up pacts to impress men with its good faith. You use [the treatises] of Ssu Nei and Kung T'ou to praise your deeds, you promulgate your dreams[66] to gladden the crowd, you kill and attack to achieve gain and to replace Yin—this is simply to replace tyranny with disorder (*i luan i pao*).

We have heard that the gentlemen of old, if they happened upon a well-ordered age (*chih shih*) did not run away from public office; but if they encountered an age of disorder, they did not try to hold on to office at any cost.[67] Now the world under Heaven is in darkness, and the virtue of the Chou is in decline. Rather than remain side by side with the Chou and defile our bodies it would be better to run away and thus protect the purity of our conduct!" The two gentlemen thereupon went north as far as the foot of Shou-yang, where they eventually died of starvation.

There are important and unimportant matters in human feelings. Important is the full satisfaction of strivings (*yü ch'üan*). What is unimportant has to be used for nourishing that which is important. Po Yi and Shu Ch'i were the men who renounced their bodies and their lives to establish their will. It means that

they decided what is of foremost importance and what
is not.[68]

The *Lü-shih* text differs from that of Ssu-ma Ch'ien. According
to Ssu-ma Ch'ien, the brothers were disappointed by Wu-wang
because his conduct, namely his military actions against the
last ruler of Yin, did not conform to the traditional pattern
of filial piety and humanity. In the *Lü-shih* text, however,
the theme of Yin's protection disappears and a completely
different thought emerges in its place: the moral inadmis-
sibility of exploiting the difficulties that confront a declining
dynasty for the purpose of self-glorification. It should be
mentioned that this approach was not adopted by later
literature, as will become apparent below. In fact, Chinese
authors used Ssu-ma Ch'ien's interpretation for the information relating to Po-i's story.

The appearance of this rival version in the *Lü-shih* text
seems to be due to the historical circumstances under which
this book was compiled, as well as by its general tendency.
As stressed by Kung-ch'üan Hsiao, this text was composed
by experts gathered by Lü Pu-wei. It has a clear anti-Legalist
tendency aimed at undermining the foundations of the traditional policy of the Ch'in state.[69] Taking this into account,
one is tempted to agree with the critics of Wu-wang who,
aware that Yin was in a state of chaos, wanted to show that
since Wu-wang was the only one who could establish order
in the Empire, he must not refrain from using any means.
The latter may have been a hint to Cheng (later Ch'in
Shih-huang), who was then preparing to proclaim himself the
Son of Heaven.

The title of the passage that tells the brothers' story reflects
a tradition, traceable to Mencius, of seeing them as the
embodiment of sincerity and purity. And, in fact, we can find
in the above passage an explanation of the brothers' conduct
which conforms to this pattern, namely that they feared
bringing shame upon themselves by collaborating with the
ruler of Chou. Whereas the idea of "purity of conduct" is
attributed to the brothers themselves, the "full satisfaction
of strivings" is, without doubt, based on a different concept
of man supplied by the authors of the *Lü-shih* text. The aim

of this concept of man is that he completely satisfy all his desires. However, if at first glance such a formula brings to mind the hedonistic philosophy of Yang Chu's style, it has another dimension in the *Lü-shih* text. In the chapter "Respect for Life" (*Kuei sheng*) it is said:

> The whole life (*ch'üan sheng*) is best, the diminished life is next best, while the life which is dedicated to the noble purpose in spite of the danger of death (*ssu*) is still less good. The harried life (*p'o sheng*) is the lowest. Therefore when we speak about honoring life we have in mind the whole life. In this so-called whole life the six desires (*liu yü*) all are appropriately satisfied. In the diminished life, appropriate satisfaction of the six desires is partially achieved. . . . In the case of what is termed the harried life, no one of the six desires is appropriately satisfied. The man receives only what he hates . . . what is shameful. There is no greater shame than injustice (*pu i*). . . . It is better to die than to live a harried life.[70]

Therefore, the interpretation of the images of Po-i and Shu-ch'i in the *Lü-shih* text is that, unable to fulfill the "whole life," they preferred to die. We can consider this conduct an illustration of the theory cited above of the four kinds of human life; as such it receives the authors' approval. This extraordinarily interesting passage raises certain questions concerning both the concept of man reflected in the evaluation of Po-i's and Shu-ch'i's behavior and the problems connected with the appearance and development of hedonism in Chinese philosophy.

The *Soviet Philosophical Encyclopedia* gives the following definition of hedonism: It is a concept which considers pleasure to be the highest value, and the striving to attain it is a principle of behavior.[71] Although the passage in "Respect for Life" does not mention pleasure, its essence is the same, for, in principle, the fulfillment of all desires is no different than attaining pleasure. We must recognize that the terminology of this passage is rooted in the hedonistic ideas of Yang Chu, even if the conclusions do not conform to the hedonist theory; on the contrary, they contradict it.

First of all, it should be mentioned that the formula "whole life" in this passage appears in this form for the first time. It does not appear in chapter 7 of the *Lieh-tzu*, where Yang Chu's views are depicted. However, Yang Chu's views are formulated in just this way in *Huai-nan-tzu*, chapter 13.[72] The fact that this theory can be attributed to Yang Chu is, furthermore, corroborated by a passage in *Lieh-tzu*, where Yang Chu's views about the fulfillment of desires are given in greater detail. The *Lü-shih* text mentions "six desires"; the same number of desires are named in the *Lieh-tzu* chapter "*Yang Chu*":

> (1) What the ears wish to hear is tones and sounds, and if these are denied them, I say that the sense of hearing is restricted. (2) What the eyes wish to see is the beauty of women, and if this is denied them, I say that the sense of sight is restricted. (3) What the nostrils wish to turn to is orchids and spices, and if these are denied them, I say that the sense of smell is restricted. (4) What the mouth wishes to discuss is truth and falsehood (*tao-che shih fei*), and if this is denied it, I say that the intelligence (*chih*) is restricted. (5) What the body wishes to find ease in is fine clothes and good food, and if these are denied it, I say that its comfort is restricted. (6) What the will (*i*) wishes to achieve is freedom and leisure, and if it is denied these, I say that its movement (*wang*) is restricted.[73]

If the above passage is considered authentic, this portion of the text may constitute very important evidence in the controversy concerning Yang Chu's views. Modern sinologists consider *Lieh-tzu*, at least in its present form, as a compilation of the third century A.D. and not of the pre-Ch'in period in which Lieh-tzu lived.[74] Based on this assumption, some authors claim that Yang Chu's views were, in reality, far from hedonism. For example, Wing-tsit Chan who, like Fung Yu-lan, considers Yang Chu to be the first Taoist, writes:

> He was not a hedonist who urged all men to "enjoy life" and to be satisfied with "a comfortable house, fine clothes, good food, and pretty women". . . . He was,

rather, a follower of Nature who was mainly interested in "preserving life and keeping the essence of our being intact, and not injuring our material existence with things."[75]

Fung Yu-lan expresses the same point of view,[76] but A.C. Graham gives the most complete statement. In the introduction to his translation of chapter 7 of *Lieh-tzu*, he writes that the historical Yang Chu, who lived about 350 B.C., was the first Chinese thinker who did not incline to take part in the struggle for wealth and power:

> He seems to have held that, since external possessions are replaceable while the body is not, we should never permit the least injury to the body, even the loss of a hair, for the sake of any external benefit, even the throne of the Empire. For moralists such as the Confucians and Mohists, to refuse a throne would not be a proof of high-minded indifference to personal gain, but a selfish rejection of the opportunity to benefit the people. They therefore derided Yang Chu as a man who would not sacrifice a hair even to benefit the whole world.[77]

Graham believes that along with texts ascribed to Yang Chu by a later hedonist author, there are in *Lieh-tzu* passages which reflect the original thoughts of Yang Chu, and these he italicizes.

W. Bauer opposes this point of view, claiming that we can already see in ancient China the beginnings of both hedonism and individualism. He writes that, in distinction to other Taoists who are to achieve the state of a "living corpse," Yang Chu aspired to the fulfillment of life not through its continuation but through its intensification: "He has discovered the Golden Now."[78] Bauer writes that there is no reason for rejecting the idea that a hedonist hero existed as early as the fourth century B.C. He stresses that this alters the entire prospect of human life, for the hope for happiness in the future appears, from this point of view, as a denial of life that fulfills itself now, at this moment.[79]

Various passages from the *Lü-shih* text are significant

proof that the idea of the essence of life as maximal fulfillment of desires already existed in the pre-Ch'in period. Were we to assume otherwise, we would have to deny the authenticity of this text, which is accepted as one of the most trustworthy of ancient Chinese sources. The concern with the fulfillment of desires is, further, significant in connection with views on the reasons for China's backwardness at the end of the nineteenth and beginning of the twentieth centuries. According to Benjamin Schwartz, Yen Fu, influenced by Western theories (primarily Spencer), concluded that China's backwardness was the result of a preference for harmony and satisfaction with minimal effort at existence. China's sages since antiquity avoided the danger of struggling for the fulfillment of desires. "To the sages . . . the prospect of strife and conflict represented the demonic—the ultimate evil. They thus shrank back from the actualization of men's potentialities, settling for peace, harmony, and order on a low level of human achievement."[80]

Although it would be incorrect to say that European philosophy is hedonistic in nature, it does, to a certain extent, contain strands of hedonism, satisfaction, and the fulfillment of desires. It is not by chance that Schwartz's description of the Chinese approach to this problem includes the famous passage from *Hsün-tzu* which warns that the unlimited satisfaction of desires leads to disorder.[81] Although Yen Fu seems to emphasize the connection between the struggle for existence and evolution, he may also imply the dilemma regarding the negative or positive evaluation of desires and their satisfaction—in other words, the stress on the *limitation* of desires or on their *fulfillment.* Concerning the latter interpretation, Bauer points to the contrast between Yang Chu and Hsün-tzu.[82]

Let us, however, return to the passage under consideration. Although its main feature is the goal of satisfying desires, this goal belongs to the moral sphere. Therefore death is preferable to a life without justice. In evaluating this point of view we can say that, even if Yang Chu's attitudes contradict Confucianism, both Confucianism and Yang Chu ultimately reach very similar conclusions. Indeed, of the "six desires" named by Yang Chu, five are aimed at satisfying the body, while only one, the sixth, is related to a nonphysical sphere. In the *Lü-shih* text, however, immediately after mentioning the satisfaction of desires, it is stated that Po-i and Shu-ch'i, who understood what is important, renounced their bodies in order to establish their will (*i*). The outcome is that "desire," which Yang Chu names *last*, becomes the *most important* in the *Lü-shih*. It is interesting to note that the term will (*i*), used by Yang Chu, does not play a significant role in *Mencius*, where it relates to intellectual rather than moral qualities. We can assume that Yang Chu's usage of this specific term reflects a deliberate departure from Confucian terminology. In fact, since self-sacrifice in favor of a neutral "will" seems to be an artificial concept, the only justification for the *Lü-shih*'s having used the term *i* in the passage mentioned above is that it was most likely taken from the text of Yang Chu. In the more general passage cited above about the four kinds of life, this inadequate terminology is corrected, and the authors use the Confucian term *i* (righteousness). On more than one occasion Confucian sources indicate that life is not preferable to death in all circumstances.[83] A passage from *Mencius* closely approximates the text quoted from the *Lü-shih.* It states: "Life is what I want, righteousness (*i*) is what I want. If I cannot have both, I would rather take righteousness, than life."[84] In accordance with this analysis, we are led to conclude that Kung-chuan Hsiao is correct in viewing the *Spring and Autumn Annals of Lü Pu-wei* as a work whose main ideas are close to the Confucian position.[85] The same evaluation is given in the *Ssu-k'u ch'üan-shu tsung-mu t'i-yao* and by Chang Hsüeh-ch'eng.[86] But Bauer opposes this view, regarding the *Lü-shih* text as a "collection of very different Taoist mix-forms."[87]

The Stupidity of Self-Sacrifice

Contrary to the above discussion, we find in ancient Chinese literature not only approval and admiration for Po-i and Shu-ch'i because they were audacious and adhered to their ideals, but also sharp criticism. This criticism emanated from a typical Taoist standpoint, namely the juxtaposition of nature's quietude, grandeur, and purity together with the vanity, self-interest, and falseness of human deeds.

Even the *Analects* criticizes Confucius and his views on the aims of human life. In chapter 18 there are dialogues between Confucius and his pupil Tzu-lu, on the one hand, and with the recluses, on the other. The latter did not believe that meaningful public action is possible; indeed, since they considered such action to be dangerous, they advocated complete withdrawal from the world. Later, both "social despair" and the striving for self-preservation as the highest aim of human life became significant elements of Taoist philosophy.

As is generally known, the *Tao-te ching* mentions neither names nor dates, which explains why there is no mention of Po-i. But in the second classical Taoist book, the *Chuang-tzu*, which, according to the opinion of many scholars, preceded the *Tao-te ching*, Po-i is mentioned five times. Each of these passages provides significant concrete examples of one of the important aspects of Taoist ideology.

The sharpest criticism of Po-i can be found in the passage where Chuang-tzu describes the image of an ideal Taoist person, "The True Man of ancient times (*ku chih chen-jen*)."[88] Chuang-tzu portrays a superman, who cares about neither life nor death and has no human feelings, "not using the heart (*hsin*) to repel the Way (*tao*), not using man to help out Heaven."[89]

Later on, the Taoist sage's (*chen jen*) opposition to the Confucian *chün-tzu* is shown in a most peculiar manner: Chuang-tzu ascribes Confucian qualities to the Taoist sage, who exists beyond good and evil: "He who has affections is not benevolent (*fei jen*), . . . he who cannot encompass both profit and loss is not a *chün-tzu*."[90] This awkward attempt to ascribe the qualities of a *chün-tzu* to the Taoist sage proves, if nothing else, the popularity and authority achieved by Confucianism. For it is evident that the Taoist philosopher did not wish to offend the reader by directly attacking the concept of humanity and the *chün-tzu*.

The following passage indicates Chuang-tzu's ideas. After naming eight persons, among them Po-i and Shu-ch'i, he concludes: "All of them slaved in the service of other men, took joy in bringing other men joy, but could not find joy in any joy of their own."[91] Obviously, according to Chuang-tzu, everybody must think only about himself; the man who cares about others and tries to help them is blameworthy because he enslaves himself. There is hardly another formula that so conclusively denies the principles of morality.

One of the methods used by Chuang-tzu to discredit morality is to show the futility of human deeds in respect to both their quality and quantity. Chuang-tzu tells the story of the Lord of the River (*Ho-po*) who was ecstatic because of the autumn flood. But when he reached the Northern Sea and saw how much bigger it was than the river, he understood that even the greatness of the flood-swollen river can in no way compete with the greatness of the sea.

> In the past, I heard men belittling the learning of Confucius and making light of the righteousness of Po Yi (*ch'ing* Po-i *chih i*), though I never believed them. Now, however, I have seen your unfathomable vastness. If I hadn't come to your gate, I would have been in danger. I would forever have been laughed at by the masters of the Great Method (*Ta-fang chih chia*)![92]

The God of the Northern Sea answers by stating that it is impossible to speak about the ocean with a well frog; then he admiringly describes the immensity of the universe and stresses the smallness of man in comparison with this vastness.

> Compared to the ten thousand things is he not like one little hair on the body of a horse? What the Five Emperors passed along, what the Three Kings fought over, what the benevolent man grieves about, what the responsible man labors over—all—is no more than this! Po Yi gained a reputation (*ming*) by giving it up; Confucius passed himself off as learned because he talked about it. But in priding themselves in this way, were they not like you a moment ago priding yourself on your flood waters?[93]

By equating Po-i with Confucius, Chuang-tzu shows an understanding of their inner closeness. Both are depicted as advocating a morality which, from a universalistic point of view, is futile and petty.

The most poisonous attack on Po-i occurs in the passage in which Chuang-tzu tries to prove Po-i's identity with Bandit Chih. After Mencius, this pair of antithetical heroes—Po-i and Chih—developed into a standard image of opposite types of men: one noble, the other evil. In order to prove the futility and unimportance of moral criteria, the authors of *Chuang-tzu* use these two images to show that, in spite of their apparent difference, their essence is alike. To illustrate this they take several examples (a petty man, a knight [*shih*], an official, a sage) and state that all are pursuing different ends, but in order to achieve these they sacrifice themselves (*hsün*—a character which, however strange it may seem, expresses both meanings), thus destroying their nature (*hsing*). The conclusion is that "the two of them died different deaths, but in destroying their lives and blighting their inborn nature they were equal."[94]

It is very interesting how the paradoxical belief, the striving for profit as an act of self-sacrifice, entered the Chinese language and, to a certain extent, the Chinese mind as well. Not only does this contradictory notion clearly defy common sense (since readiness to sacrifice oneself is a rare quality, limited to people who possess moral idealism and resolution), but it also challenges the Confucian approach, which regards striving for profit as the specific attribute of the petty man. However, as Legge has pointed out,[95] the character *hsün* originally meant "to bury along with the dead," to associate with in death as in life. In modern Chinese it has come to mean both "self-sacrifice" and "to give oneself up to passions or indulge."

In another passage, the same idea is expressed by Bandit Chih. This passage also gives examples of people who are judged very highly by the world but do not deserve it because "all of them for the sake of gain brought confusion to the Truth (*chen*) within them."[96] The first set of examples comprises mainly the exemplary Confucian rulers, Chih's purpose here being to expose their false morality. (Thus, for example, he refers to Yao as a cruel father, to Shun as a disrespectful son, and so on.) After this group comes a group of people who sacrificed themselves, beginning with Po-i and Shu-ch'i. Here Chih draws a somewhat different conclusion: "These . . . men were no different from a flayed dog, a pig sacrificed to the flood, a beggar with his alms-gourd in his hand. All were ensnared by thoughts of reputation (*ming*) and looked lightly on death."[97]

The most detailed passage about Po-i and Shu-ch'i differs from those above. I have in mind a sentence which first appears in the *Lü-shih* and is almost completely incorporated into the *Chuang-tzu*. The core of this passage is not the self-sacrifice of the brothers, but their refusal to participate in government. In contrast to the two passages cited, there is no criticism, but approval of the brothers' conduct. It is interesting, however, to analyze the terms in which this approval is formulated. Instead of the *Lü-shih*'s conclusion that the main purpose of life is the fulfillment of desires, the *Chuang-tzu* concludes that "to be lofty in principle and meticulous in conduct, delighting in one's will alone without stooping to serve the world—such was the ideal of these two gentlemen."[98] Without doubt, this conclusion contradicts the Confucian approach. We recognize in it the continuation of the dilemma that appeared previously in the *Analects*, namely: In refusing to compromise one's principles is it preferable to abandon the world for the sake of preserving one's purity? Or, since it is impossible to change the world, is it therefore preferable to refrain from interfering in the stream of universal life for the sake of not endangering one's life?

As is generally known, Taoist philosophy later played a highly significant role in the development of Chinese poetry.[99] Although the analysis of Po-i's image in Chinese poetry should be the theme of a separate study, it should be stated here already that Po-i's self-sacrifice is condemned in Chinese poetry. Thus he is characterized as follows by Tung-fang Shuo:

> For the intelligent fellow, there is nothing like living
>   by the golden mean.
> Taking it easy, he merely follows the Way.
> Po-i and Shu-ch'i were stupid to starve on Mount
>   Shou-yang;

> Liu-hsia Hui was really smart to keep his equanimity
>   when thrice dismissed from office.
> Eat your fill and walk it off;
> Better a salaried officer than a clod-hopper.
> Be a recluse, yet play the man of the world.[100]

After quoting this, Li Chi notes that "in finding Po Yi's action stupid, Tung-fang So's [sic] view reflects the Neo-Taoist preoccupation with the preservation of life as the most important consideration of all. Since dying for one's principle was folly and complete acceptance of the world was impossible, a compromise lay in seeking physical comfort while maintaining a noncooperative spirit."[101]

By no means do all Chinese poets accept this kind of compromise, nor did it conform to Chuang-tzu's ideas, who presumably refused to be "a salaried officer," for such a position posed the danger of enslavement. Li Po's poetry expresses a similar disapproval of moral self-sacrifice:

> A man should enjoy himself during his lifetime;
> Why stick to books and suffer want and sickness?
> A man should seek honors during his lifetime;
> Why stick to principles and suffer wind and dust? [102]

From this point of view, "the shining examples of moral integrity . . . are merely silly." This is the sense of Li Po's words in another poem:

> What kind of Men were Yi and Ch'i
> That they starved themselves on the Western Hill? [103]

Notes

Notes to Introduction

1. See David N. Keightley, "The Religious Commitment: Shang Theology and the Genesis of Chinese Political Culture," *History of Religions,* 17. 3-4 (1978), pp. 211–225.
2. Thomas A. Metzger, *Escape from Predicament: Neo-Confucianism and China's Evolving Political Culture,* New York: Columbia University Press, 1977, p. 197.
3. Hao Chang, "Neo-Confucian Moral Thought and its Modern Legacy," *Journal of Asian Studies,* 39 (1980), p. 260.
4. Cited in Metzger, *Escape from Predicament,* p. 250.
5. See Hsü Fu-kuan, "Hsien Han ching-hsüeh ti hsin-ch'eng" (The Formation of classical learning before the Han), in *Chung-yang Yen-chiu Yüan kuo-chi han-hsüeh hui-i lun wen-chi* (Proceedings of the Academia Sinica international conference on sinology), Ch'ien Ssu-liang, ed., Taipei Academia Sinica, 1981, vol. 8, pp. 509–540 (hereafter *Proceedings of the Academia Sinica*).
6. See E. Zürcher, *The Buddhist Conquest of China: The Spread and Adaptation of Buddhism in Early Medieval China,* Leiden: E. J. Brill, 1972, pp. 46, 230–231.
7. Arthur F. Wright, "Introduction," in *The Confucian Persuasion,* Arthur F. Wright, ed., Stanford: Stanford University Press, 1960, p. 6.
8. See Edwin G. Pulleyblank, "Neo-Confucianism and Neo-Legalism in T'ang Intellectual Life, 755–805," in *The Confucian Persuasion,* pp. 77–114. See also William H. Nienhauser, Jr., "Some Preliminary Remarks on Fiction, the Classical Tradition and Society in Late Ninth-Century China," in *Critical Essays in Chinese Fiction,* Winston L.Y. Yang and Curtis P. Adkins, eds., Hong Kong: The Chinese University Press, 1980, pp. 1–16. Nienhauser suggests a confluence between the new critical hermeneutics and developments in *ch'uan-ch'i.*

9. Wm. Theodore de Bary, "Introduction," in *The Unfolding of Neo-Confucianism*, Wm. Theodore de Bary, ed., New York: Columbia University Press, 1975, p. 11.
10. "Confucianism was only interested in affairs of this world," wrote Max Weber. See his *The Religion of China*, New York: The Free Press, 1951, p. 155.
11. Wm. Theodore de Bary, "Introduction," in *Yüan Thought: Chinese Thought and Religion under the Mongols*, Hok-lam Chan and Wm. Theodore de Bary, eds., New York: Columbia University Press, 1982, pp. 1–3; Hao Chang, "Neo-Confucian Moral Thought and its Modern Legacy," p. 266; and Hao Chang, "New Confucianism and the Intellectual Crisis of Contemporary China," in *The Limits of Change: Essays on Conservative Alternatives in Republican China*, Charlotte Furth, ed., Cambridge: Harvard University Press, 1976, p. 291.
12. James F. Cahill, "Confucian Elements in the Theory of Painting," in *Confucianism and Chinese Civilization*, Arthur F. Wright, ed., New York: Atheneum, 1964, pp. 77, 92.
13. Thomé H. Fang, *The Chinese View of Life, the Philosophy of Comprehensive Harmony*, Hong Kong: The Union Press, 1957, pp. 195–214.
14. For a discussion on the question of orthodoxy, see de Bary, "Introduction," in *The Unfolding of Neo-Confucianism*, pp. 1–32.
15. Where to locate the roots of Han Learning, and to what extent its "evidential investigations" were a reaction to either Sung or Ming Neo-Confucianism is discussed by Edward T. Ch'ien, "Chiao Hung and the Revolt against Ch'eng-Chu Orthodoxy," in *The Unfolding of Neo-Confucianism*, pp. 271–303. See also Hu Shih, "Chi-ko fan li-hsüeh ti ssu-hsiang chia" (Several thinkers opposed to li-hsüeh), in *Hu Shih wen-ts'un* (Collected works of Hu Shih), Taipei: Yuan-tung, 1961, Vol. 3, pp. 53–107. Hu argues that the age of *li-hsüeh* was from 1050 to 1600, and that the centuries 1600 onward were characterized by opposition to it.
16. Lucien Bianco, *Origins of the Chinese Revolution, 1915–1949*, Stanford: Stanford University Press, 1971, p. 1.
17. Joseph R. Levenson, *Confucian China and its Modern Fate, The Problem of Intellectual Continuity*, Berkeley: University of California Press, 1958, Vol. 1, p. xxx, and *The Problem of Historical Significance*, Berkeley: University of California Press, 1965, vol. 3, pp. 113–115.
18. Ibid., p. 113.
19. Wing-tsit Chan, *Religious Trends in Modern China*, New York: Columbia University Press, 1953. pp. 4, 20. See also H.D. Harootunian, "Metzger's Predicament," *Journal of Asian Studies*, 39 (1980), pp. 245–254. Harootunian cautions against attempts at establishing a "total history" and is, therefore, highly critical of Metzger's assumption of spiritualized Neo-Confucian continuity.

20. Clifford Geertz, "The Integrative Revolution, Primordial Sentiments and Civil Politics in the New States," in *Old Societies and New States, The Quest for Modernity in Asia and Africa*, Clifford Geertz, ed., New York: The Free Press, 1963, pp. 105–157. See also Michel Oksenberg and Richard Bush, "China's Political Evolution: 1972–82," *Problems of Communism*, 31. 5 (1982), pp. 1–19.

21. Richard Critchfield, "Science and the Villager: The Last Sleeper Wakes," *Foreign Affairs*, 61. 1 (1982), pp. 14–41.

22. Hao Chang, "Intellectual Radicalism and the Quest for Meaning—the Decade of the 1890's," in *Proceedings of the Academia Sinica*, vol. 8, pp. 371–392.

23. See Thomas A. Metzger, "Author's Reply," *Journal of Asian Studies*, 39 (1980), pp. 282–283. Metzger suggests that if the transformative vision of modernization had a source in tradition, then the May Fourth "invalidation" may itself be a "transformative way of thinking about modernization."

24. Ch'ien Mu, *Chung-kuo ssu-hsiang shih* (A history of Chinese thought), Hong Kong: Hsin Ya, 1962, pp. 7, 163–165.

25. Hu Shih, "Shuo Ju (On the Ju)", in *Hu Shih wen-ts'un* (Hu Shih's collected works), Taipei: Yüantung, 1953, Vol. 4, pp. 1–103; Fu Ssu-nien, "Hsing-ming ku hsün pien-cheng (Evidence about life in antiquity)", in *Fu Ssu-nien chüan-chi* (Fu Ssu-nien's collected works), Taipei: Lien-ching, 1980, Vol. 2, pp. 159–403; and Ku Chieh-kang, ed., *Ku shih pien* (Discussions in ancient Chinese history), reprint, 7 vols. Hong Kong: Taping, 1962–1963, see especially vols. 2 and 3.

26. Hao Chang, "New Confucianism and the Intellectual Crisis," p. 286. See also Irene Eber, "Hu Shih and Chinese History: the Problem of *Cheng-li kuo-ku*," *Monumenta Serica*, 27 (1968), pp. 169–207.

27. Tu Wei-ming, "Hsiung Shih-li's Quest for Authentic Existence," in Furth, *The Limits of Change*, p. 246.

28. Mou Tsung-san, *Li-shih che-hsüeh* (Philosophy of history), Hong Kong, 1962, pp. 164–174, 180–181.

29. The 1961–1962 brief thaw is discussed by Merle Goldman, "The Unique 'Blooming and Contending' of 1961–62," *China Quarterly*, 37 (1969), pp. 63–64.

30. Pan Zhenping, "Reassessment of Confucius," *Beijing Review*, 26.22 (30 May 1983), pp. 18–21. See, for example, Jin Jingfang, "On the Question of Methodology in the Study of Confucius", *Chinese Studies in Philosophy*, 12, no. 2 (1980–81), pp. 68–75 and Zhang Hengshou, "Theories of 'Humaneness' in the Spring and Autumn Era and Confucius' Concept of Humaneness", Ibid., 12, no. 4 (1981), pp. 3–36. In these the questions of Confucius' class and the progressive and conservative elements in his thought continue to predominate. See, however, also Julia Ching's optimistic appraisal "China's Reassess-

ment of Confucianism," *The Asian Wall Street Journal*, 15 January 1982.

31. Tu Wei-ming, *Proceedings of the Heyman Center for the Humanities*, Columbia University in the City of New York, 1982.

32. See, for example, K'uang Ya-ming, "Tui K'ung-tzu chin-hsing tsai yen-chiu ho tsai p'ing-chia" (Carry out renewed research and renewed reappraisal of Confucius), *Kuang-ming jih-pao*, 13 September 1982, p. 4. K'uang writes that inquiries into Confucius' influence must utilize "using the past for the present" (*ku wei chin yung*) and oppose "stressing the past and not the present" (*hou ku po chin*).

33. Wu An-chia, "Communist China's Current Attitudes Toward Traditional Chinese Culture," *Issues and Studies*, 19. 6 (1983), pp. 43–58.

Notes to Chapter 1

1. Vitaly Rubin, "Values of Confucianism," *Numen*, 38.1 (1981), p. 72. For a comparable interpretive position, see V. Rubin, "The End of Confucianism?", *T'oung Pao*, 49 (1973), pp. 68–78.

2. Joseph R. Levenson, *Confucian China and Its Modern Fate: A Trilogy*, Berkeley: University of California Press, 1968.

3. The term is borrowed from the title of a collection of essays in memory of Levenson, *The Mozartian Historian: Essays on the Works of Joseph R. Levenson*, Maurice Meisner and Rhoads Murphey, eds., Berkeley: University of California Press, 1976.

4. Levenson, *Trilogy*, general preface, p. x.

5. Ibid.

6. Levenson, *Trilogy*, vol. 3, p. 123.

7. *From Max Weber: Essays in Sociology*, H. H. Gerth and C. Wright Mills, trans. and eds., New York: Oxford University Press, 1958, p. 196.

8. Levenson, *Trilogy*, vol. 3, pp. 110–125.

9. *The Limits of Change: Essays on Conservative Alternatives in Republican China*, Charlotte Furth, ed., Cambridge, Mass.: Harvard University Press, 1976; see articles by Hao Chang, Yü-sheng Lin and Tu Wei-ming.

10. Guy S. Alitto, *The Last Confucian: Liang Shu-ming and the Chinese Dilemma of Modernity*, Berkeley: University of California Press, 1979.

11. Max Weber, *The Religion of China*, Hans H. Gerth, trans. and ed., New York: The Free Press, 1964, p. 235.

12. Thomas A. Metzger, *Escape from Predicament: Neo-Confucianism and China's Evolving Political Culture*, New York: Columbia University Press, 1977.

13. *Self and Society in Ming Thought*, Wm. T. de Bary, ed., New York:

Columbia University Press, 1970; *The Unfolding of Neo-Confucianism*, Wm. T. de Bary, ed., New York: Columbia University Press, 1975; *Principle and Practicality: Essays in Neo-Confucianism and Practical Learning*, Wm. T. de Bary and Irene Bloom, eds., New York: Columbia University Press, 1979; and *Yüan Thought: Chinese Thought and Religion under the Mongols*, Hok-lam Chan and Wm. T. de Bary, eds., New York: Columbia University Press, 1982.

14. Tu Wei-ming, "Confucian Ethics and the Entrepreneurial Spirit in East Asia," seminar presentation at Business Administration, National University of Singapore, 31 August 1982. Included as chapter 3 in Tu Wei-ming, *Confucian Ethics Today: The Singapore Challenge*, Singapore: Federal Publications, 1984.

15. Peter Berger, "Secularity—East and West" (typewritten manuscript), pp. 16–19.

16. See Joseph R. Levenson's argument in his *Liang Ch'i-ch'ao and the Mind of Modern China*. Cambridge, Mass.: Harvard University Press, 1953.

17. *Analects* VII, 3.

18. Han Yü, "Yüan Tao" (The origin of the Way), in *Ch'ang-li ch'üan-chi* (Complete works of Han Yü), 5 vols., Shanghai: Commercial Press, 1918, vol. 2, 11/6b.

19. *Analects* IX, 5.

20. For an example of the conflict between Confucians and Legalists, see *Chung-kuo ssu-hsiang shih* (History of Chinese thought), Hou Wai-lu et al., eds., 5 vols., Peking: Jen-min, 1957, vol. 2, pp. 172–180.

21. See Yü Ying-shih, "Han-Chin chih chi shih chih hsin-chih-chüeh yü hsin-ssu-ch'ao" (The new awakening of the literatus and new currents of thought in the transition between Han and Chin), *Hsin-ya hsüeh-pao (New Asia Journal)*, 5.1. (1959), pp. 25–144.

22. Edwin G. Pulleyblank, "Neo-Confucianism and Neo-Legalism in T'ang Intellectual Life, 755–805," in *The Confucian Persuasion*, Arthur F. Wright, ed., Stanford: Stanford University Press, 1960, pp. 77–114.

23. The locus classicus for this expression is found in *Chuang-tzu*, chapter 32. See *Chuang-tzu yin-te (Index to Chuang-tzu)*, Harvard-Yenching Institute, 1947, 91/33/15.

24. The following monographs are pertinent to this issue: Erik Zürcher, *The Buddhist Conquest of China: The Spread and Adaptation of Buddhism in Early Medieval China*, Leiden: Brill, 1959, and Kenneth K. S. Ch'en, *The Chinese Transformation of Buddhism*, Princeton: Princeton University Press, 1973.

25. Arthur Wright, *Buddhism in Chinese History*, Stanford: Stanford University Press, 1959.

26. Kenneth K. S. Ch'en, *Buddhism in China: A Historical Survey*, Princeton: Princeton University Press, 1964, pp. 471–486.

27. This is what I interpret as the implicit message in Shimada's article, "Chan-hou Jih-pen Sung–Ming li-hsüeh yen-chiu te kai-k'uang" (A survey of Sung–Ming Confucian studies in post-war Japan), *Chung-kuo che-hsüeh* (Chinese philosophy), Peking, 7(1983), pp. 146–158.
28. Levenson, *Trilogy*, vol. 1, pp. 156–163.
29. It should be noted that, although the term *"shih-hsüeh"* has often been rendered as "practical learning," its occurrence in Ch'eng I's writings, cited by Chu Hsi in his preface to the *Great Learning*, clearly shows that *shih-hsüeh* is opposed to *hsü-wen* ("ephemeral literature," referring to the literary studies required for the examinations) and to *k'ung-li* ("empty principle," referring to the Buddhist doctrine of *śūnyatā*), and that the term is also used by the Sung masters to define what Confucian learning really entails.
30. The expression is used by Mou Tsung-san to characterize the Sung–Ming Confucian approach to ultimate questions about ontology and cosmology. See Mou Tsung-san, *Hsin-t'i yü hsing-t'i* (The substance of mind and the substance of nature), 3 vols., Taipei: Cheng-chung, 1968, vol. 1, pp. 115–189.
31. *China's Response to the West: A Documentary Survey, 1839–1923*, Ssu-yü Teng and John K. Fairbank, eds., Cambridge, Mass.: Harvard University Press, 1954.
32. Mary Wright, *The Last Stand of Chinese Conservatism: The T'ung-chih Restoration, 1862–1874,* Stanford: Stanford University Press, 1957.
33. For a comprehensive study on K'ang, see Kung-ch'üan Hsiao, *A Modern China and a New World: K'ang Yu-wei, Reformer and Utopian, 1858–1927*, Seattle: University of Washington Press, 1975. See also Jonathan Spence, *The Gate of Heavenly Peace: The Chinese and Their Revolution, 1895–1980*, New York: The Viking Press, 1981, pp. 1–60.
34. Quoted from Wing-tsit Chan, *A Source Book in Chinese Philosophy*, Princeton: Princeton University Press, 1969, p. 724. For the original statement, see Liang Ch'i-ch'ao, *Intellectual Trends in the Ch'ing Period*, Immanuel C. Y. Hsü, trans., Cambridge, Mass.: Harvard University Press, 1959, p. 94.
35. Wolfgang Bauer, *China and the Search For Happiness*, Michael Shaw, trans., New York: The Seabury Press, 1976, pp. 300–329.
36. Levenson, *Trilogy*, vol. 1, pp. 107–108; vol. 2, p. 37. For a critique of Levenson's position, see Hao Chang, *Liang Ch'i-ch'ao and Intellectual Transition in China, 1890–1907*, Cambridge, Mass.: Harvard University Press, 1971, pp. 224–237.
37. For an example of this nuanced approach to modern Chinese intellectual history, see Benjamin I. Schwartz, *In Search of Wealth and Power: Yen Fu and the West*, Cambridge, Mass.: Harvard University Press, 1964.
38. Tse-Tsung Chow, *The May Fourth Movement: Intellectual Revolution*

in Modern China, Cambridge, Mass.: Harvard University Press, 1960, pp. 19–40.

39. For Hu Shih's strategy to present the dark side of Chinese culture as a way of undermining the complacency of the traditionalists, see his three essays on faith and reflection (*hsin-hsin yü fan-hsing*), in *Hu Shih lun-hsüeh chin-chu* (Recent scholarly writings of Hu Shih), Shanghai: Commercial Press, 1935, pp. 479–499.

40. Tse-tsung Chow, *The May Fourth Movement*, pp. 308–312.

41. Ibid., pp. 58–61.

42. Mao Tse-tung, "Hunan nung-min yün-tung k'ao-ch'a pao-kao" (Report on the investigation of the peasant movements in Hunan), in *Mao Tse-tung hsüan-chi* (Selected works of Mao Tse-tung), 4 vols. Peking: Jen-min, 1951, Vol. 1, pp. 32–35.

43. For Dewey, see *Tu Wei wu ta yen-chiang* (Five major lectures by Dewey), recorded by Mu-wang et al., Peking: Ch'en-pao ts'ung-shu, 1920; *John Dewey's Lectures in China, 1919–1920*, Robert W. Clopton and Tsuin-chen Ou, trans. and eds., Honolulu: University Press of Hawaii, 1973; Barry Keenan, *The Dewey Experiment in China*, Cambridge, Mass.: Harvard University Press, 1977. For Russell, see *Lo-su chi Po-la-k'o chiang-yen chi* (Collection of lectures by Russell and Dora Black), recorded by Li Hsiao-feng et al., Peking: Wei-i jih-pao she ts'ung-shu, 1921; Suzanne P. Ogden, "The Sage in the Inkpot: Bertrand Russell and China's Social Reconstruction in the 1920s," *Modern Asian Studies*, 16.4 (1982), pp. 529–600.

44. Maurice Meisner, *Li Ta-chao and the Origins of Chinese Marxism*, Cambridge, Mass.: Harvard University Press, 1967, pp. 60–70.

45. J. K. Fairbank, E. D. Reischauer, and A. M. Craig, *East Asia: Tradition and Transformation*, Boston: Houghton Mifflin Company, 1973, p. 756.

46. Lu Hsün, "Sui-kan lu san-shih-pa" (Random thoughts, No. 38), *Hsin ch'ing-nien* (*New Youth*) 5.5 (15 November 1918), pp. 515–518. For a thought-provoking analysis of Lu Hsün's "complex consciousness," see Yü-sheng Lin, *The Crisis of Chinese Consciousness: Radical Antitraditionalism in the May Fourth Era*, Madison: The University of Wisconsin Press, 1979, pp. 142–151.

47. Charlotte Furth, *Ting Wen-chiang: Science and China's New Culture*, Cambridge, Mass.: Harvard University Press, 1970, pp. 99–135. See also *Sources of Chinese Tradition*, Wm. T. de Bary, Wing-tsit Chan and Chester Tan, comps., 2 vols., New York: Columbia University Press, 1960, vol. 2, pp. 172–181.

48. Carsun Chang (Chang Chia-sen), *The Third Force in China*, New York: Bookman Associates, 1952.

49. Carsun Chang, *The Development of Neo-Confucian Thought*, 2 vols., New York: Bookman Associates, 1957–1962.

50. For Fung, see his *Hsin li-hsüeh* (New learning of the Principle),

Ch'ang-sha: Commercial Press, 1939; *Hsin yüan-jen* (New origins of man), Chungking: Commercial Press, 1943; *Hsin yüan-tao* (New origins of the Way), Shanghai: Commercial Press, 1945. For Ho, see his *Tang-tai Chung-kuo che-hsüeh* (Contemporary Chinese philosophy), Nanking: Sheng-li, 1947.

51. Holmes Welch, *The Buddhist Revival in China*, Cambridge, Mass.: Harvard University Press, 1968, pp. 51–71, 117–120.

52. Wing-tsit Chan, *A Source Book in Chinese Philosophy*, p. 743.

53. Hsiung Shih-li, *Hsin wei-shih lun* (New exposition of the Consciousness-only doctrine), 3 vols., Peking: Peking University Press, 1933.

54. Jerome B. Grieder, *Hu Shih and the Chinese Renaissance: Liberalism in the Chinese Revolution, 1917–1937*, Cambridge, Mass.: Harvard University Press, 1970, pp. 173–216.

55. Tu Wei-ming, "Confucianism: Symbol and Substance in Recent Times," *Asian Thought and Society: An International Review*, 1.1 (April 1976), 42–66; also in Tu Wei-ming, *Humanity and Self-Cultivation*, Berkeley: Asian Humanities Press, 1979, pp. 257–296. For an example of the surge in Confucian studies in the People's Republic of China, see *Lun Sung–Ming li-hsüeh* (On Sung–Ming Confucianism), Hangchou: Chekiang jen-min, 1983. This collection includes more than thirty essays originally contributed to the international conference on Sung–Ming Confucian thought held in Hangchou, 15–21 October 1981.

56. Joseph Levenson, "Communist China in Time and Space: Roots and Rootlessness," *The China Quarterly*, no. 39 (July-September, 1969), pp. 1–11.

57. Briefly mentioned in Carsun Chang, *Development of Neo-Confucian Thought*, preface.

58. For a succinct account of Professor Fang's philosophy, see Thomé H. Fang, *Creativity in Man and Nature*, Taipei: Linking Publishing Co., 1980.

59. See "A Manifesto for a Reappraisal of Sinology and Reconstruction of Chinese Culture," signed by Carsun Chang, T'ang Chün-i, Mou Tsung-san, and Hsü Fu-kuan, in *Development of Neo-Confucian Thought*, vol. 2, pp. 455–483.

60. For two recent attempts to address this issue, see Wm. T. de Bary, *The Liberal Tradition in China*, Hong Kong: The Chinese University Press and New York: Columbia University Press, 1983, pp. 91–108, and Tu Wei-ming, *Confucian Ethics Today: The Singapore Challenge*.

Notes to Chapter 2

1. Cho-yun Hsü, *Ancient China in Transition*, Stanford: Stanford University Press, 1965, p. 56, table 5.

2. Ibid., pp. 28–32.
3. See my paper, "Historical Conditions of the Emergence and Crystallization of the Confucian System," in *The Axial Age and Its Diversity*, S.N. Eisenstadt, ed., in press.
4. James Legge, trans., *The Analects*, vol. 1 of *The Chinese Classics*, reprint, Hong Kong, 1970, XIII.19.
5. Ibid. XXII.2.
6. Ibid. XV.5.
7. Kuang-ch'üan Hsiao, *A History of Chinese Political Thought*, F.W. Mote, trans., Princeton: Princeton University Press, 1979, vol. 1, pp. 87–89, 121.
8. Legge, *Analects* VII.29.
9. Ibid. VII.33.
10. Hsiao, *A History*, pp. 82–86.
11. Hsü, *Ancient China*, pp. 158–160.
12. Ch'ien Mu, *Ssu-shu shih-i* (Comments on the Four Books), Taipei: Chung-hua wen-hua, 1953, vol. 1, pp. 131–132; *Shih-chi hui-chu k'ao-cheng* (The Historical Record, with commentaries and annotations), 1932–1934 reprint, Taipei: I-wen, 67/5–47; Hsü, *Ancient China*, pp. 37–52, 92–102.
13. Hsü, *Ancient China*, pp. 34–37.
14. Legge, *Analects* III.8.i–ii.
15. James Legge, trans., *The Doctrine of the Mean*, vol. 1 of *The Chinese Classics*, reprint, Hong Kong, 1970, chap. 21.
16. Ch'ien, *Ssu-shu*, vol. I, pp. 117–151.
17. *Li chi* (Book of Rites), Ssu-pu pei-yao edition, 7/11, 9/12; *Hsün-tzu* (The works of Hsün-tzu), Ssu-pu pei-yao edition, 3/13.
18. James Legge, trans., *The Works of Mencius*, vol. 2 of *The Chinese Classics*, reprint, Hong Kong, 1970, IB.(vi)3–4.
19. Chien, *Ssu-shu*, vol. II, pp. 13–18.
20. Hsü, *Ancient China*, p. 39.
21. Vitaly A. Rubin, *Individual and State in Ancient China*, Essays on Four Chinese Philosophers, New York: Columbia University Press, 1976, pp. 33–54.
22. *Mo-tzu* (The works of Mo-tzu), Ssu-pu pei-yao edition, 3/1–3.
23. Hsiao, *A History*, pp. 243–244.
24. *Mo-tzu* 7/1–3, 10.
25. Legge, *Mencius* IIA. 3–5, VIIB.31.
26. Ibid. IA, VIB.4.
27. Ibid. VIA.4 and 5.
28. Ibid. VIIA.33.
29. Ibid. VIIB.31.
30. Hsiao, *A History*, p. 153.
31. Yu Hao-liang, "Chung-shan san chi ming-wen k'ao-shih" (Notes on inscriptions of three bronze vessels of the state of Chung-shan), *K'ao-k'u hsüeh-pao*, 2 (1979), pp. 171–183.

32. Legge, *Mencius* VIB.2.
33. Hsü, *Ancient China*, pp. 94–96, 98–100.
34. Hsiao, *A History*, pp. 205–206, n. 119; *Hsün-tzu*, 11/7–8.
35. *Hsün-tzu* 3/7.
36. Ibid. 1/2, 5/7–8; Hsiao, *A History*, pp. 190–192.
37. Rubin, *Individual and State*, p. 40.
38. *Hsün-tzu* 11/9–10, 13.
39. *Hsün-tzu* 5/7.
40. Hsiao, *A History*, p. 18.
41. Ibid., pp. 184, *Hsün-tzu*, 13/1–3.
42. Legge, *Mencius* IVA.27.
43. *Hsün-tzu*, 19/3–14.
44. Ibid. 2/13, 13/1.
45. Ibid. 4/10, 5/5–7.
46. Hsiao, *A History*, p. 206, n. 119.
47. *Shih-chi*, 6/33–47.
48. *Han-shu pu-chu* (An annotated history of the Han dynasty), Taipei: I-wen reprint, 30/51.

Notes to Chapter 3

1. This essay is one chapter of a full-length study and translation of the *KTT* now in preparation for the Princeton Library of Asian Translations of Princeton University Press.
2. See, for example, Chi-yun Chen, *Hsün Yüeh: The Life and Reflections of an Early Medieval Confucian*, Cambridge, 1975, pp. 162–177; Dan Daor, "The Yin Wenzi and the Renaissance of Philosophy in Wei-Jin China," University of London thesis, 1973, pp. 40–103; Donald Holzman, *Poetry and Politics: The Life and Works of Juan Chi, A.D. 210–263*, Cambridge, 1976. Erik Zürcher, *The Buddhist Conquest of China*, Leiden, 1959, vol. I, pp. 43–46; Etienne Balazs, *Chinese Civilization and Bureaucracy*, A. Wright, ed., H.M. Wright, trans., New Haven, 1964, pp. 187–254; Jay Sailey, *The Master Who Embraces Simplicity, A Study of the Philosopher Ko Hung, A.D. 283–343*, San Francisco, 1978, pp. 346–464; Richard B. Mather, trans., *Shih-shuo hsin-yü*, Minneapolis, 1976, pp. xiii–xxx.
3. Zürcher, *The Buddhist Conquest*, p. 45.
4. Balazs, *Chinese Civilization*, p. 195.
5. Chen, *Hsün Yüeh*, pp. 164–165.
6. Chan Wing-tsit, *A Source Book in Chinese Philosophy*, Princeton, 1963, pp. 314–315. See also Henricks G. Robert, *Philosophy and Argumentation in Third Century China, The Essays of Hsi K'ang*, Princeton, 1983, pp. 3–4.

7. *HHIWC* by Yao Chen-tsung in *Hou-Han shu*, in *Erh-shih-wu shih pu-pien*, reprint of 1936–1937 K'ai-ming ed., Taipei, 1974, vol. 2, pp. 2305–2445.
8. *SKIWC* in *San-kuo chih*, by Yao Chen-tsung in *ibid.*, vol. 3, pp. 3189–3300.
9. *PCSIWC* in *Pu Chin shu*, by Ting Kuo-chun in *ibid.*, vol. 3, pp. 3653–3964.
10. For a discussion of the "death" of Confucianism at the beginning of the Wei dynasty, see Chen, *Hsün Yüeh*, p. 164.
11. For the so-called "Mohist revival," see Zürcher, *The Buddhist Conquest*, p. 46.
12. For a discussion of Logic in third-century China, see Daor, "The Yin Wenzi," pp. 62–103.
13. *SKIWC*, p. 3253.
14. For the dating and authenticity of the *Yin Wen-tzu*, see Daor, pp. 1–38.
15. *SKIWC*, p. 3259.
16. *SKIWC*, p. 3250.
17. *Sui-shu*, Peking, Chung-hua shu-chü, 1973, p. 937.
18. Ibid.
19. Quoted in Chang Hsin-ch'eng, *Wei-shu t'ung-k'ao*, 1939, reprint, Shanghai, 1954, Vol. 2, pp. 744–745.
20. Ibid., p. 744.
21. Ibid., p. 744.
22. Ibid., pp. 747–748.
23. Chiang Chao-hsi, *K'ung-ts'ung cheng-yi*, 1720, Ho-hsi shu-wu.
24. Tsukada Tamon (Tsukada Tora), *Cho chu Kososhi*, Keishi shobo, 1975.
25. There are, of course, exceptions. Short discussions of the *KTT* can be found in R.P. Kramers, *Kung-tzu chia-yü*, Leiden, 1950, and in A.C. Graham, "Two Dialogues in the Kung-sun Tzu: 'White Horse' and 'Left and Right'," *Asia Major*, n.s., 11 (1965).
26. *K'ung-ts'ung-tzu* is translated in Needham's *Science and Civilisation*, Cambridge: Cambridge University Press, 1956, vol. 2, p. 598, as *The Book of Master K'hung Ts'hung*. David R. Knechtges, in his translation of the *Wen-xuan* (Princeton, 1982, p. 96), takes *K'ung-ts'ung* to be the name of K'ung Tsang's father.
27. For a survey of the main evidence indicating that the *KTT* is a third-century forgery by Wang Su, see Chang, *Wei-shu*, Vol. 2, pp. 744–751. See also, Lo Ken-tzu, *Ku shih pien*, Taipei: Ming-lun, 1970, pp. 184–195.
28. Chang, *Wei-shu*, vol. 1, II. 19–21.
29. *KTT*, Ssu-pu ts'ung-k'an ed. (SPTK), 3.50a/1. and 5.19b/4.
30. See Kramers, *K'ung-tzu chia-yü*, pp. 98–99, n. 323.
31. Wang Su is not even mentioned in a 10-volume history of Chinese

philosophy which surveys the thought of no fewer than one hundred philosophers. See Wang Shou-nan, *Chung-kuo li-tai ssu-hsiang-chia*, Taipei, 1978. For a list and description of Wang Su's works, see *SKIWC*, pp. 3191–3256.

32. Wang Shou-nan, *Ssu-hsiang-chia*, pp. 54–90.

33. *A Concordance to the Yi Ching*, Taipei: Chinese Materials and Research Aids Service Center, 1966, p. 1.

34. Ibid., p. 49.

35. *KTT*, SPTK ed., 2.38b/4.

36. *Mencius*, D.C. Lau, trans., Middlesex: Penguin Books, 1970, IA.1–3, p. 49. See also pp. 173–174 for a different version of the same argument.

37. *Lun-heng*, Alfred Forke, trans., Paragon: New York, 1962, vol. 1, p. 418.

38. It should be pointed out, however, that neither Wang Ch'ung nor the author of the *KTT* came to terms with the Mencian argument. Mencius was a deontologist, and his philosophy attempts to persuade us of man's autonomous morality, that is to say, man should never be affected by any considerations other than his inner moral duties. Although *li* (profit) can be given a moral connotation it is hard to see how it can become an "instrumental" concept, as inner moral duty.

39. Lau, *Mencius*, III B.9, p. 115.

Notes to Chapter 4

1. Fung Yu-lan, *Chung-kuo che-hsüeh shih*, Shanghai, 1935, introduction, pp. 8–9. English translation in Derk Bodde, *A History of Chinese Philosophy*, Princeton: Princeton University Press, 1952, introduction, p. 2.

2. Fung Yu-lan, *A History*, introduction, p. 10. The English translation is my own.

3. Ibid., p. 100.

4. Homer H. Dubs, *Hsün-tze: The Moulder of Ancient Confucianism*, London: Arthur Probsthain, 1927, Taipei reprint, 1966, pp. 162–163.

5. Ibid., p. 112.

6. James Legge, trans., *Li Ki*, vol. 28 of Sacred Books of the East series, F. Max Muller, ed., Oxford: Oxford University Press, 1885, p. 103.

7. James Legge, trans., *The Doctrine of the Mean*, vol. 1 of *The Chinese Classics*, pp. 384–385.

8. There always were those who continued to believe in a supreme personal deity, as Huang Tsung-hsi (1610–1695). See his small tract, "P'o hsieh lun" (Against perverse theories), in *Li-chou yi-chu hui-k'an*, Shanghai ed., 1910.

9. James Legge, trans., *The Book of Documents*, vol. 3 of *The Chinese Classics*, p. 202.

10. Ibid., p. 466.

11. Ibid., p. 248. Hence Confucius' answer to Tzu-chang regarding the "universal" ancient practice of three years' mourning after the parents' death is not supported by the text as we have it today. Kuo Mo-jo proposes the possibility that Wu-ting was struck with illness and could not speak. See his *Ch'ing-t'ung shih-tai* (The Bronze Age), Shanghai: Hsin wen-yi, 1951, pp. 137–141.

12. It is even possible that Confucius was absorbed in *studying* this music. See Kuo Mo-jo, *Ch'ing-t'ung* p. 200.

13. Wing-tsit Chan, "The Evolution of the Confucian Concept *Jen*," *Philosophy East and West* 4 (1955), 295–319.

14. Translation adapted from James Legge, *Analects*, vol. 1 of *The Chinese Classics*, p. 271.

15. Commentary on Hexagram No. 2. Translation adapted from James Legge, *Yi King*, vol. 16 of Sacred Books of the East series, p. 421.

16. *Chu-tzu yü-lei* (Recorded conversations of Chu Hsi), reprint, Taipei, 1970, 12.10b. English translation adapted from Wing-tsit Chan, *A Source Book in Chinese Philosophy*, Princeton: Princeton University Press, 1964, p. 607.

17. *The Interior Life*, F. Murphy, trans., New York: P.J. Kenedy, 1961, p. 118. This meaning of the word "recollection" is however little known in today's English-speaking world.

18. *Chu-tzu yü-lei*, 12.2b.

19. "Kuan-hsin shuo" (On contemplating the mind), *Chu-tzu wen-chi* (Collected writings of Chu Hsi), reprint, Taipei, 1972, 67.21b. Translation adapted from Wing-tsit Chan, *A Source Book*, p. 604. It should not be surprising that Leclerq also says: "Reflection, recollection and prayer develop spiritual aspirations and are a source of enlightenment but a life solely devoted to contemplation places the soul in danger of turning in on itself and of succumbing to a very dangerous and refined type of egotism." See his *Interior Life*, p. 18.

20. This is taken from Chu's commentary on *The Great Learning*. Translation adapted from James Legge, vol. 1 of *The Chinese Classics*, p. 365.

21. Ibid., pp. 365–366.

22. Julia Ching, *Confucianism and Christianity*, Tokyo: Kodansha International, 1977, pp. 159–160.

23. Huang Tsung-hsi, *Ming-ju hsüeh-an*, Ssu-pu pei-yao (SPPY) ed., 58.17a. The translation is by Rodney Taylor, in *The Records of Ming Scholars*, Julia Ching and Chaoying Fang, eds., in press, University of Hawaii Press.

24. *Erh-ch'eng ch'üan-shu*, SPPY ed., 6.3a.

25. Huang Tsung-hsi, *Ming-ju*, 58.17a.

Notes to Chapter 5

1. J. Cahill, *The Compelling Image*, Cambridge, Mass.: Harvard University Press, 1982, p. 119.
2. See, for example, O. Grabar, "The Visual Arts, 1050–1350," in *The Cambridge History of Iran*, J.A. Boyle, ed., Cambridge: Cambridge University Press, vol. 5, p. 655.
3. H. Honour, *Chinoiserie*, New York: Harper and Row, 1961.
4. M. Sullivan, *The Meeting of Eastern and Western Art*, London: Thames and Hudson, 1973, pp. 46–89.
5. Hsiang Ta, "European Influences on Chinese Art in the Later Ming and Early Ch'ing Period," in J.C.Y. Watt, ed., *The Translation of Art: Essays in Chinese Painting and Poetry*, Hong Kong: Chinese University of Hong Kong, 1976. This essay was first published in Chinese in 1930. See also, J. Cahill, *The Compelling Image* and his *The Distant Mountains*, New York–Tokyo: Weatherhill, 1982.
6. Cahill, *Distant Mountains*, p. 213; Hsiang Ta, "European Influences," p. 164.
7. Quoted in Hsiang Ta, "European Influences," p. 164.
8. Ibid., p. 167.
9. C. and M. Beurdeley, *Guiseppe Castiglione*, Rutland, Vt.–Tokyo: Tuttle, 1971.
10. Ibid., p. 147.
11. Ibid.
12. Ibid., p. 148.
13. Cahill, *Compelling Image*, pp. 75–83; *Distant Mountains*, pp. 176–180.
14. Cahill, *Compelling Image*, p. 94.
15. Cahill, *Compelling Image*, pp. 75–77; *Distant Mountains*, pp. 176–177.
16. J. Cahill, "The Early Styles of Kung Hsien," *Oriental Arts n.s.*, 16.1 (Spring, 1970), pp. 62 ff; Y. Woodson, "The Problem of Western Influence," in *The Restless Universe*, J. Cahill, ed., Berkeley: The University Art Museum, 1971.
17. Cahill, *Distant Mountains*, p. 40.
18. Ibid., p. 57.
19. Ibid., pp. 58–59.
20. J. Chaves, "Some Relationships between Poetry and Painting in China," in J.C.Y. Watt, *The Translation of Art*, p. 86.
21. A.S. Condivi, *The Life of Michelangelo*, A.S. Wohl, trans., Baton Rouge: Louisiana State University Press, 1976, p. 105.
22. F. Hartt, *Michelangelo: The Complete Sculpture*, New York: Abrams, 1968, p. 13.
23. J. Pope-Hennessy, *Italian High Renaissance and Baroque Sculpture*, London: Phaidon, 2d ed., 1970, p. 113.
24. A.S. Wylie and A.F. Valenstein, "Between a Hostile World and Me: Organization and Disorganization in Van Gogh's Life and Work," in

The Psychoanalytic Study of Society, W. Muensterberger and L.B. Boyer, eds., New Haven: Yale University Press, 1979, p. 104.

25. A.J. Lubin, *Stranger on the Earth*, New York: Holt, Rinehart and Winston, 1972, p. 9.
26. Ibid., p. 11.
27. Ibid., p. 252, n. 15.
28. Letter, The Hague, second half of July, 1882.
29. A. Dube-Heynig, *E.L. Kirchner*, Munich: Graphik, 1961, p. 15.
30. H.C. Chang, *Chinese Literature 2: Nature Poetry*, Edinburgh: Edinburgh University Press, 1977, p. 8.
31. Ibid.
32. E.J. Coleman, *Philosophy of Painting by Shih-t'ao*, The Hague: Mouton, 1978, and a review by P.K.K. Tong, *Journal of Aesthetics and Art Criticism* (Fall, 1979), pp. 102–104. P. Rychmans, *Les "Propos sur la Peinture" de Shitao, Mélanges Chinois et Bouddhiques*, no. 15, Bruxelles: Institut des Hautes Études Chinoises, 1970.
33. Coleman, *Philosophy of Painting*, pp. 48, 118.
34. D.C. Lau, trans., *Confucius, the Analects*, London: Penguin Books, 1979, IV.15 p. 174.
35. Coleman, *Philosophy of Painting*, pp. 38–39, 115. Rychmans, pp. 15–18.
36. Cahill, *Compelling Image*, pp. 184–187.
37. Letter of 1 May, 1778, in W. Hildesheimer, *Mozart*, New York: Farrar, Strauss, Giroux, 1982, p. 91.
38. R. Stang, *Edvard Munch*, New York: Abbeville Press, 1979, p. 15.
39. Ibid., pp. 111, 227.
40. M. Urban, *Emil Nolde: Landscapes*, London: Pall Mall Press, 1970, pp. 29–30.
41. Ibid., p. 34.
42. L. Simpson, *Three Men on a Tower*, New York: Morrow, 1975, p. 307. Williams is quoted from "I Wanted to Write a Poem."
43. C. Schorske, *Fin-de-siècle Vienna*, New York: Random House, Vintage Books, 1981, p. 363.
44. *Enneads* 5. 8.1, in A.H. Armstrong, *Plotinus*, London: Allen and Unwin, 1953, p. 149.
45. *Enneads* 6. 7.22, ibid., p. 75.
46. *Enneads* 6. 7.33, ibid., p. 149.
47. E. Panofsky, *Idea*, Columbia, S.C.: University of South Carolina Press, 1968.
48. Ibid., pp. 49, 53–54.
49. Ibid., pp. 93–95.
50. Ibid., p. 116.
51. H. Chipp, *Theories of Modern Art*, Berkeley: University of California Press, 1969, pp. 552–553.

52. *Karel Appel,* A. Frankfurter, ed., New York: Abrams, 1980, p. 107.
53. Kiyohiko Munakata, *Ching Hao's "Pi-fa chi": A Note on the Use of the Brush,* Ascona: Artibus Asiae, 1974, pp. 40–47, 51. On *ch'i* and *ch'i-yün,* see also R.B. Acker, *Some T'ang and Pre-T'ang Texts on Chinese Painting,* Leiden: Brill, 1954, pp. XXVIII–XXXIII; Liu Shou Kwan, "The Six Canons of Hsieh Ho Re-examined by a Contemporary Chinese Painter," *Oriental Arts,* n.s., 7.2,3 (Summer 1971, Autumn 1971).
54. D. Pollard, "*Ch'i* in Literary Theory," in *Chinese Approaches to Literature from Confucius to Liang Ch'i-ch'ao,* A. Rickett, ed., Princeton: Princeton University Press, 1978, pp. 64–65.
55. See especially Acker, *T'ang Texts,* pp. XXVIII–XXXIII.
56. Munakata, *Pi-fa chi,* pp. 20–21, n. 13; and pp. 24–25, n. 21.
57. Julia Ching, *To Acquire Wisdom: The Way of Wang Yang-ming,* New York: Columbia University Press, 1976, pp. 142–144.
58. Wen Fong, "Tung Ch'i-ch'ang and the Orthodox Theory of Painting", *National Palace Museum Quarterly,* 2 (1967–68), and Wen Fong, *Images of the Mind,* Princeton: Princeton University Press, 1984, p. 171.
59. S. Bush, "Lung-mo, K'ai-ho, and Ch'i-fu," *Oriental Arts,* n.s. (1962). The quotation is from G. Rowley, *Principles of Chinese Painting,* Princeton: Princeton University Press, 1947, p. 48.
60. Siu-kit Wong, "*Ch'ing* and *Ching* in the Critical Writings of Wang Fu-chih," in *Chinese Approaches,* Rickett, ed.
61. Ibid., pp. 148–150.
62. O. Ewert, "Einfühlung," and W. Perpeet, "Einfühlungsästhetik," in *Historisches Wörterbuch der Philosophie,* J. Ritter, ed. Basel: Schwabe, 1971–.
63. W.S. Sahikian, *History and Systems of Psychology,* New York: Wiley, 1975, p. 194.
64. Ch'eng Yi-ch'uan, in A.C. Graham, *Two Chinese Philosophers,* London: Lund Humphries, 1958, p. 49.
65. J. Ching, *Wang Yang-ming,* p. 127.
66. Wan-go Weng, *Chinese Painting and Calligraphy,* New York: Dover, 1978, pp. XXI–XXII.
67. To Katia (Pringsheim), early June 1904, in *Letters of Thomas Mann,* S. and C. Winston, eds. and trans., vol. 1, *1889–1941,* London: Secker and Warburg, 1970.
68. S. Spender, "The Making of a Poem," in *The Creative Process,* G. Ghiselin, ed., Berkeley: University of California Press, 1952, pp. 112–125.
69. *World Photography,* B. Campbell, ed., London: Hamlyn, 1982, p. 69.
70. *Clyfford Still,* J.P. O'Neill, ed., New York: Metropolitan Museum of Art, 1979, p. 10.
71. S. Terenzio, *Robert Motherwell and Black,* London-New York: Petersburg Press, 1980, p. 126; H. Rosenberg, *De kooning,* New York: Abrams, 1973, p. 246.

72. From an anonymous *tanka* in *Kokinshu*, in *From the Country of Eight Islands*, H. Sato and B. Watson, eds., Seattle: University of Washington Press, 1981, p. 119.

Notes to Chapter 6

1. Vitaly A. Rubin, *Individual and State in Ancient China: Essays on Four Chinese Philosophers*, Steven I. Levine, trans., New York: Columbia University Press, 1976, pp. 26–27.
2. Chu Hsi, *Ssu-shu chi chu*, reprint of Ming edition, Taipei: Chung-kuo tzu-hsüeh ming-chu chi-ch'eng, no. 18, 1979, pp. 39–41.
3. *Mencius* 1B.8; Wm. Theodore de Bary et al., eds., *Sources of Chinese Tradition*, New York: Columbia University Press, 1960, vol. 1, pp. 95–97.
4. Wm. Theodore de Bary, *The Liberal Tradition in China*, Hong Kong: The Chinese University Press and New York: Columbia University Press, 1983.
5. Chu Hsi, *Ssu-shu chi chu*, pp. 7–8 (Preface to *Ta-hsüeh chang-chu*).
6. Ibid., pp. 1–6 (Preface to *Ta-hsüeh chang-chu*).
7. Chu Hsi, *Hui-an hsien-sheng Chu Wen-kung wen-chi*, in *Chu-tzu ta-ch'üan*, Ssu-pu pei yao edition, 100.5b–7a.
8. Ibid., 74.23a–29b.
9. There has been no full and systematic discussion of the community compact in any language I know of. One illustration of the system appears in Wing-tsit Chan's *Instructions for Practical Learning*, New York: Columbia University Press, 1963, pp. 298–306. It is a translation of Wang Yang-ming's proposal for a community compact, but without any reference to its antecedents in the Sung and especially to Chu Hsi.
10. Discussed in *The Rise of Neo-Confucianism in Korea*, Wm. Theodore de Bary and JaHyun Kim Haboush, eds., New York: Columbia University Press, 1985, pp. 21–22.
11. See Ueyama Shumpei, "Shushi no Karei to *Girei keiden tsū kai*," *Tōhō gakuhō*, 54 (1982), pp. 173–256, especially pp. 221–222.
12. Ch'iu Chün, *Ta-hsüeh yen-i pu*, 160 *chüan*, 1559 reprint of 1488 edition, preserved in the National Central Library, Taipei, 13.5b.
13. Huang Tsung-hsi, "Yüan fa," in *Ming-i tai-fang lu*, Wu-kuei lou ed., 1879, 8a.

Notes to Chapter 7

1. See Rodney L. Taylor, "The Centered Self: Religious Autobiography and the Neo-Confucian Tradition," *The History of Religions*, 17 (1978), pp. 266–283; and James Olney, "Autobiography and the

Cultural Moment: A Thematic, Historical, and Bibliographic Introduction," in *Autobiography, Essays, Theoretical and Critical,* James Olney, ed., Princeton: Princeton University Press, 1980, pp. 3–27. I gratefully acknowledge Harold R. Isaacs' remarks on this subject in personal correspondence.

2. David K. Shipler, *Russia, Broken Idols, Solemn Dreams,* New York: Times Books, 1983, pp. 301–346.

3. Borys Leytzkyj, *Politische Opposition in der Sowjetunion 1960–1972, Analyse und Dokumentation,* München: Deutscher Taschenbuch Verlag GmbH and Co., 1972, pp. 9–11, 21–22, 100.

4. In the diary entry for 1 January, 1970, he further noted that a study of the people's assembly on the basis of the *Tso chuan* was a dead end. The assemblies did not play an important role in the political life of that period. I wish to acknowledge my gratitude to Inessa Rubin for making the diaries available to me and for translating the passages cited in this paper.

5. Ibid.

6. Diary, February 1964.

7. Ibid.

8. The lecture was entitled "Early Confucians and Legalists: An Appreciation of their Ideological Heritage." A brief summary of the lecture and the discussion which followed is contained in *Narody Asii i Afriki,* 5 (1964), p. 225.

9. They are "Confucianism," *Sovietskaya Istoricheskaya Entsiklopedia* (Soviet historical encyclopedia), Moscow, 1965, vol. 7, pp. 875–878, and "Confucius," ibid., p. 1014. The editor, L.I. Duman, who removed the offending portions, also signed his name to the articles.

10. Vitaly Rubin, "Tzu-ch'an and the City State of Ancient China," *T'oung Pao,* 52. 1–3 (1965), pp. 8–34.

11. Shipler, *Russia,* p. 140.

12. Inessa Rubin adds here that the turning point for those Soviet Jews who wanted to leave came in 1970 when the first exit visas were granted.

13. Vitaly Rubin, "Dva istoka kitaiskoi politicheskoi mysli (Two sources of Chinese political thought), *Voprosy Istorii,* 3 (1967), pp. 70–81.

14. Diary, January 1969.

15. According to Inessa Rubin, the book, which was printed in an edition of 6,700 copies, became something of a sensation. Within hours of its appearance in the bookstores it was sold out. No additional copies were printed. The English translation is by Steven I. Levine, *Individual and State in Ancient China.* Rubin's introduction to the English edition describes how he came to write the book.

16. *Individual and State,* pp. 27, 115, 118.

17. Ibid., pp. 89–111, 28.

18. Rubin refers especially to chapter 28 in the *Chuang-tzu.*

19. "Taoist Political Thought," ms. in the archives of Inessa Rubin, pp. 36–75.
20. *Individual and State*, pp. XXV–XXVI.
21. See his "Shen Tao and Fa Chia," *Journal of the American Oriental Society*, 94. (1974), pp. 337–346.
22. Diary, October 1979.
23. Vitaly Rubin, "The Profound Person and Power in Classical Confucianism," in *Proceedings of the Academia Sinica*, Vol. 8, pp. 339–362.
24. Several diary notations from 1979 reveal that he continued to give serious attention to the question of freedom of choice. Eremeticism, he realized, was also an exercise in freedom of choice.
25. "The Profound Person," p. 344. Rubin first mentioned Po-i in the diary in the summer of 1970 as a topic for studying "the ideal of the just in ancient Chinese ethics."
26. According to the diary, November 1969, Rubin, no doubt as a result of his growing involvement in the dissident movement, came to see his own scholarly work in terms of acts of courage.
27. "The Profound Person," pp. 361–362.
28. *Individual and State*, p. 28. In the diary, March 1970, Rubin referred to Don Quixote as the lonely fighter who goes fearlessly against the stream and does not think of his own well-being.
29. Vitaly Rubin, "The End of Confucianism?," *T'oung Pao*, 59 (1973), pp. 68–78.
30. Laurence A. Schneider, *A Madman of Ch'u: The Chinese Myth of Loyalty and Dissent*, Berkeley: University of California Press, 1980.
31. Julia Ching, "Neo-Confucian Utopian Theories and Political Ethics," *Monumenta Serica*, 30 (1972–1973), pp. 32–33.
32. Ibid., pp. 37–38, 41.
33. A diary notation to this effect is made on 10 February 1979, and in April 1981 Rubin and I talked at length about the implications of his project.

Notes to Chapter 8

1. Ssu-ma Ch'ien, *Shih Chi*, Peking: Chung-hua shu-chü, 1955, 61. 1209–1211 (hereafter SC); the translation has been modified from Burton Watson, *Ssu-ma Ch'ien, Grand Historian of China* (hereafter Watson, *Ssu-ma Ch'ien*), New York: Columbia University Press, 1958, pp. 187–190.
2. Almost a literal quotation from *Lao-tzu* (*Tao-te ching*), chap. 29: "The world under Heaven is a holy vessel," in Arthur Waley, *The Way and Its Power*, London: Allen and Unwin, 1977, p. 179.
3. Hsü Yu's rejection of the empire is mentioned in chap. 1 of "Chuang-tzu chi chieh," in *Chu tzu chi-ch'eng*, Peking, 1957, vol. 3, pp.

3–4; see *The Complete Works of Chuang Tzu,* Burton Watson, trans. (hereafter Watson, *Chuang Tzu*), New York: Columbia University Press, 1968, pp. 32–33.

4. T'ai-po is praised by Confucius in the *Lun yü* (hereafter, *Analects*), VIII.1.
5. *Analects* V. 22.
6. Ibid. VII. 14.
7. Ssu-ma Ch'ien apparently hints at the bitterness of the song which is included in the biography. This bitterness contradicts Confucius' opinion that the brothers did not feel rancor.
8. The formula about knowing how to look after the old is apparently based on *Mencius* IVA.13.
9. According to Li Chi, these names appear in this place because these rulers received the throne from their predecessors without use of force. Li Chi, "The Changing Concept of the Recluse in Chinese Literature," *Harvard Journal of Asiatic Studies,* 24 (1962–1963), p. 256, n. 3.
10. Li Chi writes that "the story of Po-i and Shu-ch'i, *whether history or legend* [italics mine–V.R.], was widely known in Confucius' day," ibid., p. 236.
11. Ibid.
12. Kaizuka Shigeki, "The Problem of Fate in the Historiography of Ssu-ma Ch'ien," *Chūgoku kodai no kokoro,* cited in Watson, *Ssu-ma Ch'ien,* p. 239, n. 23.
13. Bernhard Karlgren, *Grammata Serica Recensa,* Stockholm, 1957, item 1168, pp. 301–302.
14. Ibid., item 388, p. 110.
15. Wing-tsit Chan, "The Evolution of the Confucian Concept *Jen,*" *Philosophy East and West,* 4. 4 (1955), p. 295.
16. *SC,* 61.1211; Watson, *Ssu-ma Ch'ien,* p. 189.
17. *Analects* IX. 5.
18. In the text of the *Analects* VII. 5, Confucius regrets not dreaming about the Duke of Chou for a long time.
19. *Analects* III. 14. Unless otherwise noted the translations from the *Analects* are by Vitaly Rubin.
20. Ibid. VIII. 20.
21. Ibid. XIX. 22.
22. Wing-tsit Chan, *A Source Book in Chinese Philosophy,* Princeton: Princeton University Press, 1969, pp. 6–67.
23. *Analects* XVI. 2.
24. Ibid. VII. 1.
25. The question of whether Confucius was the transmitter of ancient tradition or a reformer who created a new doctrine began to be discussed in China as early as the Han dynasty, with the appearance of the New Text School and Old Text School. Whereas the representatives of the Old Text School of classical scholarship

maintained that it was the Duke of Chou who originated the Six Disciplines, and that Confucius was only their transmitter, the New Text School was of the opinion that Confucius, who composed the *Ch'un-ch'iu,* was the creator of a new political and moral system. See Fung Yu-lan, *A History of Chinese Philosophy,* Princeton: Princeton University Press, 1952, vol. 1, p. 56; Philip C. Huang, *Liang Ch'i-ch'ao and Modern Chinese Liberalism,* Seattle: University of Washington Press, 1972, p. 15. When the traditions of the New Text School were revived in the theory of K'ang Yu-wei, this question was raised anew. In his works, K'ang Yu-wei arbitrarily manipulated the historical material in order to prove that Confucius was a revolutionary—a thesis that he tried to defend for political considerations and that compromised to a great extent his approach; see the criticism of his methods in Kung-ch'üan Hsiao, *A History of Chinese Political Thought,* vol. 1, pp. 131–132. However, the question regarding the role of conservative and innovative elements in Confucius' doctrine is still unresolved. This precisely is the problem at the basis of Confucius' estimate in Joseph R. Levenson and Franz Schurmann, *China: An Interpretative History,* Berkeley: University of California Press, 1969. In the chapter "Traditionalist as Innovator," the authors develop the paradoxical thought that, although Confucius was a traditionalist, "yet, it is precisely here, in his traditionalism, that Confucius shines forth as the innovator. *Then if traditionalism implies this exaltation of age over youth, do we not find some of the crucial values of feudalism denied?*" (authors' italics—V.R.; p. 53). Thus, according to the authors' view, Confucius' innovation was merely his traditionalism. This standpoint is hard to accept. It is not derived from the analysis of sources, but rather from a purely theoretical examination of such vague and pluralistic terms as "feudalism." An interesting summary of the present state of this problem is given in the book by N.E.. Fehl, *Rites and Propriety in Literature and Life,* Hong Kong: The Chinese University of Hong Kong, 1971. On p. 87, Fehl writes: "The Confucius of *Lun yü,* and probably the Confucius of history, had something of both these [above-mentioned] perspectives, sometimes in tension."
26. *Analects* II. 12.
27. Ibid. VIII. 13.
28. Vitaly Rubin, "The Profound Person and Power in Classical Confucianism," in *Proceedings of the Academia Sinica,* Vol. 8, pp. 339–362.
29. *Analects* XII. 17. The problem of the role of the ruler as an example is dealt with by Herbert Fingarette, "How the Analects Portrays the Ideal of Efficacious Authority," *Journal of Chinese Philosophy,* 8.1 (1981), pp. 29–49.
30. *Analects* XII. 11.

31. Ibid. II. 13.
32. Ibid. IV. 24.
33. Ibid. XIV. 29.
34. Duke Ching is mentioned in the *Analects* on two more occasions: in XII. 11, he appears speaking with Confucius, and he admires Confucius' advice "let the ruler be ruler"; in XVIII.3, he says that, being old, he was afraid he "will not be able to put Confucius' talent to use." This caused Confucius to leave Ch'i. Lau, in his commentaries, characterizes him as being a "not particularly wise ruler"; *Confucius, The Analects*, p. 239.
35. *Analects* XVI. 11–12. I consider these paragraphs to be parts of a single whole; such an arrangement gives meaning to paragraph 12, about which Legge wrote that it "implies a reference to something which has been lost"; see *The Four Books*, James Legge, trans., reprint, New York: Paragon Books, 1966, p. 249. Obviously Po-i and Shu-ch'i are meant by the people who "seek the fulfillment of their noble aims" in the *Analects* XVIII. 8, where they are characterized as those who refused to surrender their noble aims (*pu hsiang ch'i chih*). Paragraphs 11 and 12 are to be understood as a single whole according to Liu Pao-nan, in *"Lun yü cheng i,"* in *Chu Tzu chi-ch'eng*, vol. 1, p. 363, and by Arthur Waley, *The Analects of Confucius*, New York: Allen and Unwin, 1938, p. 207.
36. That under certain circumstances the withdrawal into oblivion is a necessary and correct step in order to achieve success (for the *chün-tzu* this is tantamount to the extension of the right way) is found in the comment on the third line of the hexagram *k'un*. J. Blofeld translates this as follows: "Concealment of talent (or beauty) constitutes the right course. As to the undertaking of public affairs, though immediate success may not be achieved, their ultimate fruition is assured". See his *I Ching: the Chinese Book of Changes*, London: Allen and Unwin, 1976, p. 92. A similar thought is expressed by Yu. K. Shchutskii in his interpretation of the 5th hexagram *hsü* ("Necessity of Waiting"). He writes: "Creating the truth now, we can allow the future to realize it, in the time when it will become apparent of itself. At this stage it is important to 'possess the truth'; then its splendor and obviousness will develop on their own." See Yu. K. Shchutskii, *Kitaiskaya klassicheskaya "Kniga Peremen"* (The Chinese classical "Book of Changes"), Moscow: Izdatel'stvo Vostochnoi Literatury, 1960, p. 211.
37. *Analects* XVIII. 8.
38. Ibid. VII. 14.
39. Ibid. V. 22.
40. According to *Analects* XIV. 39, "Best of all, to withdraw from one's generation (*pi shih*)", in Waley, *The Analects of Confucius*, p. 190. Within Confucianism there are two general approaches to this question. According to one, the call for political action, in

which service to society is paramount, is the main feature. This point of view is expressed by Hao Chang. He writes that, according to Confucianism, "a man could not be called a sage no matter how morally cultivated he was, unless he fulfilled his commitment to public service"; Hao Chang, *Liang Ch'i-ch'ao and Intellectual Transition in China 1890–1907*, Cambridge, Mass.: Harvard University Press, 1971, pp. 8–9. Julia Ching states similarly: "According to Confucian teachings, self-cultivation is not so much an end in itself, as it is a basis for service to others. The Confucian is a man *for others*" (author's italics—V.R.); Julia Ching, *Confucianism and Christianity*, Tokyo: Kodansha International, 1978, p. 88. Although these authors affirm that Confucianism also advocates self-cultivation, they consider this value of secondary importance as compared with the commitment to participate actively in government and, by so doing, to serve society. Together with this approach, which stresses the primacy of the "outward" part of the famous twofold formula "sageliness within and kingliness without" (*nei sheng wai wang*) "Chuang-tzu chi shih," chap. 33; in *Chu tzu chi ch'eng*, Vol. 3, p. 216; Watson, *Chuang Tzu*, p. 364 is that of the present-day Confucians who see the center of Confucian tradition in the notion of self-cultivation. Mou Tsung-san interprets Confucianism as a "religion of moral cultivation"; Mou Tsung-san, *Hsin-i yü hsing-ti*, p. 6, cited by Hao Chang, "New Confucianism and the Intellectual Crisis of Contemporary China," in *The Limits of Change*, p. 291. T'ang Chün-i also insists that the key concept of Confucian ethics is the notion of "searching in oneself"; T'ang Chün-i, "The Development of Ideas of Spiritual Value in Chinese Philosophy," in *The Chinese Mind*, Charles A. Moore, ed., Honolulu: University of Hawaii Press, 1967, pp. 192–194. In addition a third approach should be noted where the equality of both aims of the Confucian doctrine is stressed. Benjamin I. Schwartz sees in the first two one of the polarities of Confucian thought, and he writes that "over the course of the centuries ... some men gravitated to ... one pole rather than the other in spite of their nominal commitment to both"; Benjamin I. Schwartz, "Some Polarities in Confucian Thought," in *Confucianism in Action*, David S. Nivison and Arthur F. Wright, eds., Stanford: Stanford University Press, 1959, p. 52. Frederick W. Mote notes that although Confucianism is normally associated with the ideology of participation and of public service, "there is an equally valid aspect of Confucianism ... which justifies withdrawal from public life and official services under some conditions"; Frederick W. Mote, "Confucian Eremetism in the Yüan Period," in *The Confucian Persuasion*, Arthur F. Wright, ed., Stanford: Stanford University Press, 1960, p. 206.

41. *Analects* XVIII. 7.

42. Ibid. XVIII. 1.
43. *Shang shu* (Book of Documents), in *Shih-san ching ching-wen*, Taipei: Kaiming, 1961, pp. 14–15, 16–17, 19–21.
44. *Mencius* IIB.5. Unless otherwise noted, translations from the *Mencius* are by Vitaly Rubin.
45. Ibid., VB.1.
46. Ibid.
47. Chiao Hsün's (1763–1820) commentaries provide an interesting explanation of the contradiction between the generally accepted biography of Po-i as given by Ssu-ma Ch'ien and Po-i's image as it is depicted by Mencius. Chiao Hsün writes:
    I think that if Po-i lived at the time of the [tyrant] Chou, he must have known about his crimes. It is impossible to imagine that a pure man could have helped the villain, but he did not have the strength (*fei k'o-yi li-cheng*), he lived in a small state far away, and even if he had wanted to correct the tyrant he could not have done so. He fulfilled his duties and paid his taxes, though being ashamed of it. Undoubtedly, in his heart he had long since dreamed of leaving (*p'i*), but he could not admit it [apparently, *jen yen* has to be understood as *jen yen* (see glossary)]. Therefore, he served until the end on the pretext that the mandate to rule in his appanage had been granted him by his ancestors. Since Shu-ch'i strove for the same things as his brother, Mencius does not mention him. When Mencius said that he "waited until the world under Heaven would be clean again", he meant that [Po]-i considered only how to excape from the crimes of Chou Hsin, he did not try to correct the latter through admonishing him ... but he did try to correct Wu-wang. *Meng-tzu cheng-i*, in *Chu tzu chi-ch'eng*, Vol. 1, p. 395.
    In order to make Mencius' version more plausible, Chiao Hsün interprets Po-i's attitude towards the tyrant in such a way that Po-i is turned into a dissident and an internal emigré. However, the fact that Po-i reproached Wu-wang for his disobedience contradicts Chiao Hsün's attempt to save Mencius' credibility. Po-i could not have criticized Wu-wang if Chiao Hsün's portrayal of Po-i were correct.
48. *Mencius* IB.1.
49. Ibid. VIIB.14.
50. Ibid. VA.5.
51. Ibid. IIA.9.
52. Ibid. VB.1.
53. Ibid. VIA.7.
54. Ibid. VB.1.
55. Ibid. IIA.6.
56. Schwartz, "Some Polarities in Confucian Thought," pp. 51–52.
57. *Mencius* VA.7.

58. As a rule, the character *chih* is not neutral in Confucian texts, but has a very strong and positive meaning. For this reason I can agree neither with D.C. Lau's nor with Dobson's translation "ambition"; see *Mencius*, trans. with an introduction by D.C. Lau, London: Penguin Books, 1970, p. 107, and *Mencius: a New Translation*, annotated and arranged by W.A.C.H. Dobson, Toronto: University of Toronto Press, 1963, p. 125. Nor do I agree with Legge's "desire for office"; see *The Works of Mencius*, James Legge, trans., New York: Dover Publications, 1970, p. 265.
59. *Mencius* IIIB.2.
60. Ibid. IIA.2.
61. Ibid.
62. See, for example, the title of book 7 of the Confucian anthology of the twelfth century, *Chin ssu lu chi chu*, "On Serving or not Serving in the Government, Advancing and Withdrawing" (*chin t'ui*), Ssu pu pei yao edition; in *Reflections on Things at Hand*, trans. with notes by Wing-tsit Chan, New York: Columbia University Press, 1967, p. 183. The expression *"chin t'ui"* as "advancing and retiring" became a part of the Chinese language.
63. Wm. Theodore de Bary, ed., *Self and Society in Ming Thought*, New York: Columbia University Press, 1970, p. 18.
64. *Mencius* IIIB.10.
65. *The Book of Lord Shang*, J.J.L. Duyvendak, trans., Chicago: University of Chicago Press, 1963, p. 288.
66. According to the commentary by Kao Yu, the dream which predicted the annihilation of the Yin dynasty by Wu-wang is meant here. This dream was mentioned in one of the subsequently lost parts of the *Book of Documents;* see *Lü-shih ch'un-ch'iu* in *Chu tzu chi-ch'eng*, vol. 6, p. 120.
67. This is a paraphrase of the formula depicting Po-i's conduct as given in *Mencius* VB.1, quoted earlier.
68. *Lü-shih ch'un-ch'iu*, in *Chu tzu chi-ch'eng*, vol. 6, pp. 119–120. See the translation into German, *Frühling und Herbst des Lü Bu We*, by R. Wilhelm, Jena: Diederich Verlag, 1928, pp. 149–151. The text of *Lü-shih ch'un-ch'iu* is, to a large extent, identical with the text found in chapter 28 of *Chuang-tzu*, for which I used the translation by Burton Watson, *Chuang Tzu*, pp. 321–322. As A.C. Graham proves, the text of *Chuang-tzu* was written later than *Lü-shih ch'un-ch'iu;* see A.C. Graham, "How much of *Chuang Tzu* did Chuang Tzu write?", *Journal of the American Academy of Religion*, thematic issue (supplement), 47.3 (September 1979), p. 481. Therefore, the quoted text served as source for the authors of *Chuang-tzu.*
69. Kung-ch'üan Hsiao, *A History of Chinese Political Thought*, pp. 559–560. Hsiao agrees with Ch'ien Mu's view that the book must have served as an ideological basis for the future seizure of power

by Lü Pu-wei. However, we find a strong criticism of Legalistic methods in other ancient Chinese classical works, beginning with the fourth century B.C. Thus, the hypothesis of preparing a *coup d'état* seems superfluous and insufficient as an explanation of the ideas expressed in the book.

70. *Lü-shih ch'un ch'iu* in *Chu tzu chi-ch'eng*, vol., 6, p. 15; trans. in Kung-ch'üan Hsiao, *A History of Chinese Political Thought*, p. 561.
71. *Filosofskaya entsiklopediya*, F.V. Konstantinov, chief editor, Moscow: Sovetskaya Entsiklopediya, 1960, vol. 1, pp. 338–339.
72. Fung Yu-lan, *A History of Chinese Philosophy*, vol. 1, p. 134.
73. "Lieh-tzu chu," in *Chu tzu chi-ch'eng*, vol. 3, p. 79; the translation is a modified version of that found in A.C. Graham, *The Book of Lieh-tzu*, London: J. Murray, 1960, p. 142.
74. See A.C. Graham, "The Date and Composition of Liehtzyy," *Asia Major*, n.s. 8 (1961), pp. 139–198.
75. Wing-tsit Chan, "The Story of Chinese Philosophy," in *The Chinese Mind*, Charles A. Moore, ed., Honolulu: University of Hawaii Press, 1967, p. 39.
76. Fung Yu-lan, *A History of Chinese Philosophy*, vol. 1, pp. 140–141.
77. A.C. Graham, *The Book of Lieh-tzu*, pp. 135–136.
78. Wolfgang Bauer, *China und die Hoffnung auf Glück*, München: Hanser, 1971, p. 79.
79. Ibid., pp. 80–81.
80. Benjamin I. Schwartz, *In Search of Wealth and Power*, p. 55.
81. Ibid., p. 54. This is one of the central ideas found in Hsün-tzu's writings, where this thought is expressed in several passages; see, for example, the beginning of chapter 19, *Hsün-tzu: Basic Writings*, Burton Watson, trans., New York: Columbia University Press, 1963, p. 89.
82. Bauer, *Die Hoffnung auf Glück*, p. 93.
83. *Analects* XV. 8.
84. *Mencius* VIA.10.
85. Kung-ch'üan Hsiao, *A History of Chinese Political Thought*, p. 563.
86. See Chang Hsin-ch'eng, *Wei shu t'ung-k'ao*, vol. 2, p. 1015.
87. Bauer, *Die Hoffnung auf Glück*, pp. 167–168.
88. "Chuang-tzu chi shih," in *Chu tzu chi-ch'eng*, vol. 3, pp. 103–104; Watson, *Chuang Tzu*, p. 78.
89. Ibid.
90. Ibid. p. 105; Watson, *Chuang Tzu*, p. 78.
91. Ibid. In n. 3 (p. 79) Watson writes that all the above-mentioned tried either "to reform the conduct of others or made a show of guarding their own integrity. All either were killed or committed suicide."
92. Ibid., vol. 3, p. 248; Watson, *Chuang Tzu*, p. 175.

93. Ibid., vol. 3, p. 251; Watson, *Chuang Tzu*, p. 177.

94. Ibid., vol. 3, pp. 146–147; Watson, *Chuang Tzu*, p. 102.

95. *The Works of Mencius*, J. Legge, trans., pp. 474–475, note to VIIA.42.

96. "Chuang-tzu chi shih," in *Chu tzu chi-ch'eng*, vol. 3, p. 430; Watson, *Chuang Tzu*, p. 329.

97. Ibid., vol. 3, 431; Watson, *Chuang Tzu*, p. 330.

98. Ibid., vol. 3, p. 426; Watson, *Chuang Tzu*, p. 322.

99. See the introduction by A. Cooper in *Li Po and Tu Fu*, Arthur Cooper, trans., London: Penguin Books, 1976. See also V.M. Alekseev, *Kitaiskaya poema o poete: stansy Sykun Tu (837–908)* (A Chinese poem about a poet: Ssu-k'ung T'u's verses), Petrograd: A. Dressler, 1916.

100. Quoted in Li Chi, "The Changing Concept of the Recluse in Chinese Literature," p. 242.

101. Ibid.

102. See James J.Y. Liu, *The Chinese Knight-Errant*, Chicago: University of Chicago Press, 1967, p. 66.

103. Ibid., p. 65.

Glossary

Ai

隘

Ch'an

禪

Chan Jo-shui

湛若水

Chang Chih-tung

張之洞

Chang Chün-mai

張君邁

Chang Hsin-chen

張心徵

Chang Hsüeh-ch'eng

章學誠

Chang Hung

張宏

Chang Ping-lin

章炳麟

Chang Tsai

張載

Ch'ang-yen

長彥

chen

眞

chen-jen

眞人

"Ch'en shih-i"

陳士義

Ch'en Tu-hsiu

陳獨秀

cheng

正

Ch'eng Hao

程顥

Cheng Hsüan

鄭玄

Ch'eng I

程頤

cheng-li kuo-ku

整理國故

215

Ch'eng T'ang

成湯

ch'i (instrument)

器

ch'i (vital force)

氣

Chi-hsia

稷

"Chi-i"

記義

"Chi Mo"

詰墨

Chi-tzu

箕子

Chi (Tzu-ssu)

伋 (子思)

"Chi-wen"

記問

Chi-yen

李彥

ch'i-yün

氣韻

Chia I

賈誼

"Chia-yen"

嘉言

Chiang Chao-hsi

姜兆錫

chiang-hsüeh

講學

"Ch'iang-kuo"

強國

Chiao ko

膠鬲

Chiao Ping-chen

焦秉貞

"Chieh Li"

介立

Ch'ien Mu

錢穆

Chih

跖

chih (wisdom)

智

chih (purpose)

志

ch'ih

恥

"Chih-chieh"
執節

chih i chin, luan i chin
治亦進, 亂亦進

chih shih
治世

chih tse chin, luan tse t'ui
治則進, 亂則退

Ch'in shih-huang
秦始皇

Chin-wen
今文

ching
敬

ch'ing
清

ch'ing Po-i chin i
輕伯夷之義

ch'ing-t'an
清談

ching-tso
靜坐

Ch'iu Chün
邱濬

ch'iu jen erh te jen
求仁而得仁

Ch'iu (Tzu-chia)
求 (子家)

Chou Hsin
紂辛

Chou-tzu hsin-lun
周子新論

chu-ching ch'iung-li
居敬窮理

chu-hou
諸侯

Chu Hsi
朱熹

chu-i wu-shih
主一無適

chu-tzu
諸子

Chu-tzu chia-li
朱子家禮

"Chu-wei"
居衛

ch'üan
權

Ch'uan (Tzu-kao)

穿（子高）

ch'üan-sheng

全生

Chuang-tzu

莊子

Ch'un-ch'iu

春秋

chün-tzu

君子

chung (loyalty)

忠

chung (centrality)

中

Chung-huang

仲驤

Chung-ni

仲尼

Chung-yung

中庸

fa

法

Fang Tung-mei (Thomé Fang)

方東美

fei-fa

非法

fei-jen

非仁

fei-li

非禮

feng

風

fu

福

fu-li

復禮

Fu Ssu-nien

傅斯年

Fu (Tzu-yu)

鮒（子魚）

Fung Yu-lan

馮友蘭

Han Fei-tzu

韓非子

Han shih wai chuan

韓氏外傳

Han-shu

漢書

han-yang

涵養

Han Ying

韓嬰

Han Yü

韓愈

ho

和

Ho kuan-tzu

鶡冠子

Ho Lin

賀麟

hou

侯

Hou Han i-wen-chih

後漢藝文志

Hsia

夏

hsiao

孝

hsiang-yüeh

鄉約

"Hsiao Erh-ya"

小爾雅

hsien hsing ch'i yen

先行其言

hsin

心

"hsin-lun"

刑論

hsing (action)

行

hsing

性

hsing-ch'a

省察

hsing-hsing

惺惺

hsing ho

行貨

hsing-ming chin-hsüch

性命之學

hsiu-shen chih-jen

修身治人

hsiu-yang

修養

Hsiung Shih-li

熊十力

Hsü Fu-kuan

徐復觀

Hsü Heng

許衡

hsü-shih

虛實

Hsü Yu

許由

hsüan-hsüeh

玄學

hsüeh

學

hsün

殉

"Hsün-shou"

巡狩

Hsün-tzu

荀子

Hu Shih

胡適

Huang

黃

Huang T'ing-chien

黃庭堅

Huang Tsung-hsi

黃宗羲

Hui

惠

Hung Mai

洪邁

i (righteousness)

義

i (will)

意

i (proper)

宜

i luan i pao

以亂易暴

I-yin

伊尹

jen (to bear)

任

jen (humanity)

仁

jen-ch'üan

人權

jen-yen (admit)

認言

jen-yen

忍言

ju-chiao

儒教

"Ju-Fu"

儒服

Ju-lin wai-shih

儒林外史

ju-shu

儒術

"k'ang-chih"

抗志

K'ang Yu-wei

康有為

Kao P'an-lung

高攀龍

Kao-tsung (Wu-ting)

高宗（武丁）

ko-wu chih-chih

格物致知

k'o

可

K'o (Tzu-chin)

樈（子直）

k'o-chi

克己

Ku Chieh-k'ang

顧頡剛

ku chih chen-jen

古之眞人

Ku shih pien

古史辨

Ku Yen-wu

顧炎武

Kuan Chung

管仲

Kuang Wu-ti

光武帝

"kuei sheng"

貴生

kung

公

k'ung

空

K'ung An-kuo

孔安國

Kung Hsien

龔賢

"Kung-i"

公儀

"Kung-sun Lung"

公孫龍

K'ung Ts'ang

孔臧

K'ung-ts'ung-tzu

孔叢子

K'ung-tzu chia-yü

孔子家語

Kuo Mo-jo

郭沫若

Lao Lai-tzu

老萊子

li (ritual)

禮

li (profit)

利

li (pattern, principle)

理

Li-chi

禮記

Li Chi

李祁

li-ch'i

理氣

Li Kung-lin

李公麟

Li (Po-yü)

鯉 (伯魚)

Li Ssu

李斯

Li Ta-chao

李大釗

Liang Ch'i-ch'ao

梁啓超

liang-chih

良知

Liang Shu-ming

梁漱溟

"Lien-ts'ung-tzu hsia"

連叢子下

"Lien-ts'ung-tzu shang"

連叢子上

Lin

琳

Lin-tzu

臨淄

Liu Hsia-hui

柳下惠

liu yü

六欲

Lu Chiu-yüan

陸九淵

Lu Hsün

魯迅

Lü Ta-chün

呂大鈞

Lü Pu-wei

呂不韋

Lü-shih Ch'un Ch'iu

呂氏春秋

Lun-heng

論衡

"Lun-shih"

論勢

"Lun-shu"

論書

Lun-yü

論語

Mei Ssu-p'ing

梅思平

Men Ying-chao

門應詔

meng (pact)

盟

Meng k'o

孟軻

min

民

min-ch'üan

民權

Ming-chia

名家

Mo-tzu

墨子

Mou

茂

Mou Tsung-san

牟宗三

Mu

穆

nei-sheng wai-wang

內聖外王

Ou-yang Ching-wu

歐陽竟無

pao

暴

Pi-kan

比干

pi-shih

避世

Pien Sui

卞隨

Po-i

伯夷

p'o sheng

迫生

Po (Tzu-shang)

白（子上）

Pu-chin-shu i-wen-chih

補晉書藝文志

pu i

不義

pu-ju ch'i shen

不辱其身

pu-li wen-tzu

不立文字

Ren Jiyu

任繼愈

san kang

三綱

San-kuo i-wen-chih

三國藝文志

shang mou

上謀

Shang-ti

上帝

Shang Yang

商鞅

shao (music)

韶

Shao-kung

召公

shen

神

Shen Chou

沈周

shen-hsin

身心

Shen-nung

神農

Shen Pu-hai

申不害

shen-tu

慎獨

Shen Tsung-hsien

沈完騫

sheng

聖

sheng-sheng

生生

sheng-tung

生動

shih (bureaucracy, knight)

士

shih (real, solid)

實

shih (timely)

時

Shih-chi

史記

Shih-ching

詩經

shih-hsüeh

實學

Shih-t'ao

石濤

shou-lien

收斂

shu (considerate)

恕

shu (administrative techniques)

術

Shu-ch'i

叔齊

Shu-ching

書經

Shung

舜

Shou Ju

說儒

ssu (death)

死

ssu (selfish)

私

Ssu-ma Ch'ien

司馬遷

Ssu-ma Kuang

司馬光

ssu-wen

斯文

Su Shih (T'ung-p'o)

蘇軾（東坡）

Sui-shu ching-chi-chih

隋書經籍治

Sung Hsien

宋咸

ta chang fu

大丈夫

Ta fang chih chia

大方之家

ta fu

大夫

Ta-hsüeh

大學

Ta-hsüeh yen-i pu

大學衍義補

"Tai wen"

答問

Tai Chen

戴震

T'ai-chou

泰州

T'ai-hsü

太虛

T'ai-kung

太公

Tan

旦

T'an Ssu-t'ung

譚嗣同

T'ang

湯

T'ang Chün-i

唐君毅

T'ang Shun-chih

唐順之

T'ang Yin

唐寅

tao-che shih fei

道者是非

tao chih pu hsing

道之不行

tao-t'ung

道統

te

德

te chih

得志

Teng Hsi-tzu

鄧析子

t'i

體

t'i-yung

體用

"T'ien-chih"

天志

t'ien-hsia

天下

t'ien-jen ho-i

天人合一

t'ien-li

天理

t'ien-ming

天命

t'ien-tzu

天子

"Tsa-hsün"

雜訓

tsa-shuo

雜說

Tsang

臧

Tsang Lin

臧林

Tseng Ching

曾鯨

Tseng Tsan

曾參

Tseng-tzu

曾子

Tso-chuan

左傳

Tso-chuan i-chieh

左傳義詁

tso-wang

坐忘

tsu ch'iu erh pao wei

阻丘而保威

Tsui (Tzu-ch'an)

㝡 (子產)

ts'un

存

ts'un tien-li, ch'u jen-yü

存天理, 去人欲

"Tu chih"

獨治

"Tui Wei-wang"

對魏王

Tung Ch'i-ch'ang

董其昌

Tung Chung-shu

董仲舒

Tung-fang So

東方朔

Tzu-ang

子昂

Tzu-ch'an

子產

Tzu-chang

子張

Tzu-chien

子建

Tzu-feng

子豐

Tzu-ho

子和

Tzu-hsia

子夏

Tzu-hsiang

子襄

Tzu-kung

子貢

Tzu-kuo

子國

Tzu-li

子立

Tzu-shun

子順

Tzu-wen

子文

Tzu-yu

子游

tzu-yu

自由

tzu-yu chu-i

自由主義

Tzu-yüan

子元

wan-fu lien, no-fu yu li-chih

頑夫廉，懦夫有立志

wang

往

Wang Ch'ung

王充

Wang Fu-chih

王夫之

Wang Hsi-chih

王羲之

Wang Mang

王莽

Wang Su

王肅

Wang Wei

王維

Wang Yang-ming

王陽明

wei-hsüeh

為學

Wei-shu t'ung-k'ao

偽書通考

Wei-tzu

微子

Wei-tzu K'ai

微子開

Wei Yüan

魏源

wen

文

Wen Cheng-ming

文徵明

"Wen chun-li"

問畢禮

Wen Wu chih-tao

文武之道

Wu Ching-tzu

吳敬梓

Wu Kuang

務光

Wu Li

吳歷

wu-pao

伍保

Wu Pin

吳彬

Wu T'ai-po

吳太伯

wu-ts'ung Chou

吾從周

Wu-wang

武王

wu-wei

無為

yang (male vital force)

陽

yang (nourish)

養

Yang Chu

楊朱

Yao

堯

Yen Fu

嚴復

Yen Hui

顏回

Yen-tzu

晏子

yin (retirement)

隱

yin (female vital force)

陰

yin chü i ch'iu ch'i chih,
hsing i i ta ch'i tao

隱居以求其志
行義以達其道

Yin-wen-tzu

尹文子

Yu chih-fa erh hou yu chin jen

有治法而後有治人

Yü

禹

Yü

虞

Yü Ch'ing

虞卿

yü ch'üan

欲全

Yüan Shih-k'ai

袁世凱

Yüeh

約

yüeh

樂

yung

用

Index

Aesthetic universal, xvi, 81–82, 90
Aesthetics: in Europe, 99, 101, 104; in Medieval
 Europe, 100; in China, 102, 103
Alberti, Leone Battista, 91, 100–101
Alitto, Guy, cited, 5
Analects (Lun-yü), 29, 32, 36, 41, 117, 139, 166, 180,
 183; Po-i and Shu-ch'i mentioned in, 161; chün-tzu
 described in, 162; on Po-i and Duke Ching, 171
Appel, Karel, 101–102
Art: Chinese and European, 82; universal in, 83;
 Chinese, 84; and aesthetic present, 85; Buddhist of
 India, 86; Renaissance, 86; Mughal, 87; tendency
 to pantheism in, 94; ontology of, 96; separate and
 individual, 99; local and variable, 107
Artistic interaction, 82; of European and Chinese
 painting, 87

Bandit Chih, 171, 182
Bauer, Wolfgang, cited, 177, 178, 179
Benevolence, see Humanity
Bernini, Giovanni Lorenzo, 92, 93
Blake, William, 91
Book of Changes (I Ching), 27, 57, 171; mention of
 reverence in, 72; and brushstroke of painting, 96
Book of Documents (Shu-ching), 27, 70, 77, 156, 159,
 165, 166, 169; discussed in KTT, 44–45; mention of
 reverence in, 72
Book of Poetry (Shih-ching), 27, 77, 156, 160; in
 KTT, 45
Book of Rites (Li Chi), 27, 68, 112
Buddhism, xiv, xxii, 10, 12, 64, 69, 114, 122; and
 Neo-Confucianism, 11; and Yogācarā
 (Consciousness-only) School, 18; influence of, 71,
 74, 78; human nature in, 123

Castiglione, Guiseppe, 88
Ch'an (Zen) Buddhism, 74, 123, 128
Ch'an Buddhists, 95
Chan Jo-shui, 129
Chan, Wing-tsit, 6; cited, xix; quoted, 160, 176–177
Chang Chih-tung, 8, 15
Chang Chün-mai (Carsun Chang), 17
Chang Hao, xxiii, cited, xv, xx, 207n40
Chang Hsüeh-ch'eng, 179
Chang Hung, 90
Chang Ping-lin (T'ai-yen), 14
Chang Tsai, 9, 19, 128

Chang-yen, 44t
Ch'en Tu-hsiu, 15
Ch'eng Hao, 78, 79, 128
Cheng Hsüan, 112
Ch'eng I, 78, 125, 128; and doctrine of reverence, 73
Ch'i, 102, 104; of mind, 78; and Tao, 103
Chi-tzu, 165
Chi-yen, 43, 44t, 50
Ch'i-yün, 102, 103
Chia I, 151
Chiang Chao-hsi, 52
Chiao Ping-chen, 88
Ch'ien Mu, cited, xx; and Confucian learning, 19;
 and Confucian Classics, xxi; Lectures cited,
 123–124; on Lü Pu-wei, 209–210n69
Ching, see Reverence
Ch'ing, see Purity
Ching, Julia, cited, 151–152
Ch'iu Chün cited, 128–129
Chou Hsin, 165, 208n47
Chou-tzu hsin-lun, 42
Christianity, xxii, 12, 64, 77, 80, 89
Chu Hsi, xvii, 8, 18, 71, 78, 123, 124–130 passim; and
 KTT, 51, 52; and reverence, 72–73; and Confucian
 meditation, 74; and "pursuit of principles," 75–76;
 and rites, 124; on ritual and education, 127
Chu-tzu chia-li, see Family Ritual of Chu Hsi
Ch'ü Yüan, 151
Chuang-tzu, 142–143, 151; and sitting and forgetting,
 74; Chuang-tzu, The, 159, 180, 183; and Taoist
 sage, 180; on Po-i, 181; on Po-i's identity with
 Bandit Chih, 182
Ch'un-ch'iu, see Spring and Autumn Annals
Chun-tzu (superior man, gentleman), 25, 26, 57, 112,
 165, 166, 169; Rubin on, 142; and withdrawal, 147,
 162; and Taoist sage, 180
Chung, see Loyalty
Chung-huan, 44t
Chung-ni, see Confucius
Chung-yung, see Doctrine of the Mean
Civility and propriety (wen and li), 24
Community compact (hsiang-yüeh), 125–127, 128,
 131, n9; in Korea, 127
Confucian asceticism, 71
Confucian Classics, xiv, xv, 10, 12, 27, 70; in KTT, 50;
 and spirituality, 77; see also Thirteen Classics;
 Three Classics of Li

Confucian conservatism, 5, 111, 112, 161
Confucian ethics, 6, 7, 9, 10; and warlords, 16
Confucian heritage, 4; and May Fourth, 15, 16; and
   Joseph Levenson, 19
Confucian humanism, xxiii, 4, 17, 20, 154; and Vitaly
   Rubin, 3; and Joseph Levenson, 4; second epoch
   of, 6, 11; development of third epoch, 8; and Han
   Yü, 10; in Taiwan and Hong Kong, 19; future of,
   20–21; and humanity, 117; and Rubin, 138–139
Confucian learning, xiv, 9, 20
Confucian method (*ju-shu*), 10
Confucian scholarship, xiv; in Wei-chin era, 42
Confucian socialism, 17
Confucian symbolism, 8, 16, 19
Confucian tradition, xi, xii, xiv, xxiii, xxiv, 5, 6, 8, 13,
   79; survival of, xxi, 20; and K'ang Yu-wei, 14; and
   May Fourth, 16
Confucian values, xx, 13, 27, 122; internalization of,
   28
Confucian Way (Tao), 7, 9, 10, 57
Confucianism: revival of, xv, 3, 8, 17, 122; and quest
   for sagehood, xvi, 79; in Korea, Japan and
   Vietnam, 12; and Marxism, 18; and Confucius'
   disciples, 26; and Mencius' incorporation of
   righteousness, 31–32; as rationalistic of Hsün-tzu,
   37; in Wei-Chin era, 39, 56; and legalism, 45;
   limitations of, 80; and human rights, 109, 111; and
   humanity, 117; and family-centered outlook, 119;
   Rubin's work on, 139; human nature in, 167;
   Hsün-tzu as forerunner in establishment of, 168;
   and Yang Chu, 178
Confucius, xi, 13, 23–24, 28, 36, 44t, 47, 55, 70, 96,
   105, 138, 142, 147, 149, 157, 164, 167, 168, 172,
   180, 181; teaching of, 25–26, 64–66; and humanity,
   30, 31, 70; discussed in *KTT*, 43–45, 48, 50; and
   Tzu-ssu and Mencius, 52–53; on reverence, 72;
   and reverence, 117; and the *chün-tzu*, 118, 150,
   153, 162, 163, 165, 166; and timeliness, 146, 168;
   and praise of Po-i and Shu-ch'i, 147, 157, 160–161,
   162–163, 165; on filial piety, 160; as transmitter,
   204 n25
Contemporary art, 83
Cultural Revolution, 111, 130

Dark Learning (*hsüan-hsüeh*), 40
David, Jacques Louis, 84
de Bary, Wm. T., 6; quoted, xv
Delacroix, Ferdinand Victor Eugene, 84
de Machant, Guillaume, 91
Dewey, John, 16
Dhyāna (meditation), 74, 114
Doctrine of the Mean (*Chung-yung*), 27, 68; in *KTT*,
   46; on human nature, 123
Don Quixote and Po-i, 146–147, 155–156
Duke of Chou, 9, 161, 205 n25

Empathy in art, 104
Erh-ya, 47
European influence on Chinese painters, 89–90

Fa, *see* Law
Fairbank, J.K., cited, 17
Family Ritual of Chu Hsi (*Chu-tzu chia-li*), 126, 128
Fang, Thomé (Fang Tung-mei), cited, xvi, 19
Filial piety (Filiality; *hsiao*), 119, 158, 160, 174
First Emperor (Ch'in Shih-huang), 36, 49, 141, 174
Freedman, Jill, 107
Freedom of choice, 144, 151
Fu Ssu-nien, xxi
Fung Yu-lan, xxi, xxii, 17, 176, 177; quoted, 63–64;
   cited, 116
Fusion: concept in art, 82; in Buddha image, 86; of
   European and Chinese styles, 88; idea of, 90; and
   love, 92; desire for, 94; as cosmic and social
   principle, 94, 96; and creation, 99; impetus for, 105

Ghiberti, Lorenzo, 91
Graham, A.C., quoted, 177
Great Learning (*Ta-hsüeh*), 75, 124

Han Fei-tzu, 36, 138; attacked in *KTT*, 49, 51, 57
Han Learning, xviii
Han shih wei-chuan (Han Ying), 150
Han-shu, 43
Han Yü, 9
Heaven, xiii, xiv, xv, 29, 69, 79, 117, 120, 169; and
   Earth, 55, 67–68, 78, 79, 96; and Confucius, 65; will
   of, 66; all (or world) -under, 68, 167, 169, 170, 173;
   as impersonal force, 69; service of, 77; mandate
   of, 123, 161; and the moral nature, 128; injustice
   of, 151
Heavenly principle (*t'ien-li*), 67, 70, 74, 78; and
   humanity, 71; and Confucian mysticism, 79; and
   human nature, 122
"Herdboy with Bamboo and Rock" ("Su Shih and Li
   Kung-lin"), 91
Herder, Johann von, 102, 104
Hinduism, xxii, 64
Ho kuan-tzu, The, 53
Ho Lin, 17–18
Hoffman, E.T.A., 91
Hou-Han i-wen-chih, 40
Hsiang-yüeh, *see* Community compact
Hsiao kung-ch'üan, 174, 179
Hsieh Ho, 102
Hsing, *see* Human nature
Hsiung Shih-Li, 7; and Buddhism, 18
Hsü Fu-Kuan, xxi, 7, 20; cited xiii; and Confucian
   learning, 19
Hsü Heng, 127
Hsü Yu, 157, 159
Hsün-tzu, xii, 9, 19, 168; quoted, 32; critical of
   Confucius, 33; and interdependence of humanity,
   righteousness, propriety, 35; and legalist theory,
   36; and rites, 66–67; *Hsün-tzu*, The, 178
Hu Shih, xxi, 15, 18
Huang T'ing-chien: poem quoted, 91
Huang Tsung-hsi, xviii, 70, 131–132; and laws and
   institutions, 131
Human nature (hsing), 182; Mencius on, 32, 123;
   and Sung philosophers, 122; Chu Hsi on, 124
Human rights, 113, 114–115, 117, 122, 123; and
   Vitaly Rubin, xxiii, 109–110; and Confucian
   tradition, xviii, 111, 113; Chinese and Japanese
   terms for, 113; and the West, 110, 111, 113; as
   rites, 120, 129; Ch'iu Chün on, 128
Humanity (*jen*), xxii, 23, 25–26, 36, 57–58, 145, 158,
   160, 164, 174; discussed by Mencius, 29–30, 120;
   and righteousness, 31, 37, 57; in the *Analects*, 36;
   transformed by Confucius, 65; as spiritual growth,
   71; and empathy, 104; and cosmic connotations,
   105–106; and the *chün-tzu*, 180
Hundred Schools of Philosophy, 39, 41, 50
Hung Mai, 51

I, *see* Righteousness
I Ching, *see* Book of Changes
I-yin, 167, 168, 169, 170
Identity of mind and nature (*liang-chih*), 103, 105
Ideology and Culture in Ancient China, *see*
   Individual and State in Ancient China
Individual and State in Ancient China (Vitaly
   Rubin), 110, 111, 140, 142, 143, 149
Islam, xxii, 12, 64, 77

Jen, *see* Humanity
Ju-lin wai-shih (The Scholars) (Wu Ching-tzu), 7
Judaism, xxii, 12, 64, 77, 80

Kaizuka Shigeki, quoted, 159
Kandinsky, Vasili, 101
K'ang Yu-wei, xx, 13–14; and New Text school,
   205 n25
Kao P'un-lung, quoted, 78–79
Kirchner, Ernst Ludwig, 92, 94
Ku Chieh-kang, xxi
Ku, shih pien (Discussions in ancient Chinese
   history), xxi
Ku, yen-wu, xviii

Kuan Chung, 36
Kuang Wu-ti, 150
K'ung An-kuo, 44t, 49
K'ung Family, 43, 48, 52; genealogy of in *KTT*, 49; anecdotes about, 50; world view of, 51; and author of *KTT*, 55–56; described in *KTT*, 57
K'ung-Family-Masters' Anthology (*K'ung-ts'ung-tzu*), 39, 43–59 passim; mentioned in *Sui-shu*, 42
Kung Hsien, 90
Kung-sun Lung, 47, 50
K'ung Tsang, 44t, 49, 50
Kupka, Frank, 101

Lao Lai-tzu, 47
Law(s)(*fa*), 114, 121; Buddhist concept of, 122; study of, 124; and Huang Tsung-hsi, 131
Legalism, 41, 143; attacked in *KTT*, 57; and view of law, 121
Legalists, xii, 36, 138; and Confucians, 141
Levenson, Joseph, 6, 21; cited, xix, 4, 5, 7, 8
Li, *see* Principle
Li, *see* Profit
Li, *see* Rites, Ritual
Li Chi, cited, 158–159, 184, 204 n9, 204 n10
Li Chi, see *Book of Rites*
Li Po, 184
Li Ssu, 36
Li Ta-chao, 16
Liang Ch'i-ch'ao, 13, 14, 17
Liang-chih, *see* Identity of mind and nature
Liang Shu-ming, 5; and Yogācarā methodology of, 18
Lieh-tzu, The, 176, 177
Lipps, Theodor, 104
Liu-hsia Hui, 167, 168, 169, 184
Loyalty (*chung*), 144, 146, 152
Lu Chiu-yüan, 76
Lu Hsün, 7, 15, 17
Lun-heng (Wang Ch'ung), 150
Lun-yü, see *Analects*
Lü Pu-wei, 174
Lü-shih ch'un-ch'iu, see *Spring and Autumn Annals of Lü Pu-wei*
Lü Ta-chün, 125, 128

Madman of Ch'u (Laurence Schneider), 151
Malevich, Casimir, 101
Manet, Edouard, 84
Mao Tse-tung, 15
May Fourth (1919): movement, xx, xxi, 14–15; and Confucius, 16
Meditation, xvi; Confucian, 68, 69, 74–75; 79; Taoist and Buddhist practice of, 74; Kao P'an-lung on, 78; *see also* Dhyāna
Mei Ssu-p'ing, xxi
Men Ying-chao, 88
Mencius, xii, 9, 10, 18, 28, 32, 37, 59, 146, 149, 166, 172, 182; and Mo-tzu compared, 29–31; and Hsün-tzu compared, 34, 35; *Mencius, The*, 42, 58, 77, 122, 171, 179; and Tzu-ssu, 46, 57–58; and knowing the good, 105; quoted, 120; and goodness of human nature, 123; and personal purity, 145, 153, 174; on Po-i, 148, 167, 168–171, 208 n47; on I-yin, 169–171; on Confucius, 170; on autonomous morality, 196 n38
Metzger, Thomas, cited, xii, 5–6
Michelangelo, 92, 93, 101
Mo-chia, *see* Mohism
Mo-tzu, xii, 59, 142; and Heaven, 29; influence on Hsün-tzu, 33; *Mo-tzu, The*, 48; criticized in *KTT*, 51, 57; *see also* Mohism; Mohists
Mohism, 29, 143; revival of, 41; school of, 40, 41t
Mohists, 29, 177
Mondrian, Piet, 101
Motherwell, Robert, 107
Mou Tsung-san, xxii, 7, 20; and Confucian learning, 19; cited, 207 n40
Mozart, Wolfgang Amadeus, 97

Munch, Edvard, quoted, 97
Mysticism, 77; and enlightenment, 78; Confucian, 79; and European artists, 101–102; and the New York School, 101; in Chinese aesthetics, 102

Neo-Confucian thought, 17
Neo-Confucianism: xenophobic culturalism of, 11; complexity of term, 11–12; and autonomy of individual, 124; autonomy and self-government in, 126; and rites, 130–131
Neo-Confucians, 6, 9, 69, 100; and quest for the ultimate, 77–78; and human nature, 122; and reality, 123
Neo-Platonism, 92, 101; and the Neo-Platonic, 99; and Neo-Platonic themes, 100
Neo-Taoism, 10, 122
New Text, 13, scholars of, 49, 51, school of, 57; and Old Text schools, 204 n25
Newman, Barnett, 107
Nolde, Emil, 97; quoted, 98
Non-being, 96, 100
Nonconformity, 144, 159; protest and, 150, 153; and dissent, 152
Novalis, 104

Okada Takehiko, 6
Ou-yang Ching-wu, 18

Pattern (*li*), xvii, 128
Pi-kan, 165, 166
Pien Sui, 157
Plato, 99–100, 105
Plotinus, 99, 105; and art, 100
Po-i and Shu-ch'i, xxiii, 144–151 passim, 153, 159–172 passim, 173, 174, 175, 179–184 passim; compared to Ch'ü Yüan, 151; biography of, 157–158; and purity, 164
Po-yu, 44t
Principles (*li*), 72, 76
Professional bureaucracy (*shih*), 26, 27
Profit (*li*), 30, 196 n38; according to Tzu-ssu, 57; and benevolence and righteousness, 58
Protest: and dissent, 144, 154; as nonconformist position, 147; and withdrawal, 153, 165, 166
Pu Chin-shu i-wen-chih, 40
Pure Conversation (*ch'ing-t'an*), 40
Purity (*ch'ing*), 145, 153, 164, 167, 168, 183; and humanity, 146; and responsibility, 147, 148, 170

Quiet-sitting (*ching-tso*), *see* Meditation

Reciprocity (*shu*): and filiality, xvii, 119; and propriety, 120; and mutuality, 125
Record of the Historian (*Shih-chi*), 43, 150, 156
Responsibility, xvii, 125, 147, 169; and rights, 124; and Chuang-tzu, 143; Mencius on, 145, 148; and action, 154
Reverence (ching): defined by Chu Hsi, 72–73; according to Ch'eng I, 73; according to Confucius, 117
Righteousness (i), 23, 36, 57–58, 179; defined and developed by Mencius, 30, 34, 36–37; as universal principle, 32; affirmed and developed by Hsün-tzu, 34, 37; in *KTT*, 45; and deeds of Po-i and Shu-ch'i, 163, 181
Rites, Ritual, Propriety (li), 23, 36, 65, 70, 120, 130; defined by Hsün-tzu, 34–35; according to Confucius, 65; and music, 66, 67; as correlative responsibilities, 124; Chu Hsi's view on, 127; and social order, 128; and law, 129; practice of, 131
Rossetti, Dante Gabriel, 91
Rubin, Vitaly, xxiii, 21, 136–154 passim; cited, 29, quoted, 112–113; and Marxist categories of analysis, 137, 138; and Marxist interpretation of Chinese history, 141
Russell, Bertrand, 16

Sage Kings (Emperors), 35, 36, 45, 124; in *KTT*, 46; and Heaven, 77

San-kuo chih, see *Three Kingdoms Chronicle*
San-ku i-wen-chih, 40
Schoenberg, Arnold, 97
School of Names (Ming-chia), 41t, 42
School Sayings of Confucius (k'ung-tzu chia-yu), 43,
    56; similarity to *KTT,* 52
Schopenhauer, Arthur, 101
Schwartz, Benjamin, 14, 178; quoted, 207 n40
Self-cultivation, xv, xvi, 64, 130, 131; and humanity,
    xiii, 25; and social service dilemma of, 5; and rites,
    124; advocated by Confucianism, 207 n40
Self-examination, 66; practiced by Neo-Confucians,
    10
Shang Yang, 36, 142
Shen Chou, 91, 106
Shen Nung, 158, 173
Shen Pu-hai, 36
Shen Tsung-hsien, 103
Shih-ching, see *Book of Poetry*
Shih-t'ao (Tao-chi), 94, 95–96; and creative fusion,
    96–97
Shimada Kenji, cited, 12
Shipler, David, cited, 136, 139
Shu, see Reciprocity
Shu-ching, see *Book of Documents*
Six Classics, 156; *see also* Confucian Classics;
    Thirteen Classics
Soviet scholarship, 140, 143, 152
Spender, Stephen, 106–107
Spirituality: Confucian, 10, 66, 69, 75, 77, 79–80; and
    theology, 64; Neo-Confucian, 69, 76; of Buddhism,
    69; Christian, 73, 75; in Judaism, Islam and
    Christianity, 77; and "inner sageliness and outer
    kingliness," 80
Spring and Autumn Annals, (*Ch'un-ch'iu*), 48, 55
*Spring and Autumn Annals of Lü Pu-wei (Lü-shih
    ch'un-ch'iu),* 148–149, 174–178 passim, 179, 183;
    on Po-i and Shu-ch'i, 172–174
Ssu-k'u ch'üan-shu tsung-mu t'i-yao, 179
Ssu-ma Ch'ien, 150, 159, 160, 164, 174; and Heaven's
    injustice, 151; quoted, 156–158; and Po-i
    biography, 208 n47
Ssu-ma kuang, 128
Still, Clyfford, 107
Su Tung-p'o (Su Shih), 91
Sui-shu, 51
Sung Hsien, 52
*Supplement to the Extended Meaning of the Great
    Learning (Ta-hsüeh yen-i-pu)* (Ch'iu Chün), 128

Ta-hsüeh, see *Great Learning*
Ta-hsüeh yen-i pu, see *Supplement to the Extended
    Meaning of the Great Learning*
Tai Chen, 7
T'ai-chou school, 129
T'ai-hsü, Abbot, 18
Ta'i-po, 157
T'an Ssu-t'ung, xx
T'ang Chün-i, xxi, 6, 7, 20; and Confucian learning,
    19; cited, 207 n40
T'ang Codes, 122
T'ang Yin, 91
Tao-te ching, 96, 143, 180
Taoism, 12, 122, 128; naturalism of, 33, 37; in
    Wei-chin era, 41; School of, 40, 41t; Rubin's view
    of, 143
Teng Hsi-tzu, The, 53
Thirteen Classics, 10; *see also* Confucian Classics,
    Three Classics of Li
Three Classics of Li (*San-li*), 41; *see also* Confucian
    Classics; Thirteen Classics
Three Kingdoms Chronicle (San-kuo chih), 56
Tsang Lin, 52
Tseng Ching, 87
Tseng Tsan, 26, 27
Tseng-tzu, 46, 66
Tso chuan, 24, 137, 138
Tso chuan i-chieh, 50
Tsukada Tora, 52

Tu Wei-ming, cited, xxii
Tung Ch'i-ch'ang, 84; on compositional principles,
    103
Tung Chung-shu, 18, 121
Tung-Fang Shuo, 183, 184
Tzu-ang, 44t
Tzu-ch'an, 44t
Tzu-ch'an (kung-sun Ch'iao), 137, 138, 139
Tzu-chia, 44t
Tzu-chien, 44t
Tzu-chih, 44t
Tzu-feng, 44t, 49–50
Tzu-ho, 44t, 50
Tzu-hsia, 27; school of, 34
Tzu-hsiang, 44t
Tzu-kao, 44t, 47, 48, 50
Tzu-kung, 161
Tzu-kuo, 44t
Tzu-Li, 44t
Tzu-lu, 118, 180
Tzu-shang, 44t, 46
Tzu-shun, 44t, 48, 50
Tzu-ssu, 27, 44t, 45–47, 50, 55, 58; quoted, 54
Tzu-wen, 44t
Tzu-yu (K'ung Fu), 44t; school of, 34; in *KTT,* 49, 50;
    and *KTT,* 51
Tzu-yüan, 44t

Uzzle, Burke, 107

Van Gogh, Vincent, 92, 93–94, 106
Velasquez, Diego Rodriguez de Silva y, 84

Wang Ch'ung, 19, 150, 151, 196 n38; and criticism of
    Mencius, 58
Wang Fu-chih, xviii, 19; cited, 103–104
Wang Hsi-chih, 94; quoted, 95
Wang Mang, 150
Wang Su, xiv, 52, 195 n31; author of *KTT,* 42; as
    Confucian philosopher, 56
Wang Wei, 91
Wang Yang-ming, 7, 18, 76, 129; quoted, 105–106;
    and community compact, 127
Weber, Max, cited, 4–5, n10
Wei shu t'ung-k'ao (Chang Hsin-ch'eng), 53–54
Wei-tzu, 165
Wei-Yüan, 13, 15
Wen Cheng-ming, 91
Wen-wang, 9, 157, 161, 171, 172
Whitman, Walt, quoted, 97
Williams, William Carlos, 97, 98
Withdrawal, 144, 145, 146, 164; as nonconformist
    position of protest, 147; Confucius' and Mencius'
    attitudes on, 148; as protest, 162; as oblivion, 206
    n 36; F.W. Mote on, 207 n40
Wright, Arthur F., cited, xiv
Wu An-chia, cited, xxii
Wu kuang, 157, 159
Wu Li, quoted, 89
Wu Pin, 89; European influence on, 90
Wu-wang: Po'i's refusal to serve, xxiii, 147, 150;
    unfilial conduct of, 145, 157–158, 159–160;
    Tzu-kung on, 161; Po-i and Shu-chi'i's meeting
    with, 164; Po-i's criticism of, 168, 208 n47;
    discussed in *Lü-shih,* 172, 174

Yang Chu, 59, 177; and hedonism, 149, 153, 175,
    176; and Confucianism, 178–179
Yao, 157
Yao and Shun, 156, 169, 182; Way of, 170
Yen Fu, 14, 178
Yen Hui, 27
Yin and yang, 88, 121
Yin Wen-tzu, 42, 46; *Yin Wen-tzu, The,* 42, 53, 55
Yü, 156, 158
Yü Ying-shih, cited, 10
Yüan Shih-K'ai, 16

Zen Buddhism, *see* Ch'an Buddhism